Articles of
Resistance

Articles of Resistance

Paul Foot

BOOKMARKS

London, Chicago and Sydney

Articles of Resistance – Paul Foot
First published 2000
Bookmarks Publications Ltd, c/o 1 Bloomsbury Street, London WC1B 3QE,
England
Bookmarks, PO Box 16085, Chicago, Illinois 60616, USA
Bookmarks, PO Box A338, Sydney South, NSW 2000, Australia
Copyright © Bookmarks Publications Ltd

ISBN 1 898876 64 9 (Paperback)

Printed by Redwood Books
Cover by John Henry Barac

Bookmarks Publications Ltd is linked to an international grouping of socialist organisations:
- **Australia:** International Socialists, PO Box A338, Sydney South
- **Austria:** Linkswende, Postfach 87, 1108 Wien
- **Britain:** Socialist Workers Party, PO Box 82, London E3 3LH
- **Canada:** International Socialists, PO Box 339, Station E, Toronto, Ontario M6H 4E3
- **Cyprus:** Ergatiki Demokratia, PO Box 7280, Nicosia
- **Denmark:** Internationale Socialister, PO Box 5113, 8100 Aarhus C
- **Germany:** Linksruck, Postfach 304 183, 20359 Hamburg
- **Greece:** Socialistiko Ergatiko Komma, c/o Workers Solidarity, PO Box 8161, Athens 100 10
- **Holland:** Internationale Socialisten, PO Box 92025, 1090AA Amsterdam
- **Ireland:** Socialist Workers Party, PO Box 1648, Dublin 8
- **New Zealand:** Socialist Workers Organization, PO Box 13-685, Auckland
- **Norway:** Internasjonale Socialisterr, Postboks 9226 Grønland, 0134 Oslo
- **Poland:** Workers' Democracy, PO Box 12, 01-900 Warszawa 118
- **Spain:** Socialismo Internacional, Apartado 563, 08080 Barcelona
- **United States:** International Socialist Organization, PO Box 16085, Chicago, Illinois 60616
- **Zimbabwe:** International Socialist Organisation, PO Box 6758, Harare

Campaigning journalist of the decade

On 25 February 2000 Granada's What the Papers Say *awards ceremony was broadcast on television. The compere, who introduced the winners with quotations from their work, was Clive Anderson.*

Anderson: 'Our final award goes to a journalist who has stuck closely to his principles and, to the chagrin of the authorities, has been proven right time and again. In the 1990s there have been successful outcomes to many of his campaigns against injustice. He has had some illustrious support along the way.'

Evening Standard, 1999
Hello, this is John Lennon. Can I talk to you about the Hanratty case?

The call came through to my office at *Private Eye.* I assumed someone was joking, and begged him to leave me alone. A few moments later, in great embarrassment, I realised this really was John Lennon. And he really did want to talk about the Hanratty case.

This happened 30 years ago in the summer of 1969.

This week, 38 years after the murder, the Criminal Cases Review Commission has referred the case to the court of appeal. As I savour this decision, and rejoice for Hanratty's consistently loyal brother Michael, I feel sad that it comes far too late to save the young man's life.

Anderson: 'Because of the abolition of the death penalty, not all of our winner's campaigns have been resolved too late to save lives, as in the case of the Bridgewater Four, finally cleared in 1997.'

Guardian, 1997, 'Justice 18 Years Too Late'
Jubilation is the first emotion. But the jubilation swiftly turns to anger. Why has it taken so long for this grotesque injustice to be righted? The answer is that the judicial and police authorities are extremely reluctant to admit even the possibility that their system can go terribly wrong.

Anderson: 'This journalist returns to the same story time and again, relentlessly building up evidence until the judiciary and even the government have to take note. Here he writes about his fight to print the story of Lynn Siddons' murder.'

Independent, 1996
I tussled with the evidence and with Hugh Corrie, the experienced libel lawyer at the *Mirror*. The proofs were sent up to the *Mirror* chairman, Tony Miles. He yelled that we had taken leave of our senses and were hell-bent on ruining the *Daily Mirror* forever. We went through the whole argument again. The piece appeared across two pages on 8 April 1981. No one who read it could have any doubt about its thrust: that Michael Brookes murdered Lynn Siddons.

Anderson: 'Brookes was finally brought to book in 1996. Many of the so-called great and good also had reason to regret this journalist's relentless pursuit. Archer and Aitken both came under his scrutiny and his analysis of the arms to Iraq affair took up a whole issue of *Private Eye*.

'At the end of the 1990s we look back and see how many times Paul Foot's campaigns have made a difference. His persistence is a lesson to all journalists who want to do likewise.

'Paul Foot is the What the Papers Say *Campaigning Journalist of the Decade*.'

Contents

The system • 269

Index • 313

Introduction

This is the second book of my journalism. The first, *Words as Weapons*, was published in 1990 by Verso, with the indispensable help of Mike Marqusee. In the introduction to that book, I recalled remonstrating with my uncle Michael about a similar compendium of his work. I protested that journalism of its essence was transitory and could only suffer from any attempted conversion into literature. He agreed, but insisted that such collections of journalism could be defended on three grounds. First, they could be put together with little or no extra work. Secondly, they were invaluable to the journalist's conceit. Thirdly, they were 'a lot of fun'. All three points were vindicated with the publication of that first volume. So I was delighted when the socialist publisher Bookmarks suggested a second volume, especially as they made it clear that I would get no money for it, and that all the hard work would be done by Judith Orr, who runs the Bookmarks shop, Judy Cox, Clare Fermont, Emma Bircham, and John Rees, editor of *International Socialism*.

When the last volume was published I was working as a weekly columnist on the *Daily Mirror*. I got the job from the editor Mike Molloy in 1979. The unwritten agreement was that I would seek out and submit stories based on facts which were not widely known. Mike knew perfectly well, and regretted, that I was 'a Trot'—a member of the newly-formed Socialist Workers Party. He knew that my column would be heavily weighted against the Thatcher government, but he hoped that I would stick to the facts and not stray into propaganda. I hope I achieved this not merely in Mike's time but also under the two editors who succeeded him, Richard Stott and Roy Greenslade.

In 1984, when Mike was still editor, the *Mirror* was bought by Robert Maxwell, a sale approved by Thatcher ('A dose of Maxwell will do you good,' she told the new political correspondent Julia Langdon) and almost everyone else in authority, despite the verdict by Department of Trade inspectors in 1971 that Maxwell was not fit to run a public company. The inspectors were right, and almost at once the spirit of the old *Mirror* began to sink under Maxwell's enormous and corrupt ego. John Pilger, for instance, the outstanding reporter who had won numerous awards for the paper, was sacked in 1986. Maxwell hated my column. He did his best to curtail it. In 1985, in a profoundly embarrassing and bad-tempered interview, he told me that I was not neutral and devoted far too much space to the views and experiences of shop stewards. I told him that if he wanted a neutral columnist the world was full of them and he should hire one instead of me. My job, I explained, was not to be neutral, but in a profoundly unfair and prejudiced world to stand up for the poor against the rich, workers against employers, wrongly convicted prisoners against the judicial establishment, and so on.

He backed off, and to my great relief I hardly ever saw him again. I posted a list in my office of his closest friends, warning my colleagues that if we planned an attack on any of them we should guard ourselves from his inevitable interventions by getting the articles passed in advance by lawyers and by forewarning the editor. Maxwell demeaned everyone who worked for him, myself included, but I was able by sheltering behind the editor to protect myself from his more monstrous excesses. On the one occasion after 1985 when I was called in for a personal interview, he was good enough to tell me that as I was 51 I was too old to join the *Mirror* pension scheme.

On a glorious Guy Fawkes day in 1991 Maxwell was found dead in the sea after falling off his yacht near the Canary Islands. As the news leaked out about his plunder of the pension fund and his dubious flotation of Mirror Group Newspapers earlier in the year, the relief among *Mirror* journalists at Maxwell's death was overwhelming. For an exhilarating year the editor, Richard Stott, ran the paper as he thought fit, with the willing and enthusiastic support of his staff. For the first time for more than a decade the circulation gap between the *Sun* and the *Mirror* started to close. It would have closed altogether had it not been for a boardroom coup at the *Mirror* in October 1992. The coup was organised by David Montgomery, a former editor of the *News of the World* and *Today*, with the help of Maxwell's aides, former *Times* editor Charlie Wilson and *Mirror* chairman Robert Clark. By three to two on the defunct *Mirror* board, and against the strongly-expressed views of the journalists and staff, the board voted to make Montgomery chief executive. As soon as he came into the building, Montgomery raged through it, sacking anyone who he thought represented the 'old *Mirror* culture' or the 'idea of jobs for life'. The chief victim of this cull was the National Union of Journalists chapel that had somehow survived the Maxwell era. In a bitter six month dispute, including demonstrations, pickets and endless meetings on the newsroom floor, the NUJ chapel wrestled with the consistent union-bashing of the new management. At one stage we voted by a clear majority to go on strike, but miserably failed to do so, almost certainly because of the enormous redundancy payments on offer to those who were sacked. By the end of March 1993, it seemed to me that the industrial battle, in which I had been heavily engaged, was lost. My role as *Mirror* columnist was hopeless. Richard Stott had been sacked. So had most of my union colleagues. My column, a lot of which was devoted to assaulting employers like Montgomery, seemed hypocritical. I therefore submitted a column for publication which dealt exclusively with the state of affairs at the *Mirror,* the sackings of trade unionists, Montgomery's share options, the complicity of Clark and Wilson, etc, etc. The editor, David Banks, a cipher flown in from a Murdoch paper in Australia, refused to publish it. I wrote to him telling him he was a disgrace and so were all the members of his board. He sent out a press release to every newspaper except his own implying that I was off my rocker and needed 'professional help'. This was the first column in 14 years which was censored. My former editor Roy Greenslade helped me lay it out in proper style. I printed it at my expense and handed it out to the public outside the *Mirror* building. I left the *Mirror* for good on 31 March 1993. My friends and colleagues Margaret Renn and Bryan Rostron, both of whom had been active in the union, were sacked soon afterwards. Margaret, who was mother of the chapel, later gave evidence to the Commons Employment Committee. A Tory member of the committee later described her testimony as evidence of the worst treatment of a trade union he had ever come across. My unpublished column for the *Mirror* appears in this collection.

Some weeks later, I resumed writing 'Footnotes' for *Private Eye,* two pages I had written from 1967 to 1972. In those days the editor was my old friend Richard Ingrams. In 1986, Ingrams threw up the editorship and handed over to a bumptious 26 year old called Ian Hislop. Old *Eye* stalwarts such as Peter Mackay, Nigel Dempster and Auberon Waugh were shocked at this appointment, and a rather feeble attempt was made to stop Hislop. My own feeling at the time was that anyone whom Richard thought worthy of the post deserved at least a chance. In the following years I was endeared to Ian by his habit of printing almost anything I submitted. When I went to work for him full time I found him a tougher editor than Richard. I had to fight for my stuff more strenuously than previously, but it was none the worse for that. Moreover, much more than in the earlier period, the *Eye*, whose circulation had grown enormously to nearly 200,000, was a powerful magnet for combustible information from everywhere. The point about the *Eye*, which no one seems to grasp, is that it has no proprietor and therefore no one to act as financial or commercial bully over the editor. It is just about the only substantial publication in Britain that can claim to be part of a free press.

Soon after I started work again at the *Eye* a young man called Tim Laxton walked into the office. He had been an accountant for a reputable firm, but had resigned his post and effectively his profession in protest at the suggestion that he should help fiddle the books. He had become absorbed by the proceedings of the Scott inquiry into the export of arms and arms-related equipment from Britain to Saddam Hussein's Iraq. He had, he said, attended every session of the Scott inquiry without being paid a penny. He quite obviously understood the proceedings far more clearly than most of the journalists who were sent to the inquiry only when it was expected that there might be something dramatic to report. Fortnight by fortnight, Tim would come in with the latest news from the inquiry which turned out to be a goldmine of ministerial and civil service hypocrisy and double talk. We wrote many articles together and, when the proceedings finished in May 1994, we produced a *Private Eye* pamphlet, *Not the Scott Report: Thatcher, Major, Saddam and the Merchants of Death*, which sold some 40,000 copies and won the Orwell Prize for Journalism. Our concluding article on the Scott report when it finally came out in 1997 is included here.

The experience of the Scott inquiry taught me the huge journalistic advantages of public inquiries. Information and confidences which would normally be buried deep are suddenly, if reluctantly, made public. I had the same experience with the Waterhouse inquiry into child abuse in North Wales and the Macpherson inquiry into the racist murder of the black teenager Stephen Lawrence. The latter inquiry, which was nothing like as thorough as it should have been, led to a long string of articles in the *Eye*, some of which are published here.

In September 1993, after a series of discussions with Alan Rusbridger, editor of the *Guardian*, I started a fortnightly column for that paper. I wrote that column and the 'Footnotes' in the *Eye* for six years, 1993 to 1999. Very early on Good Friday morning 1999, I was carted off to hospital with a leaking aorta, a rather important artery. The artery burst when the surgeons opened me up. I was left for dead on several occasions, but was somehow patched up so that I survived. My brain came back, apparently intact, but my legs didn't. I came out of hospital lame, I fear permanently, in October 1999, and started my *Guardian* column again in November. In January 2000 I went back for a much-reduced stint at *Private Eye*.

All through the 1990s I continued to write for the publications of the Socialist Workers Party. I had a fortnightly column in the weekly *Socialist Worker*, edited by Chris Harman, until 1999, and wrote regularly in *Socialist Review*, edited by Lindsey German, where I was for more than 12 years a member of the editorial board. I have been lucky, also, to be published often in the *London Review of Books*, edited by Mary-Kay Wilmers and, more recently, in the *Evening Standard*, edited by Max Hastings. Plenty of examples from both are included here.

That's enough intro, I think. (Quite enough, ed.)

Heroes and heroines

Reaching across the centuries

The best thing about Christmas was Janet Suzman's *Othello* on Channel 4.

I have been a Shakespeare freak from a very young age, largely because I never did a Shakespeare play for any examination, and so could read the stuff (and speak it) for pleasure.

For years and years I puzzled over Othello. I couldn't understand why Iago was so keen to do him down.

I read the conventional criticism, including a man called Bradley, who wailed on about a 'tragic flaw' in Othello's character, which was mirrored by a 'tragic flaw' in Iago's character.

The whole play, said Bradley, was about jealousy. Othello was jealous of Desdemona, and Iago of Othello. Not very convincing. I always thought the play more haunting and overpowering than any other.

One cold night about twelve years ago I spoke to a socialist meeting in Nottingham and stayed with a comrade who was interested in drama.

The next day, as I was about to leave, he pressed into my hands a Pelican book called *Shakespeare in a Changing World*. I flicked through it as the train pulled out.

It was written by people who were once Marxists or who might (at that time) admit to be Marxists, but on the whole were trying to avoid letting their readers know they were Marxists.

I was about to put it down when I came across a chapter entitled 'Othello and the Dignity of Man' by G M Matthews.

Passion

I got to know Geoffrey Matthews later. He was, for all too short a time, a friend and a teacher. I shared his passion for the revolutionary poet Shelley.

Socialist Worker 7 January 1989

Geoffrey read Shelley not as a dead poet but a living revolutionary, and so he understood him.

He also read and enjoyed Shakespeare, not just as the greatest poet and dramatist of them all, but also as a creature of revolutionary times who took a deep interest in the world about him.

Suddenly, I read two sentences which laid Othello bare.

> Iago hates Othello because he is a Moor. This irrational but powerful motive, underlying the obsessive intensity of his feeling and the improvised reasons with which he justifies it, continually presses up towards the surface of his language.

Yes, but what of the 'tragic flaw' in Othello? Geoffrey explains:

> The theory is a nuisance because the potentialities of men are infinite and any number of potential 'flaws' can be found or invented to account for his downfall. Yet in all Shakespeare's tragedies, except perhaps *Macbeth*, the determining 'flaw' is in society rather than in the hero's supposed distance from perfection.

Adultery

Tragedy does not occur in Hamlet because the hero has a bad habit of not killing at once, but because the power of the Danish Court is founded on violence and adultery....

> The 'tragic flaw' theory means that it is a punishable offence to be any particular kind of a man. Moreover it shifts the emphasis from men in conflict to the private mind.

Othello all becomes very, very clear in this magnificent essay—but where to see it on stage?

Othello is usually played by some fruity-voiced RADA graduate, rather apologetically blacked up.

Extracts about racism, 'human nature' and prejudice are quietly shoved into the background.

I don't know if Janet Suzman ever read Geoffrey Matthews, but the two seemed to come together most miraculously in her production—which was devised especially for the Market Theatre in Johannesburg, and greeted with sustained delight there by packed audiences of every colour, night after night.

Othello here is 'rude of speech' (though his language is magnificent).

He is a South African black warrior marrying the daughter of a prominent white businessman.

And Iago, though he recognises the Moor for a decent, generous, brave, open-hearted and friendly man, hates him with a consuming, irrational and all-devouring passion because he is a Moor.

The play throws its passions and its problems through 400 years, and means something at last. It is also triumphant.

As Geoffrey Matthews wrote:

> All that Iago's poison has achieved is an object that 'poisons sight': a bed on which a black man and a white woman, though they are dead, are embracing. Human dignity, the play says, is indivisible.

Icon, icon in the wall…

What makes an icon out of an iconoclast?

Perhaps the greatest iconoclast of all time was Vladimir Ilyich Lenin. He was an incurable atheist before the Russian Revolution and after it. He went to extravagant lengths to make sure no one in the new revolutionary leadership of Russia was worshipped while alive or when dead.

He observed how hierarchical class society indulged in unashamed ancestor worship. Ruling class mandarins became infatuated with the terror of death. Many could not believe that they would ever die, but they compensated for their mortality by fantastic rituals after death.

Their religions reassured them that in some way or other their soul or spirit would live on in even greater glory than on earth. To make sure of it they embalmed, buried or entombed each other's dead bodies in grandiloquent ceremonies.

As the acknowledged leader of revolutionary Russia, Lenin insisted on living the life of an ordinary citizen, wholly unadorned with pomp or ceremony. He wrote and spoke often about the importance of a secular approach to life and death and castigated the very notion that the dead were in any way at all more important than the living.

Worship

When he died in 1924, a furious argument broke out among his followers about what should be done with his body.

The immediate, Leninist reaction was published in *Pravda*: 'We must not venerate the corpse of Comrade Lenin, but his cause.'

This was the standard Bolshevik view argued vociferously by Trotsky and Bukharin.

Lenin's widow, Krupskaya, pleaded: 'Don't make an icon out of Ilyich.'

Socialist Worker 15 July 1989

It seemed for a day or two that this conventional Leninist view would prevail. But the Communist Party had already slipped into the hands of Stalin and his allies. They unleashed an orgy of adoration for the dead hero.

'Under no circumstances can we give to the earth such a great and intensely beloved leader as Ilyich', argued one leader in the Moscow newspaper *Rabochaya Moskva*.

'We suggest his remains be embalmed and left under glass for hundreds of years.'

Stalin agreed. As Lenin's will proved, Lenin himself had been extremely suspicious of Stalin in the early 1920s. Above all, Lenin was disgusted by Stalin's religiosity. Stalin loved ornaments, symbols, icons. He believed people should worship their leaders.

He set to work with consummate skill to turn the Russian people's love and respect for Lenin into post-mortem corpse worship.

He set up a body, horribly entitled the Immortalisation Commission, which threw up a makeshift mausoleum into which Lenin's embalmed body was moved only six days after his death.

In 1930 it was moved into the great granite monstrosity where it has been ever since (except for a break during the war when, in fear of invasion, it was moved with great difficulty and expense to a safe hiding place in the Urals).

Glasnost

There, millions of people from all over the world have come to pay their respects to the mummified and petrified body of a man whose whole life was dedicated to the ending of mummification and petrification.

Only a handful of 'splitters and sectarians' were suitably disgusted.

Now that more and more Russians are beginning to think for themselves, one or two people who imagine that glasnost means what it says have expressed doubts about the whole ghastly business, and even suggested that poor old Lenin might be afforded the humble burial or cremation he would have wanted.

Not many weeks ago Mark Zakharov, director of the Leninsky Komosol theatre, went on an increasingly popular late night television show called *Vzglyad*. 'No matter how much we hate or love a person,' he said mildly, 'we don't have the right to deprive him of burial.'

How did this very moderate and unsuperstitious idea go down with the unsuperstitious moderates who, we are told, run Russia today? It was immediately ostracised and denounced in terms of which Stalin would have been proud.

Advice

A former political commentator, Georgi A Zhukov, asked: 'Why is our state television tolerating such statements?' The party leader in Vladimir, Ratmir S Bobovikov, described any argument at all about whether to downgrade Lenin's body to the miserable status of that of any other mortal as 'simply immoral'.

However much 'freedom' is being introduced into the Russian system, its rulers know perfectly well that the icon Lenin is of much more use to them than the iconoclast Lenin.

They need Lenin as a symbol of hierarchy and immortality more than ever before.

For them the great advantage of having Lenin embalmed and worshipped is that it deflects his adorers from reading him, understanding him and, worst of all, acting on his advice.

Revolutionary necrophilia

The *Observer* has decided to celebrate the 200th anniversary of Thomas Paine's *Rights of Man* (1791) with a lecture for children.

Nothing in itself could be more appropriate. From the moment when he first sailed for America in 1768 (at the ripe old age of 39), Thomas Paine dedicated himself to the education of children, and even founded one of the first girls' schools in history.

Who is to give this historic lecture in honour of this great man? The *Observer* has strained every muscle to get it right. It has come down in favour of someone very famous: the Princess Royal, Princess Anne.

No doubt some fatuous fool at the *Observer* felt that the occasion would be better acclaimed if it was graced by so famous a dignitary. But has anyone at the *Observer* even read a word of Tom Paine's? For that matter, has Princess Anne, who, for some astonishing reason, has accepted the invitation?

Thomas Paine arrived in America in the nick of time to take part in the great revolutionary agitation which was to end with the British being finally deposed as the imperialist government of America.

Paine fanned the embers of revolt with his tough, translucent prose. When the War of Independence—dubbed by Paine the American Revolution—finally broke out, he sustained the morale of Washington's flagging army with his *Crisis Papers*.

Their central theme was that the British had no business to rule the American states, and that the British king, George III, had no right to rule anywhere, especially not in Britain.

Furious

Paine's furious onslaught on the British monarchy (and on monarchy in general) made the rebel armies determined that they would for all time banish the name and concept of king from the United States of America—a resolution which has been sustained ever since.

Socialist Worker 1 June 1991

Thomas Paine was honoured by the victorious armies and the new Republican government, but he soon grew tired of honours, and returned to his native Britain. There he threw himself into the furious arguments that followed the French Revolution.

His *Rights of Man* was an answer to Edmund Burke, who had written a poisonous attack on the revolution. At the centre of Burke's argument was the preservation of the monarchy. The *Rights of Man* replied with a furious denunciation of monarchy.

> Hereditary success is a burlesque upon monarchy. It puts it in the most ridiculous light, by presenting it as an office which any child or idiot may fill. It requires some talents to be a common mechanic; but to be a king requires only the animal figures of a man, a sort of breathing automaton. This sort of superstition may last a few years more, but it cannot resist the awakened reason and interest of man.

Alas, apparently it can. For 200 years later we still have to put up with the same posturing figures whom Thomas Paine reviled in almost everything he wrote.

Paine was exiled from Britain and sentenced to death in his absence. It became a capital crime after 1792 to read the *Rights of Man*. He died in 1806, despised, forgotten and hated.

What fun he would have had with the editor of the *Observer* and all his prigs and courtiers, bowing and scraping before this latest representative of the Hanoverian dynasty!

And how he would have appreciated and lambasted the latest example of the old English disease, revolutionary necrophilia—the love and worship of revolutionaries long after they are safely dead.

Man's unconquerable mind

Who abolished slavery? That is a simple question which anyone with an O level in history can answer. William Wilberforce did it, almost on his own. This grand Christian gentleman, Tory MP and factory owner who had a reputation among his factory workers for treating them, well, like slaves, goes down in history as the man who was responsible, more than any other, for ridding the world of slavery. His chief accomplice, so runs standard history, was the youngest ever prime minister of Britain—William Pitt. Pitt and Wilberforce drafted the Abolition Bill which was first voted on—and defeated—by the House of Commons almost exactly 200 years ago.

Do Wilberforce and Pitt deserve all this credit? To find out we can start with another simple historical question: who discovered America? Surely everyone knows the answer. Christopher Columbus, an adventurer from Spain 'discovered' America, though there were, apparently, several hundred thousand people living there at the time who may have discovered it before him.

Columbus also 'discovered' Hispaniola, the largest island in what later became known as the West Indies. There were about a million people living there when Columbus arrived. So friendly were they that they saved one of Columbus's shipwrecked galleys and mended it for him. Columbus remarked on the 'paradise' which he bequeathed to the Spanish Empire. In return, the imperialists went about their business with such ferocity that in 250 years the entire native population was exterminated.

The exterminators, to continue their trade, came to rely increasingly on the slave trade from Africa. Between 1500 and 1800, 30 million slaves were taken by force from Africa to work the plantations of the West Indies and North America. They were captured by violence or trickery, forced to row their death ships across the Atlantic, starved and beaten into submission by white Christian gentlemen, most of whom were British.

Socialist Review July/August 1991

By 1789 Hispaniola had been divided and renamed. The eastern half, Santo Domingo, destitute and desolate, was still governed from Spain. The population was 125,000, of whom 15,000 were slaves. The western half, St Domingue, was run by France. It was heavily populated. In 1789 there were 30,000 whites in St Domingue, 40,000 mulattoes of mixed race, and half a million black African slaves.

This island is now known as Haiti, and is one of the poorest places on earth. In 1789 St Domingue was the richest place on earth. It produced sugar, coffee, cotton, indigo and tobacco in huge quantities. The value of its exports made up two thirds of the gross national product of all France. The French cities of Nantes and Bordeaux were entirely dependent on trade with St Domingue and, at the beginning of the 1790s, it looked to those Frenchmen who benefited from it that the golden goose would go on laying eggs for ever and ever.

The whole of this vast surplus was entirely dependent on slave labour. The lucky slaves were the ones who died in the boats. In the fields they worked an 18 hour day from 7am until 2am. The rules that they should be fed by their owners were almost everywhere ignored or flouted. Most slaves got no food at all and had to spend their few precious hours of 'free time' cultivating vegetables.

Childbirth was not encouraged among the slaves. It wasted time which was better spent in the field. Religion was banned, except only for baptism which was allowed as long as it was done collectively and quickly. The Roman Catholic church happily accepted this fleeting chance to make new converts. In exchange, the church agreed to shut up about slavery.

The slaves were allowed no education, no independent thought, no rights of any kind. This was a savage, brutalised society, held together by fear and sadism. When the liberal French writer Baron de Wimpffen went to St Domingue in 1790, he marvelled at the beauty of his hostess at one of the interminable banquets. He was less impressed when she ordered her cook, who had annoyed her with some message about the food, to be thrown into the oven alongside the next dish. Such atrocities were not the exception. They were the rule.

Between 1783 and 1789 production in St Domingue doubled. There seemed no end to the fabulous riches which could be wrung from this beautiful island and its brutalised slaves. No one worried very much about revolts. It was not just that discipline and order were enforced with such savagery. It was more that the slaves seemed to be exploited beyond the possibility of revolt. Eleven percent of them died every year—a higher percentage, for instance, than in Britain during the First World War—but that did not matter. There was an apparently inexhaustible supply of new labour in Africa.

The French Revolution started to change all this—but not too drastically. Many of the writers of the Enlightenment, whose ideas spawned the revolution, were opposed to slavery. But many of the people who took office immediately after the revolution were themselves beneficiaries of the wealth of St Domingue: not directly as slavers or planters, but indirectly as merchants and tradespeople. They hated slavery in principle but benefited from it in practice.

So the French Assembly, confronted with a demand from the idealists to abolish slavery, sought refuge in a compromise. It decreed that 500,000 black slaves must stay slaves. French citizenship was extended to any mulattoes who could show that their father and mother were born in France. There were about 400 of these, about 1 percent of the mulatto population of St Domingue.

No one was satisfied with this tiny concession. It infuriated the planters, patronised the mulattoes and ignored the slaves. But the concession opened a chink of light. Some people in France, it was obvious, cared enough about slavery in St Domingue to do something about it. The decree for the 400 mulattoes broke the log-jam of slavery and paved the way to the great revolt.

It broke out on 14 August 1791 in a plantation in the north. In a great wave of savagery, slaves slaughtered their masters and burnt their mansions—and were slaughtered in return. By the end of the year a huge leaderless slave army had established itself in the mountains of the north.

It was joined there by a coachman from the small plantation of Breda. Unlike almost all his fellow slaves, the coachman, called Toussaint because he was born on All Saints Day, could read and write. He was 46 years old. He joined the army as a medical auxiliary because (again unlike almost everyone else) he knew some first aid. Very quickly he became the acknowledged leader of the slave army, and remained in charge for 12 years of war.

His first enemies were the planters, whose governor was appointed in Paris. As soon as he took control, Toussaint signed treaties with Spain, which enthusiastically gave him arms in the hope that he might defeat the French, and hand the whole island and its riches to

Madrid on a platter. Within months Toussaint's army had captured and fortified all the ports on the north of the island.

Very quickly he realised that negotiations with the planters were useless. There would be no concessions. Messengers sent to negotiate with planters were executed before they could speak. The result was the slogan which dominated the entire slave campaign: 'Liberty or death.'

The slave revolt, which lasted more than 12 years, was inextricably intertwined with the French Revolution. In September 1792, as the revolution shifted to the left, the new convention sent three commissioners and a new general, Laveaux, to St Domingue. The commissioners declared before they left that they had 'no intention of freeing the slaves'—so they remained Toussaint's enemies.

Yet all through 1793, as the French Revolution built up to its climax, the argument between Laveaux and Toussaint continued. The French general, a Jacobin who hated the royalist planters, tried to persuade the slave leader to throw in his lot with revolutionary France against its enemies—the reactionary empires of Spain and Britain. Toussaint was suspicious. In every Frenchman he saw a slave owner. Even when, in August 1793, the commissioners, on their own initiative, issued a decree abolishing slavery, Toussaint held his army at a distance from the French and his ports for the Spaniards.

In the first six months of 1794, for two reasons, he changed sides. First came the news of a further shift in the French Revolution: proof positive that for the first time in history the common people were playing a part in government. On 3 February 1794 three delegates from St Domingue took their place in the French Convention, controlled now not by traders, but by the working people of the cities, especially Paris. The delegates were a freed black slave, a mulatto and a white man. The very sight of the black and 'yellow' man sent the convention into prolonged applause. It was moved, seconded and carried without discussion that the 'aristocracy of the skin' should be tolerated no longer and that slavery should be abolished.

This historic news reached Toussaint (who had taken a second name: L'Ouverture, the opening to liberty) in the mountains of St Domingue some time in the spring of 1794. Now he knew that not all Frenchmen were slave owners, planters or racialists. There were many in France too who wanted to break the bonds which lashed them to their exploiters, and he made common cause with them.

At the same time a British expedition of 6,000 men, which was to grow into the greatest expedition ever to have left British shores, arrived spoiling for a fight, in St Domingue. The British Prime Minister Pitt was on record, as we have seen, against slavery. One reason was that the most profitable fruits of slavery—in St Domingue—were flowing only to France. Now Pitt and his class were looking at a different picture. There was a chance that the French might be dislodged from the island by a slave revolt; and that the British might seize St Domingue, restore slavery there and make good British profits from it.

The British war against Toussaint's armies in St Domingue lasted four years—from 1794 to 1798. During this period the Abolition of Slavery Movement in Britain almost petered out. There were two more desultory attempts to get a bill through the Commons—in 1795 and 1796. In the three years after 1795 the Abolition Society met twice. From 1797 to 1804 it did not meet at all. During the eight years after 1792, moreover, a million slaves were carried from Africa to the 'New World' in British ships.

Toussaint saw at once that the French (at the high tide of revolution) had abolished slavery, while the British intended to restore it. In June 1794 he made up his mind, threw in his lot with Laveaux, joined the French, seized from the Spaniards in seven days the same ports he had conquered on their behalf, and directed all his military skill and all his army's speed, strength and courage to the war against the British.

The British lost 80,000 men in St Domingue: more than in all the Peninsular Wars. It was one of the greatest military disasters in all British history, so official history conveniently forgets it. In April 1798 Toussaint led his victorious army into the capital, Port-au-Prince, and the British never returned.

But by now the revolutionary tide had rolled back in France, and the new rulers, the Directory, were weighing up the prospects of restoring slavery in St Domingue. A new commissioner, Hedouville, bribed the mulatto generals who had fought valiantly for the slaves against the British against Toussaint. A bloody civil war ended in 1801, when Toussaint marked his triumph over the mulattoes by marching into the Spanish half of the island and conquering it.

The slave army had beaten off the first counter-attack against the slaves by the new French Republic; had beaten the mulattoes, beaten the Spanish, and in the process abolished slavery. But now, after a short peace, it was faced with a new threat: from yet another, different ruler in France, the First Consul, Napoleon Bonaparte.

Napoleon was told (rightly) by his scout General Vincent that St Domingue was 'the happiest place in your dominion'. The whip had been abolished. Hours were regulated and the new society was struggling to restore the ravaged plantations and the lost production. But Napoleon determined to undermine this short peace.

The British, united with their enemy Napoleon in their determination to put down the slave revolt, obliged with a short peace so that Napoleon could devote his full attention to Toussaint L'Ouverture. In charge of his huge expedition Napoleon appointed his son in law, Le Clerc, who predicted that 'all the niggers, when they see an army, will lay down their arms'. He had at his side all the great generals of Napoleonic France. Yet in the first six months of 1802 the French lost 10,000 men—half to disease, half to the enemy. The French soldiers were confused. As they attacked the black army, they were greeted with familiar songs: the *Marseillaise*, the *Ça Ira*, the very revolutionary hymns to whose strains they had conquered most of Europe.

On 7 June 1802 the beleaguered French generals offered Toussaint a treaty if he would appear in person to discuss it. Against the advice of his generals, he did so, was swiftly captured, taken to France and banged up in a freezing prison in the Jura. To French astonishment, however, the slave army in St Domingue fought with even greater ferocity without their leader. In a matter of months, the French were driven out of the island, never to return. Imperialist government in St Domingue was over—forever.

This is perhaps one of the most remarkable stories in all human history but because it turns history upside down it is not told in history books. The story of Toussaint L'Ouverture is almost entirely obliterated from British (and even French) culture. There is a film about Spartacus—he lost, after all—but none about Toussaint. There is a wonderful book by C L R James—*The Black Jacobins*—which is reinforced now by Robin Blackburn's comprehensive history: *The Overthrow of Colonial Slavery*. In general, though, important people everywhere have been reluctant to disclose too much about Toussaint L'Ouverture and his army, lest some rather obvious lessons might be learnt—and acted on.

What happens in real life is not determined by what great men or gods think is right or wrong. It is determined by the greed of ruling classes and the resistance to it. Slavery could have gone on for countless decades (as it did in North America) if the slaves had not fought for their freedom with the most implacable violence.

White people are not always racialist. Napoleon, Le Clerc, Hedouville were racialists. Laveaux was not—nor were the Jacobins in the convention who abolished slavery. For them, the aristocracy of the skin was yet another horrific manifestation of the aristocracy of class and religion.

William Wilberforce did not abolish slavery. The slave army of Toussaint L'Ouverture started the process—which was not finished until the slaves of America had to join white people in the North and fight a civil war to abolish slavery. The emancipation of the slaves was fought for and won by the slaves themselves.

The lowest, most debased and exploited people are capable of resisting their oppressors—and beating them.

Toussaint was himself a most humane and peace-loving man. He refused, for instance, to execute prisoners. But he knew the alternative was liberty or death, and fought accordingly. His message comes down loud and clear over these 200 years, in spite of all the attempts to silence it.

When in 1803 William Wordsworth, his own revolutionary enthusiasms already in decline, heard that Toussaint had died of pneumonia in his prison, he dedicated to the dead slave leader perhaps his finest sonnet—and one that will certainly not be taught by rote at school since it is not about daffodils:

> Live and take comfort, thou has left behind
> Powers that will work for thee—air, earth and skies—
> There's not a breathing of the common wind
> That will forget thee. Thou hast great allies.
> Thy friends are exultations, agonies and love
> And man's unconquerable mind.

Right as pie

In Melbourne prison, Australia, in November 1906, Tom Mann, socialist agitator, aged 50, was visited by J Ramsay MacDonald, newly elected Labour MP for Leicester, aged 40. Nothing is recorded of what was said. MacDonald may have expressed his enthusiasm at the advance of the Labour Party. He had trebled his vote at Leicester, and the party now had 29 MPs. He may well have looked forward to the 'century of the great hope' which so many new social democrats believed was certain to follow the triumph of socialist ideas at the polls. Tom Mann, who was in prison for 'obstructing the police' by speaking at a socialist meeting in a Melbourne suburb, would certainly have put his visitors at their ease. He had a natural gaiety about him and an unquenchable sense of humour, especially when in prison. But it is unlikely that Ramsay MacDonald left without at least one of Tom Mann's celebrated jibes at parliament ringing in his ears. At any rate, Mann did not forget the visit.

Twenty six years later, at the ripe old age of 76, he was in prison again—in Brixton, London—for refusing to be bound over after a National Unemployed Workers' Movement demonstration. The prime minister at the head of the right wing National Government of the day was J Ramsay MacDonald. Tom Mann started his socialist life, as MacDonald did, by assuming that socialist goals could be achieved through the vote. He was growing up as that vote was quickly extended to the majority of British men, and he started his political life as north-east organiser and agitator for the Social Democratic Federation. It was cruel work, and he found the narrow, sectarian approach of the SDF unconvincing and unattractive. Before long he was on his way south to take part in the event which shaped the rest of his long political life—the Great Dock Strike of 1889. This strike was won not, as most socialists thought likely, by the 'aristocracy' of labour, the men (like Tom Mann) who had served their time and read Shakespeare in the local institute libraries, but by the 'lowest of the low', the impoverished casual labourers of the London docks. Tom Mann revelled in this activity, which kept him up night and day for the whole month of the strike. He was by a long way the strike's outstanding leader, rushing from place to place, calling the workers onto the streets to raise their spirits with jokes, demonstrations and stunts. The dockers' victory and its consequence, an astounding surge in the self confidence of the British working class, was a lesson to Tom Mann all his life. He saw how the workers, in the course of their own action, changed from hopeless down and outs into enthusiastic, disciplined and rational human beings. It was a change, he reckoned, worth fighting for.

Tom Mann became a syndicalist. He placed his faith in the ability of the working class through strikes and agitation to shake the employers' economic system to its foundations. A new socialist society could only be built, he argued, by stoking up workers' organisations and exerting power until capitalism could not continue any longer. This approach made him extremely unpopular not just with employers and governments, but also with the new middle class socialists. Beatrice Webb held a sumptuous dinner to celebrate the first Independent Labour Party election victories in 1895. One of the guests was Tom Mann, who made his position quite plain. Mrs Webb was indignant: 'He is possessed', she wrote, 'with the idea of a "church" or a body of men all professing the same creed and all working in exact uniformity to the same end... And, as Shaw remarked, he is deteriorating. This stumping the country, talking abstractions and raving emotions, is not good for a man's judgment, and the perpetual excitement leads, among other things, to too much whisky.' There were things even worse than whisky lying in wait for this monster raving loony. Two years later, Tom Mann was flung out of the ILP because it was rumoured he was going round with a woman who was not his wife. It was true, as he readily admitted. He left his wife, and went to live with Elsie Harker in happiness and love for nearly half a century.

Tom Mann was not deteriorating. All this stumping the country for socialism was so exhilarating that he determined to stump some other countries too. All his life he was a committed internationalist, declaring that the basic needs and aspirations of ordinary people were the same the whole world over. When MacDonald met him in Melbourne, he was in the middle of the most ferocious agitation, which laid the foundation stone for strong trade unionism in Australia for the rest of this century. During all his long life, Tom Mann travelled ceaselessly, especially in the old commonwealth—from South Africa, where, rather to the distaste of the 'mature' labour movement there, he spoke up for the blacks, to Canada, where he spoke up for the French, to Russia, where he interceded with Lenin for imprisoned anarchists, and even to China. He always managed to get back for the big labour upheavals in Britain. In 1911, his base was Liverpool, where he became the leader of another great shipping and dock strike. In five weeks the National Union of Dock Labourers, which was based in Liverpool, grew in membership from 8,000 to 26,000. 'The whole of Liverpool,' Mr Tzuzuki tells us, 'was like an armed camp.' For printing in his new paper, the *Syndicalist*, an appeal to soldiers not to shoot at striking workers, Mann was sent for two months to Strangeways prison. 'Don't worry, Mam,' he wrote to Elsie. 'This won't hurt me and I shall be as right as pie.'

Explaining the basis of his syndicalism in a pamphlet written with his friend and fellow dock strike leader Ben Tillett in 1890, Mann said: 'The political machine will fall into our hands as a matter of course as soon as the educational work has been done in our labour organisations.' Politics, it followed, was trivial enough to be left to the parliamentarians. The view served him well through the labour 'high' of 1911 and 1912. It was not so valuable in 1914. Returning from South Africa, Tom Mann reflected: 'I extremely regret that the workers of the world are at one another's throats.' A year later, however, he was writing: 'I am really of the opinion that the war ought and must be fought out.' For the first three years of the war he buried himself in simple trade union work, cutting himself off from the anti-war activists, especially on the Clyde. Though he never became a warmonger like his friend Tillett, he did not oppose the war. This cannot have been for lack of courage—Tom Mann never shirked any battle he believed in. His apolitical syndicalism left him without independent political answers when the workers, on whose industrial strength he depended exclusively, stampeded to the colours.

After the war, his old energy revived. After a short term as general secretary of the engineering workers' union (which was merged in that time to become the AEU, as it is known today), he threw himself into the Red International Labour Union, which was founded in Moscow in 1921. Lenin's aim was to set up revolutionary trade unions to counter the 'reformist' trade unions which were being set up in the capitalist world. This policy led in Britain to the National Minority Movement, which flourished in British trade unions between 1924 and 1926. Nearly a million trade unionists were represented at the NMM conference in March 1926. Its policy was unrelieved industrial militancy, and it played a considerable part in the early success of the 'triple alliance' of miners, railwaymen and transport workers. When the General Strike of 1926 was defeated, however, the NMM quickly withered away.

Tom Mann joined the Communist Party soon after it was formed in 1922, but he never played a central role in party activities. He was not elected to the Central Committee until 1937, when he was 81. He always preferred industrial agitation to political organisation. He supported the Russian Revolution throughout the 1920s and by the time Stalin started to extirpate every revolutionary vestige of that revolution, Tom was an old man. In the late 1920s he was appointed to a three man RILU commission to China. His two companions were Earl Russell Browder, a young American Communist, and Jacques Doriot, one of the most popular Communist leaders in France. The three men were sent to 'monitor' the Chinese workers' revolution, which had seized the centre of many of the big cities. The commission was in China during the crucial weeks of 1927, and saw and faithfully reported the terrible defeat and massacre of the Chinese workers. They did not see and did not report that the defeat was plotted in the Kremlin, and that the new Stalinist foreign policy ('socialism in one country') condemned the fighting Chinese Communists to the most horrible fate. It is a strange and sobering experience to read the reports of these three devoted Communists as they chronicle the disaster for which their beloved Stalin was chiefly responsible. Once more the abstentionism inherent in the syndicalist case—the abandonment of 'difficult' political decisions to 'them upstairs'—had blinded Tom Mann to the cause of this most awful horror.

Tom Mann's particular genius was speaking in public. No one can test this out, because little if any of him is on film—but Tom Mann was probably the finest public speaker in British labour history. Like many good speakers, he yearned in his youth to be an actor, and always loved the theatre. His supreme gift was his humour. My witness is Harry McShane, who died in 1988 aged 97 after a lifetime's agitation not unlike Tom Mann's. Harry heard them all: Hyndman, Maclean, Grayson, Wheatley, Cook, Maxton, Bevan, Pollitt—yes, even MacDonald. 'None of them was a patch on Tom Mann,' he would say. He described a meeting in Mansfield in which Mann ridiculed the parliamentary aspirations of the day. 'He fell on his knees on the front of the stage, imploring parliament, beseeching, begging parliament to do the job. We were all in stitches, screaming with laughter.' Harry also told me about 'this Japanese chap who's written a very good book on Hyndman, and another on Eleanor Marx. He's been asking about Tom Mann and the New Unionists. He's writing a book about it, I hear. Make sure you get it when it comes out.'

Chushichi Tsuzuki probably set out to write a book about the three dock strike leaders, Tom Mann, Ben Tillett and John Burns. At some stage, he presumably plumped for Mann because he is so much more consistent than the other two. Burns ended up in the Liberal government and Tillett became a TUC mandarin and a shameless spokesman for the collaborationist Mond-Turner proposals in the late 1920s. But there is still too much Tillett and Burns in the book, not enough Tom Mann. In these days when, as in the 1870s and early 1880s, everyone says that the working class doesn't exist and socialism is a dangerous fantasy, we could have done with much more of Tom Mann's experience in both matters. His life should have been dovetailed more into his times, his syndicalism woven more carefully into the rise and fall of working class confidence, and his submission to Russian foreign policy more carefully and critically explained. All that said, we've got a marvellous glimpse of a British working class hero from a professor of international relations at the International University of Japan, Niigata-Urasa. Few things would have pleased old Tom more.

First published as a review of Tom Mann, 1956-1941: The Challenges of Labour by Chushichi Tsuzuki (Oxford 1992).

At last

Crows peck the eagles

For 30 years I have been searching for a performance of William Shakespeare's *Coriolanus* which understands what the play is about—and now I have found it.

The Renaissance Company's production with Kenneth Branagh as the tyrant and Judi Dench as his mother Volumnia has got it right at last.

The simple point which was missed in every single one of the 12 productions I have seen plus one I acted in—as the second senator, who had one and a half lines—is that the play is about the class war.

The scene is set in the Roman Republic, where the patricians and their senate concede to the people a couple of their own kind to act as 'tribunes'.

But no one in the English audience of 1608 could have missed the parallel, as an arrogant and ambitious king, James I, started to challenge the growing influence of the merchants and, beneath them, the angry cry of the common people.

William Shakespeare was not a revolutionary. His instincts and sympathies were with the patricians, and even with the king, though almost all his history plays about English kings show how rotten the kings were.

To that extent, Nigel Lawson's classically imbecilic comment that 'Shakespeare was a Tory' had some truth in it.

But Shakespeare was not just a 'Tory'. His greatness came not just from his command of the English language, unrivalled before or since, but from his ability to listen to how and why the language was used to express people's fears and hopes, doubts and certainties.

'The people' might well be a rabble, fickle in their choice of favourites and easily moulded by a skilful orator. But they had a point.

Socialist Worker 27 June 1992

The arrogant kings who ignored them might be high and mighty, even honest and admirable characters. But if they ignored their subjects they were tyrants.

Coriolanus is a patrician who believes so passionately in the right of his class to rule over the masses that he refuses to compromise.

He would rather drag his class into open civil war with the 'rabble' than address a kind word to them.

His pride, his valour in war, his glorious use of language are all so dominant that director after director has fallen into the trap of reducing all the other characters in the play to foils to the Great Man.

Coriolanus becomes just another personal tragedy, a tragedy of a great man done down by the stinking mob. The excitement of the play, the ebb and flow of the class struggle, is entirely missed.

In this awful directional censorship the victims have been the tribunes, Sicinius and Brutus.

Now at last the balance is struck right. Kenneth Branagh is a wonderful Coriolanus, but the reason he is the best yet—better by far, for instance, than Laurence Olivier—is that he and the director, Tim Supple, understand and, I suspect, sympathise with what the crowd represent.

The crowd, many of whom have been picked from the Sussex unemployed, are magnificent. As the initiative shifts from the oppressed to the oppressors and back again, the excitement never stops.

The scene in which the tribunes, Jimmy Yuill and Gerard Horan, gently but forcefully persuade the people to resist the dictator, a scene traditionally ignored or gutted by patrician directors, is one of the most exhilarating pieces of theatre I have ever seen.

I hope this production will soon move from the unlikely surroundings of Chichester so that all socialists can go to see it and enjoy it.

'I jolly well would have'

Did Shelley have sex with Claire Clairmont? I first heard this central question debated with great solemnity at a meeting of the Byron Society in Albemarle Street way back in 1978. I went with three fellow Shelleyans, Geoffrey Matthews, Claire Tomalin and Judith Chernaik, to hear Marion Stocking talk about Claire. Marion Stocking's beautifully edited *Journals of Claire Clairmont* had just come out, and she knew more about Claire than all the brains of the Byron Society put together. This did not stop those brains from working away at the Central Question—the sexual relations of Shelley and Claire. The Byron-worshippers were torn between those who were quite certain that anyone who had had sex with Byron (as Claire unquestionably had) could never settle for anything inferior, and those who regarded Claire as an impudent trollop who had dared to seduce the great genius and then pester him about the consequences. On and on the debate rumbled, until Beatrice Haas, then in her late seventies, rose to rebuke the academics. 'If I had been with Shelley at Byron's villa at Este in the spring of 1818,' she said, 'I jolly well would have slept with him.'

That seemed to be the end of the matter, but not quite. Marion Stocking summed up with a plea for an assessment of Claire Clairmont not as lover or hanger-on but in her own right. Not that Stocking ducked the Central Question. She ended by reading (or rather reciting, for she plainly knew the whole poem by heart) 'To Constantia Singing', which Shelley wrote to Claire in 1817. She read it with such affection and verve that it seemed to me she had crossed the Atlantic for no other purpose.

Whether or not Shelley had sex with Claire, he certainly thought about it and yearned for it. In 'To Constantia', he wrote:

> My heart is quivering like a flame;
> As morning dew that in the sun dies,
> I am dissolved in these consuming ecstasies

London Review of Books 20 August 1992

Judith Chernaik's novel is a series of fictional diary entries for 1816 and 1817 by four women—Mary and Fanny, the daughters of Mary Wollstonecraft; Claire, their step-sister; and Harriet, Shelley's first wife, who drowned herself in 1816. In an entry (entirely fictional, it must be stressed) dated 9 October 1817, she solves the Central Question in a meeting between Claire and Shelley in the woods near where they were living at Marlow. They fondle each other a little, and then:

> ...he spread his cape on the fallen leaves, and when we lay together it seemed very natural and inevitable. We were entirely private and what passed between us had nothing to do with anyone else, it was between the two of us only, and I felt loving and content.

That is probably as close to the truth as it is possible to get, not least because it clears the way for the discovery of Claire Clairmont as a real person rather than a plaything of the poets.

Byron and Shelley have suffered grievously from their detractors, but far worse from their worshippers. The awful Jane St John, who married Shelley's son and established for her dead father-in-law a ghastly shrine at Boscombe, solved the 'Claire problem' by writing her out of the record. This almost permanent friend, sister and companion of Shelley and Mary during their eight years together vanishes into the hot air of Jane Shelley's preposterous 'biography', *The Shelley Memorials* (1859).

In the slightly more honest but no less absurd Shelley-worship of the late 19th century, Claire is recognised, but only irritably, as an infuriating wallflower, eavesdropping on the glorious beauty of Shelley's marriage to Mary. Richard Holmes's unsurpassable biography, *Shelley: The Pursuit*, written in the 'golden years' of the early 1970s, was the first to rescue Claire from the patronage of the Shelley-worshippers and to introduce her as a political thinker, who not only learnt from Shelley but taught him a few things as well. This rescue was carried on by Marion Stocking, and has now been triumphantly completed by Robert Gittings and Jo Manton.

They have not much to add to the familiar part of the story—Claire's life with the Shelleys until the poet's death at the age of 29 in 1822. It is in their account of Claire's long, tough life after Shelley's death—nearly 60 years—that she emerges at last in the clear light of what Shelley called her 'alternating attraction and repulsion'.

Though she never lost touch with them, she moved away from the other members of the Shelley circle: Mary Jane Williams, who husband had drowned with Shelley, Jefferson Hogg, Trelawny, Hunt. Her work as governess and teacher took her to Tsarist Russia into the employ of a nobleman who would rather have perished than known he had taken into his home a companion of that vile atheist Shelley and even viler free-lover Byron. Claire kept her past quiet and stuck to her work. She did not, however, abandon the ideas she had discussed with Shelley. They emerge again and again, not so much in the *Journals*, which are sparse, but in her letters, whose richness, variety and humour are expertly deployed in this exhilarating book.

The strict Russian bourgeoisie could never understand why Claire was such a good teacher for their children. The reason was that she utterly rejected conventional ideas about education. Writing to Mary about her Russian employers, she said:

> They educate a child by making the external work upon the internal, which is, in fact, nothing but an education fit for monkeys, and is a mere system of imitation. I want the internal to work upon the external, that is to say that my pupil should be left at liberty as much as possible, and that her own reason should be the prompter of her action.

Reading this in the week that the education secretary John Patten presents his ideas for British education in the next 20 years, I feel bound to offer him a new title for his white paper: 'An Education Fit for Monkeys'.

By assiduous and cheerful practice of her principles, Claire worked miracles with the 'brawling, squabbling' brats of her employers, most of them incurably infected by the tyranny of serfdom. 'I have not attained two or three people of my own way of thinking', she complained in one letter, but in others she let her radical mockery loose on her unsuspecting employers:

> One thing is certain that Mr B is a Malthusian… He groans over the chestnut trees loaded with nourishing fruit and sighs over the fields of Indian corn and the hedges full of blackberries, thinking how easily the poor will get food and how that facility will set them on marrying… I believe he sees in every blossom that blows, in every blade of grass that sprouts, a newborn babe.

In the same mood, she wrote to Mary of a sparkling evening with a French couple:

> Our conversation at table was very amusing. We agreed to found a state upon the Turkish model, only that the tables should be turned and the men shut up in harems and kept by the women.

She was a women's liberationist of the Shelleyan school, looking forward to a world, as Robert Gittings and Jo Manton put it, of 'universal sexual freedom, with a personal revenge for the humiliations of Byron's contempt'. Writing to Mary in a desperate plea to stop her from 'resting on her laurels', she argued: 'There has not been nor ever will be one so calculated as yourself to raise our sex…if you would but know your value and exert your powers you could give the men a most immense drubbing.'

The tone of letters like this flatly contradicts the conventional image of the two half-sisters petulantly and jealously bickering their way through their long relationship. Mary is a constant witness to her intense irritation with Claire. While Shelley was still alive Mary wrote in her diary:

> Heigh ho, the Claire and the Ma
> Find something to fight about every day

Several times in the long years after his death, she expressed in different ways her dream: 'My idea of heaven is a world without Claire.' But Robert Gittings and Jo Manton have set the record straight here as well. Mary may often have been irritated by Claire. Few who knew her were not. But Mary was devoted to her half-sister, and in Claire's long periods of absence yearned for news of her. 'When I think of your life,' Mary wrote, 'how, left to your own resources, you courageously took your fate upon yourself, supported yourself for years, refusing to be a burden to anyone, making dear and valued friends wherever you went through your own merit—I feel sure you ought to meet with some reward.' Claire for her part remained intensely loyal to Mary, and though Jane Williams and Trelawny later let slip some of the truth about the fading passions in Mary's marriage to Shelley, especially after the two children had died, Claire held her tongue. In spite of many temptations, she never split on her sister.

The real difference between the two women was not so much

personal as political. Even before Shelley died, Mary had lost a lot of the revolutionary passion she shared with him in that frantic, whispered love affair in the Charterhouse Gardens or over Mary Wollstonecraft's grave in St Pancras churchyard. Her reforming zeal shines out brightly from *Frankenstein*—though her doubts and worries are clear too. (What happens, she wondered, when brilliant young upper class men like Shelley and Byron turn their minds to revolution, and then, just as the 'people monster' is unleashed, abandon it?) With Shelley's death, the last lingering flicker of revolutionary hope went out of Mary. Her novels, which she wrote to earn money to offset the meanness of the everlasting miser Sir Timothy Shelley, are almost impossible to read. She cut out sections of Shelley's atheism from the first collected edition, though she repented later, and did admit in her notes that all his life Shelley 'eagerly ranged himself on the people's side'. For herself, as she wrote to Trelawny: 'I have no wish to ally myself to the Radicals—they are full of repulsion to me.' Mary went firmly down the well-worn path which leads so many middle aged people to conformity and reaction.

Claire was quite the opposite. Again and again in her letters and journals there are flashes of the revolutionary convictions she shared with Shelley. Of Russia she prophesied with startling accuracy:

> Through the strawberry picking and the mushroom expeditions, the sledge drives by moonlight and the rides to drink milk at the estate sawmills, those who had ears might have heard the clang of hammer and sickle.

Nor was she hoodwinked or hypnotised, as Mary was, by the apparent security and comfort of middle class early Victorian England. She saw, understood and supported what was happening down below. While Mary and her friends fled London or signed up for the yeomanry at the climax of the Chartist agitation, Claire stayed in the city, willing the Chartists on. She wrote to Mary about the adored young Queen Victoria:

> The Queen's offer of £50 to all who convict others of fomenting rebellion is a most immoral proclamation and a downright premium to calumny, malice and all uncharitableness.

Perhaps she remembered the scorching pamphlet written by Shelley at Marlow in which he contrasted the death of English liberty in the execution of the leaders of the 1817 Pentridge Uprising with the death of a brainless young princess. The latter had been mourned in every church in the kingdom; no one had noticed the death of liberty.

Though she could not restrain all her radical opinions in her letters to Mary, Claire well understood the political gulf between them, and sought not to exaggerate it. She was, however, for these reasons, adamant that Mary should not write a life of Shelley, which she constantly threatened to do. 'Do not think of writing the memoirs', she wrote anxiously, using Mary's ill-health as an excuse. The real reason, as Robert Gittings and Jo Manton suggest, was her anxiety to protect Shelley's political convictions.

Sadly for all who share those convictions, Claire herself never wrote her own book about Shelley and Byron. Her rage against Byron went on and on into her old age. Byron-worshippers of all ages have sprung to his defence against Claire, pleading that 'the world he lived in' left him no alternative but to pluck his daughter from her mother's arms and parcel her off to a convent. This is nonsense. As Shelley advised at the time, there was a perfectly obvious alternative—to leave the little girl with Claire, who was far better equipped to bring her up than any convent.

Claire's fury against Byron is utterly just, though it would hardly have assisted her in her judgment of his poetry or his politics. Her reflections on Shelley, however, would have been invaluable. Perhaps the most remarkable feature of this book is the way Shelley keeps rising up out of the past to haunt, make love and converse with Claire all over again. A summer storm in Russia brought back the melancholy of the ghastly villa at Lerici where they were all living when Shelley was drowned. When she read Medwin's rotten pot-boiler about his cousin, or when she heard what Jane Shelley was planning, she mourned: 'It is cruel to think how Shelley's merit was lost upon the world.'

In Florence, where she finally settled, Claire could not rid herself of 'this genius extinct, the greatest ever known, and the noble system he would have established therewith fallen for many ages to the dust'. This may read like sentimental hero worship or calf-love. But it came from a genuine understanding of the poet, and what drove him on.

The point is clearly illustrated in Judith Chernaik's novel. She imagines an argument between Claire and her suitor, Thomas Love Peacock, whose conservatism did not affect his admiration for Shelley.

Peacock makes a powerful point:

> Shelley has never even attended a meeting of a Hampden Club; it did not occur to him to go to Spa Fields for the great meetings last year, though he was in London at the time. He is a dreamer, not a revolutionary... Our poet prefers reading about society to entering it. He is a scholar of revolution, not an agitator.

Claire replies:

> I do not agree with you at all. I think he is utterly reckless of himself, and plunges into dangerous activity without giving any thought to the consequences. The only reason he does not go to the northern mill towns is that he knows he would be the worst Luddite of them all; he would probably shoot the factory owners on sight. He is actually a very good shot.

Claire was not quite right. Shelley did flinch from action, and he was (who wouldn't be?) terrified of prosecution and imprisonment. But her version is much nearer the truth than Peacock's.

'Thou, too, O Comet, beautiful and fierce' was how Shelley addressed Claire in 'Epipsychidion': it was the combination of qualities in her which most attracted him, and contributed most to the contempt with which she has been treated by generations of (mainly masculine) Shelley-worshippers. Many have testified to Claire's beauty, or rather her sexual attraction. Shelley had written about that at length in 'To Constantia'. No doubt he was turned on by her looks, as every other man she met seems to have been. But the quality which attracted him above all was her ferocity. Others saw this as plain bad temper, intolerable in women. Shelley thrived on it. Claire would not accept an answer unless she agreed with it. She would answer him back, contradict him, argue with him. Ferocity was a quality he admired in others and wanted for himself:

> Be thou, Spirit fierce,
> My spirit! Be thou me, impetuous one!

Ferocity and impetuosity were his ideals. Claire brilliantly sustained them, not just when Shelley was around to help, but in herself in poverty and loneliness and humiliating employment for more than half a century after his death.

Shelley-worshippers will not, I think, like either of these books. They expose their idol too much as a red and an atheist, with a weakness for beautiful women with the same strong views. Shelleyans of the revolutionary variety, however, will enjoy them very much indeed.

Originally published as a review of Claire Clairmont and the Shelleys *by Robert Gittings and Jo Manton (Oxford 1992) and* Mab's Daughters *by Judith Cernaik (Pan 1992).*

Inspiring memory

I doubt if the Socialist Workers Party will ever put on a better memorial meeting than the one held last Friday in celebration of the restless, bustling and inspiring life of Dave Widgery.

The chief problem for the organisers was the enormous range of Dave's interests, friends, heroes and admirers.

There was no problem about his commitment to the Socialist Workers Party. I first met Dave in the middle of the 1968 'revolution' on York station. He had come from speaking at the university which he denounced, his eyes shining, as a 'great middle class fun palace'. He glowered at me. 'They don't need you there at all. They need the proletariat.'

Even when he used an old fashioned word like proletariat he had a way of making it sound ultra-modern, like something from the lyrics of a popular rock band. And in his last book (and his best, by the way, in case anyone thinks that revolutionaries get stale as they get older), *Some Lives!*, he used the word 'proletarian' quite naturally again and again.

Knew better

Dave was a party man. He loved and admired Peter Sedgwick, and had a lot in common with him. But when Peter finally dropped out of the International Socialists (forerunner of the SWP) some time in the mid-1970s, Dave would not let him go without a ferocious argument.

Dave knew better than most of his friends and contemporaries that you cannot be a socialist on your own.

Dave was all those things which so many of his 1968 generation ended up denouncing. He was a Leninist and a vanguardist. He was not in the SWP because it was the 'best of the bunch' or because he 'had to be in something' (two explanations I've heard for his commitment). Nor even was his reason for membership his agreement with

the basic policies which distinguished the SWP from other left organisations.

The chief reason was that he agreed with the sort of party the
SWP was trying to build.

Socialist Worker editor Chris Harman's speech last Friday ended
with a sharp attack on the left paper *Tribune* for a sectarian assault on
an obituary in *Socialist Review*. 'He didn't sell enough papers,' scoffed
Tribune.

In fact there are few people alive today who have sold more copies
of *Socialist Worker* (over 25 years, remember—Dave was at the very
first *Socialist Worker* editorial board meeting in 1967). He knew that
if socialist papers are not sold directly, hand to hand, they do not sell
at all (*Tribune* I cite as an example).

The majority of the speakers last Friday were not members of the
SWP. Sheila Rowbotham spoke of Dave's abiding solidarity with the
women's and gay liberation movements. Anna Livingstone, a fellow
doctor in the East End, enthused us with her stories of Dave's battle
for the health of the working class.

In particular

After a moving and quite brilliant speech which reminded me of his,
my, and Dave's hero C L R James, Darcus Howe ended by saying he
had fathered five children in Britain.

Four, he said, had grown up black and angry, battling all the time
against the awful racism around them. The fifth, he said, grew up
'black at ease'. She had 'space' to develop her own personality.

Darcus ascribed this 'space' to the work of the Anti Nazi League
in general and Rock Against Racism and Dave Widgery in particular. There could not have been a more powerful tribute to this fire-
cracker of a revolutionary whom we have lost far too soon.

A hero of Labour

Good political biography is rare enough, and even rarer in the labour movement, so I gleefully report my enjoyment of Caroline Benn's book on Keir Hardie, the first leader of the Labour Party.

This is not in any way a hagiography.

Indeed, by constantly sizing up Hardie from the vantage point of the women he knew and loved—his wife and daughter whom he expected to live on a pittance of a pound a week, and his numerous lovers, including Sylvia Pankhurst—Caroline Benn draws a picture of a vain, self regarding and slightly unpleasant man.

This is most definitely not the saintly hero painted by so many sentimental socialists.

Nor, however, is this Hardie the villain of conventional revolutionary historians, who indicate that he was politically indistinguishable from his notorious successor as leader of the Labour Party, Ramsay MacDonald.

As the book proves beyond doubt, Hardie was at every twist and turn in the story preferable to MacDonald.

He was contemptuous of and uneasy in high society, which MacDonald loved. He was suspicious of Liberals, whom MacDonald constantly cuddled. Above all, Hardie kept his working class roots, while MacDonald was always trying to tear them up.

As so often emerges from biographies of the central figures of British labour history, Keir Hardie seems a mass of contradictions.

Olive branches

On the one hand, he is accommodating, seeking to make alliances, holding out olive branches to the other side.

On the other, he is trumpeting his deep hostility to all things Liberal, insisting on the purest of pure Labour and denouncing Liberal ministers, especially Winston Churchill, whom he called a charlatan and a liar.

Socialist Worker 1 May 1993

On the one hand he is telling his colleagues that parliament is all that matters.

On the other hand, he is the consummate campaigner, never stopping his endless, lifelong stomp round the country, speaking at more meetings in a month than most of us active socialists would expect to address in a year.

How to resolve these contradictions? Caroline Benn has a go with this:

> As so often happened in Hardie's life when he found himself drifting towards Liberalism (as he had been since 1908) it was events in the industrial field which re-radicalised him.

The astonishing and quite unexpected strike wave of 1911, which awoke the railwaymen and the miners and the Irish countryside from which so many of them had come, brought Hardie quickly back to the politics of his youth.

He toured the mining areas, speaking with great passion about the hardship and courage of the strikers and their families. He denounced the bosses and Churchill with the most ferocious passion. He was all his life an internationalist, an anti-militarist, a supporter of women's liberation and an opponent of British rule in Ireland.

Of course, it is easy over all these years to pick out juicy examples of Hardie's reformism: his pettifogging parliamentarianism, his sentimentality, his endless appeals to higher values.

But he emerges from this marvellous biography as a proletarian socialist who believed in his class, who wanted to improve it through parliament. But he realised that, whatever the possibilities of parliament, little or nothing would be achieved unless the workers acted for themselves.

From young trade union organiser to veteran agitator, he was always aware that strikes make trade unions, not vice versa.

Seize the time

We socialists are always saying that workers change in struggle—but what a joy and a relief it is when we can test the theory in flesh and blood. When I drew back the curtains in Tayport at 6.30am on Thursday 20 May, the sun streamed in—it was a glorious spring morning. Half an hour later, across the river and through the city of Dundee, the picket line at Timex was revelling in the sunshine. There were 60 to 70 people there, their numbers alone a great shout of mockery at the Tory anti-union laws' insistence on six pickets. There was laughter and anger in equal measure—laughter among the pickets themselves, anger as the scabs' lorries came up the hill and turned into the gate. Inside the lorries, and inside the private cars of the supervisors, strike-breakers cowered, some of them hiding their face in balaclavas, others making a pathetic show of defiance, especially after they passed the gates. Each vehicle was greeted with a great roar of rage.

Afterwards, some pickets went home. Many others lingered in the sun. There were tea and ham rolls galore. The women crossed the road, laid out their chairs, sat down and talked.

Margaret Thompson had just come back from Norway where she picketed the headquarters of the Olsen line. She's been to London, Manchester, Newcastle, Brighton on delegations. She said:

> I've been a shop steward for 20 years but I never felt half what I feel today. I think it's because I realise my capabilities. I'm not just a worker at Timex. I've got a brain. If you do the same thing for 20 years, your brain goes soft. When I went into Timex as a girl, I was quiet as a lamb. Now I feel like a rottweiler.
>
> I think the best thing about this is you suddenly realise you have friends everywhere. At a factory in Newcastle they had exactly £110 in their coffers. After they heard us speak they gave us…£110, and I suddenly realised I was crying. They'd never met us, and they gave us everything.

Socialist Review June 1993

Jessie Britton joins in:

> They are always complaining about outside agitators. But where would we be without the people from outside who support us? When Campbell Christie (general secretary of the STUC) was here the other day, he came up to talk to me. He asked a young Militant supporter standing next to me: 'Do you work at Timex?' He knew the lad didn't. When the lad said no, Campbell looked at me knowingly, as if he knew I disapproved. But I told him straight we could never have got where we have without these young people selling papers and whipping up support for us.

Jessie doesn't think much of the constant advice from her union leaders to obey the law. 'They are worried about their assets,' she says, 'but we aren't worried about our assets. We haven't got any. What use are union assets to us if we lose the strike and can't have a union?'

I asked gingerly about the role of women in the strike. 'Oh', she laughed, 'right here the men do the dishes and the women do the fighting.'

All morning, the wit and banter were interrupted with furious shouts of invective whenever a scab lorry (usually from a firm called Scottish Express) delivered supplies. Debbie Osborne sums up the mood:

> When I was in there [contemptuous jerk of the head at the factory gates] I felt like a nobody. Now I feel a somebody. In fact I feel ten times more important than anyone in there.

I first went to Dundee as a reporter for the *Daily Record* in 1963 on an assignment to cover a by-election. John Strachey, who had only just won Dundee West in 1959, had died, and the Labour candidate was a nondescript Labour councillor called Peter Doig. Labour's campaign concentrated on the new prosperity of the city, one of the worst hit by the 1930s slump. Labour boasted, with some reason, of the enormous success of their post-war policy of shifting new industries into the unemployment blackspots of the 1930s. Nowhere was that policy more successful than in Dundee.

Boosted by huge grants and tax concessions, industry after industry settled in the purpose-built industrial estates round town. The old precarious industrial base of jute and shipbuilding was transformed by sparkling new modern factories making the consumer goods of the future, office equipment, wristwatches, fridges. The names most associated with this success were National Cash Register and Timex, each employing thousands of workers, each recognising trade unions whose stewards came to Labour's platforms glowing in their new-found confidence and strength. Labour won handsomely and won again just as well in the 1964 general election.

My reports for the *Daily Record* were all for Labour, all hostile to the cocksure jute manufacturer who stood for the Tories. But I was unimpressed by Labour's confidence. The huge corporations which owned these new industries were not Labour corporations. Labour had no control over, nor even a representative on, these distant capitalist boardrooms. What would happen if the post-war boom petered out? Would the first factories to suffer not be the ones which had been set up as outposts, the ones with strong unions in foreign countries?

So it proved. The two huge recessions of 1981 and 1990 played havoc with the new industry so lovingly and expensively redistributed to Dundee. National Cash Register and Timex are still there, pathetic shadows of what they used to be. Timex, for instance, now makes no watches at all. The strong union agreements of the 1960s have been replaced by 'sweetheart deals', even including no-strike deals, which left the stewards and rank and file permanently on the defensive.

A former president of the engineering union, Hugh Scanlon, once said in a famous TUC speech that every scratch on the trade union movement can lead to gangrene. The sweetheart approach of his successors led to gangrene soon enough.

Every concession by the unions was greeted by the employers with cries for more. In Dundee, like everywhere else, the employers, led on this occasion by the Engineering Employers Federation, started to yearn for the day when they would not have to deal with unions at all. True, the unions were a pushover. But how much more of a pushover would the workers be, how much more clear profit was there to be made, if the unions were utterly broken once and for all?

This is the fashionable thinking which led the US corporation which runs Timex to select an ardent Thatcherite from Surrey, Peter Hall, as the new president of their Scottish enterprise. Hall came armed with all the anti-union claptrap of US Timex's Human Resources Department. He started 'conversations' with selected workers which, they soon realised, were aimed at seeking out 'unhelpful elements'. He placed his own 'loyalist' spies in crucial positions.

Shortly before Christmas last year, he announced layoffs. On 5 January the workers all got letters—some 'thick' (the sack), others 'thin' (not the sack). They refused to accept the letters, and occupied the canteen. Hall promised negotiations. The workers went back to work, effectively accepting the principle of layoffs, though they balloted (92 percent) for a strike. From 8 to 29 January they worked rotating shifts to cover for their laid-off workmates, and waited for the negotiations which never came. There was no whisper of negotiation from Hall. A plea to go to ACAS was vigorously snubbed. On 29 January, frustrated by the constant prevarication, the workers came out on strike. On 17 February they reported en masse for work. They were told they could return only if they accepted a 10 percent cut in wages and other humiliations, including pension reductions. When they refused, they were locked out, and have been ever since.

The tactics of Hall and his Human Resources henchmen are familiar enough in this recession. Since the reaction of the Timex workers has been described by many commentators as 'old fashioned', it is worth recalling that Hall's union-busting dates back to the stockyards of Chicago in the first decade of the century, and even earlier. Now as then, success for them depends exclusively on workers' submission. All those in the trade union movement who have encouraged or tolerated such submission have played into the hands of the employers. Complete union organisations have been laid waste without even a gesture of revolt.

Timex, on the other hand, has become a byword in the whole British labour movement because the workers there refused to submit, and have set up a picket and a campaign so powerful that the Timex bosses are split. A historic, old fashioned victory is on the cards.

Only on the cards, however. The Engineering Employers Federation and their friends in the government will not decide one day simply to pack it in and let the workers back. They know full well what a disaster such a victory would be for employers all over Scotland.

The bosses want to win. They have the usual powerful allies. The Timex strike has the unanimous support of both local councils—Dundee City and Tayside. But the Dundee police still see it as their central duty to protect a rogue employer's inalienable right to hire scab labour and break strikes. The police behaviour on the mass demonstration on Monday 17 May was abominable. One young woman had her arm broken during arrest, was taken to hospital to have it set, hauled back to the cells, and kept behind bars for 27 hours until finally she was released without charge. Here is the classic outcome of total reliance on support from the Labour Party. Labour supports the strikers—in the councils, in the TUC, in its penetration of almost half the Scottish electorate. But Labour cannot prevent the police, whom they theoretically control, from protecting scabs or breaking the arm of a young woman who came to Dundee to express her solidarity with a cause Labour supports.

Almost everyone in Dundee supports the strike, but the machinery of the state in Dundee is determined to break it. If the momentum of the strike is lost even for a week, the EEF and its state will get its breath back, reassert itself, reorganise its newspapers (which have been curiously wobbly on the issue) and launch another offensive.

At the strike committee in the AEEU halls where I went after my morning on the picket line, the talk was all of keeping up the momentum, of boosting further the pickets and the delegations, of calling another mass demonstration outside Timex and seeking the help of more outside agitators.

These men and women are out to win. They deserve to win and they need to win. Above all, they can win. The entire resources—human and financial—of the labour movement should be put at their disposal.

How history comes alive

I met the historian Christopher Hill once, last summer. I went with BBC producer Fiona Maclean to interview him in his Warwickshire home for a programme about poetry and revolution.

He took us into his garden on a bright summer afternoon and questioned us closely on how much time he had on air. He ascertained that he had a quarter of an hour.

He then vanished upstairs and re-emerged staggering under a huge pile of books.

The tape recorder was switched on and he spoke, uninterrupted except by an infernal bee, referring to and quoting freely from his books for an hour. He spoke about Shakespeare, Andrew Marvell and above all John Milton, and their relationship to the English Revolution.

He spoke with such power and persuasive passion that we wondered, as we made our dazed way home, whether we should devote our whole 50 minutes to him alone.

After the interview I told him I had been searching everywhere for his *Milton and the English Revolution*, first published in 1978. Did he have a spare copy? No, he said nervously, he had none left.

So the search went on. It ended a year later on the top rung of a ladder in a second hand bookshop in Chicago.

Quaint and absurd

A book like this cannot be absorbed in snatched moments—it has to wait for a holiday. And so my summer holiday has been enriched beyond description by this wonderful book—the best, in my judgement, of all Christopher Hill's long lifetime's work on the English Revolution.

'I am arguing a case', he writes in his introduction.

That was a dangerous enough confession from the Master of Balliol College, but far more subversive when the 'case' was that

Socialist Worker 9 September 1993

John Milton, the academics' darling, the source of endless textual nitpicking from A level students to classical English Literature scholars, 'got his ideas not only from books but also from talking to his contemporaries'.

In other words a lot of *Paradise Lost*, *Paradise Regained*, and especially *Samson Agonistes* has more to do with the 'loony left'—known in the mid-17th century as Levellers, Diggers, Ranters, Muggletonians etc—than with any classical text or Latin scholarship.

Christopher Hill's great genius as a historian is not just that he can think himself back 300 years, and translate what often seem quaint and absurd religious discussions into the politics of the time.

The relationship of the Son to the Father, the Trinity, the destination of the soul after death, the Serpent and the Apple, Adam and Eve—all these dead notions come alive in the revolutionary forces of the time.

Some of this is hard to follow but, thanks to Christopher Hill's dry humour and unbending commitment, never difficult to read. For example:

> When a modern theologian writes 'it would no longer seem appropriate to speak of a God existing apart from man, or a human self existing apart from God', we may dismiss this as an attempt to adapt Christianity to the modern world, to preserve a God who is in fact dead.
>
> But we should not let our scepticism about trendy modern theologians reflect back upon the fantastic daring of the 17th century thinkers, who expressed their hard won belief in the importance of human beings through the medium of theology.
>
> For them it was not a trick, not a last hope of drawing a congregation: it was a tremendous and tremendously new concept, won through spiritual torment and exaltation.

Defiant laughter

In the prevailing gloom one or two lights shine out brightly. One of them is Ken Loach. Another is Ricky Tomlinson.

The other day Ken was interviewed by Melvyn Bragg on *The South Bank Show*. Bragg's light does not shine at all. He is one of the new millionaires, after cashing in on the share options in London Weekend Television which were granted by the directors and 'personalities' to each other with the single purpose of making each other rich.

Still, Bragg gave up a lot of his programme to Ken Loach, whose film about the miners' strike he had once censored.

Explaining the censorship, Bragg said he had wanted 'art' not politics. He accused Ken Loach of having a 'political agenda'.

'Yes', came the reply, modest but firm. 'I am not ducking that at all.'

'What do you mean?' asked Bragg, who is still a strong supporter of the Labour Party.

'I mean', said Ken Loach, 'that the future lies in common ownership and democratic control of the society by the people who work in it.'

Bragg shut up and went on to discuss art.

He did not comment on the courage and strength of a film-maker who has dedicated all his huge talent to what he believes in.

Special genius

Ken made films to expose the world we live in—in particular *Cathy Come Home*, a classic about homelessness.

But his special genius was to capture the reality of working class life—the pathos and anger which lies behind the bare political anger. He went on making these films as more and more of his formerly radical friends and colleagues fell away into glamour and success.

In the early 1980s he was horrified by the trade union leaders' surrender to the Thatcher onslaught. His four programmes, *Questions of*

Socialist Worker 16 October 1994

Leadership, have been banned ever since they were made by every television channel.

The ban held up Ken's film-making for half a decade, but he never flinched from his insistence that there should be no political censorship, especially in the name of 'art'.

Bragg asked him about his new film *Raining Stones* and chided him about the sentimental 'happy ending' to the film.

Ken's reply was that what needs stressing now is not just the wretchedness of working class life, not just the constant failures and dashing of hopes, but the resilience. If there were unhappy endings to his films when we were winning, there should be happy endings when we are losing, to remind us of our strength and potential.

Ken Loach has always used a small group of actors whom he trusts and who think the same way he does. I'm not sure when he stumbled on Ricky Tomlinson, but it was a glorious meeting. Ricky's uproarious defiant performance in Ken's film about the building trade in London, *Riff Raff*, was magnificent.

I haven't seen *Raining Stones* yet, but the clips are all of Ricky Tomlinson defying and laughing.

I have no doubt that the most exhilarating journalistic assignment I ever had was to travel at five in the morning to Leicester in the summer of 1975 to welcome Ricky Tomlinson as he came out of prison.

He had got two years after a prosecution inspired and masterminded by the McAlpine family for holding together the 1972 building workers' strike in Shropshire and North Wales.

When Ricky came out of the prison he was laughing. His message to the reporters was that even prison could be defied.

It was a great performance, but he was not acting. And, in partnership with Ken Loach, he still isn't.

Up the Levellers

'The poorest he that is in England hath a life to live as the greatest he.'
This assertion by Colonel Thomas Rainborowe in November 1647
seems almost a cliché, as much part of the democratic history of England
as the Magna Carta or the Tolpuddle Martyrs or Paine's *Rights of
Man*. Yet for two and a half centuries after Rainborowe said his piece,
no one knew anything about it. The colonel's controversial view was
expressed in the middle of a furious debate at the General Council of
the New Model Army, which was meeting in Putney at the height of
the English Revolution. The debate was scribbled down in shorthand
by the army secretary, William Clarke, who had a remarkable knack
for appearing at and recording decisive historical events. He was, for
instance, on the scaffold at Westminster 14 months later, on a cold January
morning in 1649, when King Charles had his head cut off.

Clarke carefully bound his record of the Putney Debates with all
his other voluminous notes, and left them to his son George. George,
a solid Restoration Tory, was also a Fellow of All Souls College,
Oxford. He quarrelled with the college authorities, and sulked off to
Worcester College, to which he bequeathed his huge library. His
father's record of the Putney Debates lay buried, unseen and apparently
unnoticed, in the bowels of the college library for the whole of
the 18th and most of the 19th centuries. During that time, historians
of the English Revolution had to make do with state papers and
memoirs. When, in old age, William Godwin came to write his four-
volume *History of the Commonwealth*, he had no idea that the Putney
Debates had ever taken place. His surprising hostility to the Leveller
Party of the 1640s was founded on his deep suspicion of any political
activism which went further than words or argument. His stern
approach to the Levellers, who were in truth his ideological ancestors,
might have been seasoned—and his account enormously improved—if he could have savoured in full one of the most passionate
and crucial arguments in English history.

London Review of Books 9 December 1994

In the late 1880s, a young history don at Oxford, Charles Firth, called on Mr H A Pottinger, the librarian at Worcester, who'd revealed that he had uncovered something remarkable. To Firth's excitement, the librarian produced William Clarke's bound volumes, including his record, carefully transcribed from his own shorthand, of the debates at Putney. Firth worked on the manuscript, trying to make sense of the innumerable gaps, the hasty insertions, the wrongly-numbered pages. He handed the first results of his endeavours to his hero and mentor, the historian Samuel Rawson Gardiner, who was just completing the first edition of his monumental *History of the English Civil War*. Delighted at the discovery, Gardiner crammed into his third volume a typically fair and faithful account of the Putney Debates. In 1891, 244 years after it was spoken, Colonel Rainborowe's declaration was published.

The democratic significance of the Putney Debates was not fully appreciated, however. Firth's version of the Clarke papers was published only in a scholarly edition by the Camden Society. Even as the poorest he, and, much later, the poorest she won the right to vote, the arguments and aspirations of the Levellers, who were the first to demand a widespread franchise, were confined to a small circle. The few scholars who took the Levellers seriously—G P Gooch, say, or the American Theodore Pease—restricted themselves to short sections on the Putney Debates. In 1938, a new edition of the debates was published by A S P Woodhouse, with a foreword by the radical Oxford don, A D Lindsay, who had stood in a famous by-election that year as an anti-Tory candidate. Woodhouse's version gave life and spirit to the debates, and became popular reading in the rising radical tide of the late 1930s and 1940s. It inspired many of the debates that took place in the British army at the end of the Second World War—debates which laid much of the foundation for the Labour landslide of 1945.

In 1645 the New Model Army, under Oliver Cromwell and Thomas Fairfax, had successfully defended parliament against the King. Charles I, licking his wounds, was determined not to concede an inch of his divine right or a penny of his royal income. The majority of the landed gentlemen in parliament were determined to do a deal with the king. They were delighted that the army had cut Charles down to size but, terrified of the new and efficient military power they had created, they demanded that the army be disbanded, or, better still, packed off to slaughter Catholics in Ireland. What they overlooked was that the army they were trying to disband consisted of young officers and a rank and file who knew their power and were determined not to let it slip back into the hands of the Presbyterian parliament. The more that reactionary majority and their friends in the City demanded that the army disband, the closer the army moved to London. In August 1647 it entered the City, forced its arrears of pay from a suddenly compliant City and persuaded parliament to reverse all its demands for disbandment. Only then did the army retire, but not far away, to Hammersmith and Putney.

For months the army had seethed with democratic ideas. The troops elected 'agitators': 'At the time,' Ian Gentles reassures his readers, 'the word "agitator" had none of its modern pejorative ring, and meant simply one who has been empowered to act on behalf of others.' There was, however, nothing remotely 'simple' about such a proposition. The idea that a rank and file soldier could represent and make decisions for his fellows was as alarming to the men of property in the 1640s as it is today. Even worse, the rank and file, once they sniffed democracy, were determined to keep it and extend it. They demanded, and got, a printing press. They insisted, and got, representatives on a new executive, the General Council of the army. Above all, they linked up with the Leveller Party, the first ever 'left wing' party in Britain, which had its own elected executive and its own regular newspaper. The Levellers and their new recruits in the army proposed something even more alarming than agitation. They proposed that parliament be elected by the people.

The General Council of the army was due to meet on 28 October 1647. On 27 October a document was delivered to the Putney headquarters. It was called 'An Agreement of the People', and was signed by agitators from five regiments. It was most certainly written by the most persuasive of the Leveller leaders, William Walwyn. It was simple and concise. Its central demand was that the very next year 'the people do chuse themselves a parliament.' This was a central issue in the Putney Debates, which took place under Cromwell's chairmanship the next day, and spilled over into further angrier sessions on 1 November and 2 November. The council was dominated by agitators who favoured the extended franchise. The opposition was left to Cromwell, who tried to refer the more controversial questions to a committee and to his son-in-law, the Commissary General, Henry

Ireton. 'I think', Ireton said, 'that no person has a right to an interest
or share in the disposing of the affairs of the kingdom and in deter-
mining or choosing those that shall determine what laws we shall be
ruled by here—no person has a right to this that hath not a permanent
fixed interest in the kingdom.' After all, he went on (and on and on)
was there not a danger that a parliament elected by the people might
confiscate property? And if that could happen, was this not taking
away a 'fundamental part of the civil constitution'?

Ireton's main opponent was Colonel Rainborowe, who followed up
his famous remark about the poorest he with something even more
important:

> And therefore truly, Sir, I think it's clear that every man that is to live
> under a government ought first by his own consent to put himself
> under that government.

Back and forth the argument raged between the rank and file, who
argued for a representative democracy, and the grandees, who could
not understand how any political system could survive which threatened those whom Ireton called 'the persons in whom all land lies, and
those in corporations in whom all trading lies'.

It is an argument which has been raging ever since. The vote
started to be conceded, reluctantly and gradually, more than 200
years later, but its democratic impact was skilfully and comprehensively
contained by the persons in whom all land lies and the corporations
in whom all trading lies. Rainborowe and his allies won the vote in
the army council that misty November afternoon in Putney.

They won again in the Whitehall Debates the following year,
after the second civil war. Once again, the majority who wanted to
establish a freely-elected parliament with most men voting was
coolly ignored, and went on being ignored until the Levellers were
crushed in 1649. Eleven years after that, in 1660, the entire revolution was overthrown, another even more ridiculous king was en-
throned, and the franchise for almost everyone postponed for two
and a half centuries.

There is no more exciting period in English history than 1647 to
1649. No wonder so many historians have swarmed around it. No
wonder that Woodhouse's rendering of the Clarke papers was reprinted
in 1951, 1955, 1966, 1974 and 1986. No wonder that the arguments
of the time are mirrored by similar squabbles among scholars, some

of whom pretend to be free from bias. Charles Firth's *Cromwell's Army* (1902) is a careful, rather tedious, study of minutiae about provisions, discipline, artillery, etc. Mark Kishlansky's *The Rise of the New Model Army* was published in 1979, the first year of the Thatcher government, an appropriate time for his revelation that there was nothing very political about the New Model Army and indeed nothing very revolutionary about the 1640s. Ian Gentles is not dull like Firth or reactionary like Kishlansky. He tells his story with relish and verve. At times he gets so caught up in the debates that he invents reactions to them:

> Rainborowe's sardonic comment, 'I see that it is impossible to have liberty but all property must be taken away,' must have prompted a murmur of approval. Encouraged, he continues…

The murmurs and the encouragement can be put down to Enthusiastic Historian's Licence, by no means a fault. Mr Gentles knows his feelings and does not disguise them. He is excited by the revolutionaries he describes, but on the whole he does not approve of them. He finds the Leveller leader John Lilburne 'long-winded and conceited'; Rainborowe 'truculent' and 'sour'; William Thompson, who fought to a heroic death in the 1649 Leveller mutiny, 'at bottom was one of those figures who is familiar in all revolutions; the man of violent or criminal propensities who for a time camouflages his lawlessness beneath the rhetoric of resistance to unjust authority'.

Gentles pooh-poohs the demands for universal suffrage with the (irrelevant) projection that it would have led to a Royalist majority in parliament, ridicules the idea that the army could have been paid by soaking the rich, and is on the lookout all the time for 'extremists'. I think I detect in certain tell-tale Gentles phrases (most notably, 'the locomotive of history') a Marxist training. If so, as so often, the training has been abandoned for something much safer. He is back on track with Gardiner and Firth, adoring respectable revolutionaries like Cromwell and Fairfax, excited by the revolution but suspicious and frightened of its consequences.

Yet his account is so comprehensive and fair that it cannot suppress the truth about the achievement and the political daring of the Levellers. There was never more solidarity in the army than at the height of debate and discussion. John Lilburne may or may not have been a bore, but it was his astonishing personal courage and persistence that dragged a prisoner's 'right to silence' from reluctant authorities: a right considered so important by American revolutionaries in the 1770s that they wrote it into their new constitution. It lasted in Britain for nearly 350 years. The Levellers wrote some of the greatest political pamphlets in our history. When George Orwell picked out his plums of English pamphlets, he included *Tyranipocrit*, a glorious outpouring of invective against the twin monster—the Tyrant who oppresses and his chief ally, the Hypocrite, who justifies the oppression. Until recently, it was assumed that this was written by William Walwyn, though the editors of a recent anthology of the *Writings of William Walwyn* (Georgia, 1989) ascribe it to an anonymous Leveller in exile.

There is no doubt at all who wrote *The Hunting of the Foxes*, an ever-topical assault on revolutionary grandees who betray and persecute the people who fought for them:

> Was there ever a generation of men so apostate, so false and so perjured as these?… You shall scarce speak to Cromwell about anything, but he will lay his hand on his breast, elevate his eyes and call God to record, he will weep, howl and repent even while he doth smite you under the fifth rib.

The author was Richard Overton, the father of all challenging journalism.

Overton had neither the wisdom of Walwyn nor the maniacal courage of Lilburne. His most precious weapon was his wit, which he wielded savagely against hypocrites of all kinds, especially clerical hypocrites. He could see both sides of an argument as clearly as he could make up his mind on one of them, and he could always, even when his colleagues were infuriated by it, see the joke. There was no more eloquent representative of the spirit and achievement of these Levellers. For all his suspicion of these 'extremists', Ian Gentles cannot keep them down.

First published as a review of The New Model Army in England, Ireland and Scotland 1645-53 *by Ian Gentles (Blackwell 1994).*

A passionate prophet of liberation

In London in the 1790s, like in London today, it was commonplace to see a woman being beaten up in the street, and equally common for embarrassed or irritated bystanders to pass by on the other side. William Blake had a short temper and often lost it. Walking in the St Giles area, and seeing a woman attacked, he launched himself on the scene with such ferocity that the assailant 'recoiled and collapsed'. When the abuser recovered, he told a bystander that he thought he had been attacked by the 'devil himself'. At around the same time Blake was standing at his window looking over the yard of his neighbour when he saw a boy 'hobbling along with a log tied to his foot'. Immediately he stormed across and demanded in the most violent terms that the boy should be freed. The neighbour replied hotly that Blake was trespassing and had no business interfering in other people's property (which included, of course, other people's child labour). The furious argument which followed was only resolved when the boy was released.

Some years later, in 1803, Blake was living in a country cottage in Sussex when he came across a soldier lounging in his garden. Blake greeted the soldier with a volley of abuse, and frogmarched him to the local pub where he was billeted. The soldier later testified that as they went, Blake muttered repeatedly, 'Damn the king. The soldiers are all slaves.' In the south of England in 1803, when soldiers were billeted in every village for fear of a Napoleonic invasion, such a statement was criminal treachery. The soldier promptly sneaked to his superiors. Blake was tried for sedition, and escaped deportation and even possibly a death sentence largely because the soldier made a mess of his evidence and because no one in court knew anything about Blake's revolutionary views which had been openly expressed ten years previously. He was found not guilty, and went on writing for

International Socialism Summer 1996

another 23 years until his death. He never once swerved from his intense loathing of king, soldiers and slavery.

These are two of the hundreds of anecdotes in Peter Ackroyd's glorious biography which will warmly commend Blake to any reader even remotely committed to reform. This warmth enthuses the whole book. Ackroyd revels in Blake's 'exuberant hopefulness' which grew out of his passionate rage at the world he saw around him. The *Songs of Innocence* and the *Songs of Experience* which he wrote in the first fine careless rapture of the French Revolution are presented here not just in scholarly textual analysis but in admiration and wonder. Here is Blake's disgust with slavery in 'The Little Black Boy':

> My mother bore me in the southern wild,
> And I am black, but O! my soul is white;
> White as an angel is the English child:
> But I am black as if bereav'd of light.

The English child might indeed be 'white as an angel' but, if unlucky enough not to be born rich, he or she was likely to be a victim of the vilest exploitation. Ackroyd sets out the whole of Blake's *Song of Innocence* called 'The Chimney Sweeper', which moves in six short verses from utter misery:

> When my mother died I was very young
> And my father sold me while yet my tongue
> Could scarcely cry weep weep weep weep
> So your chimneys I sweep and in soot I sleep.

To hope, in a dream which first sees all the sweeps in coffins, until:

> And by came an angel who had a bright key
> And he opened the coffins and set them all free.
> Then down a green plain leaping laughing they run
> And wash in a river and shine in the Sun.

And back again to a last verse which seems like an anti-climax:

> And so Tom awoke and we rose in the dark
> And got with our bags and our brushes to work.

Tho' the morning was cold, Tom was happy and warm,
So if all do their duty, they need not fear harm.

When I first read that last verse, I took it for what it seemed: a sell out of the indignation which sets the poem off. How does Peter Ackroyd explain it?

> It has been suggested that this closing line is in sharp contrast to the rest of the poem, but in fact it maintains precisely the same note; the innocence of the speaker, and of Tom himself, is a destructive and ignorant innocence because it actively complies both with the horrors of the climbing trade and of the society that accepts it without thought. It is the 'unorganised innocence' that can persuade a deformed or dying sweep that he is happy, after all, while confirming the credulous or the sanctimonious in their belief that 'duty' is all that needs to be, or can be done. Blake has dramatised a 'state' or an attitude without in the least acceding to it; then in the companion poem within *Songs of Experience* that shares the same title, he emphasises his disgust:

And because I am happy, and dance and sing,
They think they have done me no injury:
And are gone to praise God and his Priest and King
Who make up a heaven of our misery.

The point that the *Songs of Experience* often harden up the *Songs of Innocence* is also made by Edward Thompson, who does what Ackroyd has done for 'The Chimney Sweeper' for the 'Song of Experience' called 'London'.

I wander thro' each chartered street
Near where the chartered Thames does flow
And mark in every face I meet
Marks of weakness, marks of woe.

In every cry of every man,
In every infant's cry of fear
in every voice; in every ban,
The mind-forged manacles I hear.

How the chimney sweeper's cry
Every blackning Church appalls;
And the hapless soldier's sigh
Runs in blood down palace walls

But most thro' midnight streets I hear
How the youthful harlots' curse
Blasts the new-born infants' tear
And blights with plague the marriage hearse.

Edward Thompson traces the use of the word 'chartered' to the controversy between Edmund Burke (against the French Revolution) and Thomas Paine (for it). The 'chartered' towns excluded from any vestige of control what Burke called 'the swinish multitude'. The soldier gave his blood for the palaces, and the chimney sweep his life and limbs for the churches. Prostitution was the other side of the coin to marriage. The swinish multitude crops up again in a savage poem about a 'chapel all of gold' from which Blake sees a serpent turning away:

Vomiting his poison out
On the bread and on the wine.
So I turned into a sty
And laid me down among the swine.

Blake could see more clearly than most of his contemporaries the rising consciousness of a new class which was being robbed as ruthlessly as any of its predecessors, and he sided unequivocally with the exploited and the poor. This commitment was never dull, never repetitive. It was invigorated and complemented by Blake's illustrations and engravings. He annotated the books he read with neat and powerful notes which still survive and disclose his ideas and how he expressed them. The smooth talking, smooth painting and very fashionable Sir Joshua Reynolds was dealt with like this:

Reynolds: I felt my ignorance, and stood abashed.
Blake: A Liar. He never was abashed in his life and never felt his ignorance.
Reynolds: I consoled myself by remarking that these ready inventors are extremely apt to acquiesce in imperfection.

Blake: Villainy. A lie.

Reynolds: But the disposition to abstractions is the great glory of the human mind.

Blake: To generalise is to be an idiot. To particularise is the alone distinction of merit. General Knowledges are those knowledges that idiots possess.

Reynolds: The great use in copying, if it be at all useful, should seem to be in learning to colour.

Blake: Contemptible.

Reynolds: But as mere enthusiasm will carry you but a little way...

Blake: Damn the fool. Mere enthusiasm is all in all.

Thompson calls this Blake's 'robust contempt' for the high and mighty, which he held in common with the other great iconoclastic poets of his time, notably Byron. Like Byron, Blake's first reaction to the pretensions of great men was to laugh out loud. Byron's view of his former foreign secretary Lord Castlereagh was succinctly expressed over the great man's grave:

Posterity will ne'er survey
A nobler scene than this.
Here lie the bones of Castlereagh.
Stop traveller, and piss.

And here was Blake on the subject of the most respected philosopher of his day (and his devotion to the classics):

A ha to Dr Johnson
Said Scipio Africanus
Lift up my Roman petticoat
And kiss my Roman anus.

Add to all this Blake's enduring belief in sexual liberation as a necessary condition of human freedom. 'Enjoyment and not abstinence is the food of intellect' was his motto. Most sex was shut up in private fantasy:

The moment of desire! The moment of desire! The virgin
That pines for man shall awaken her womb to enormous joys
In the secret shadows of her chambers; the youth shut up from

Lustful joy shall forget to generate, & create an amorous image
In the shadows of his curtains and in the folds of his silent pillow.

One answer was 'lovely copulation, bliss on bliss', a regular theme
for Blake, especially in his paintings and engravings. None of this was
poetic licence for the release of male libido, as it plainly was for the
Swedish theologian Emmanuel Swedenborg, whose church Blake
joined. Blake, a bitter enemy of monogamy when applied as a church
and state edict, lived all his life in apparently harmonious monogamy.
He was at his testiest when official theorists and priests argued for discrimination against and/or seclusion of women. His views on these matters were close to those of his great contemporary, Mary Wollstonecraft.

Perhaps it was his constant harping on these sexual questions which
explains another feature of Blake's life common to many other reforming writers of the time. As Ackroyd points out, 'He remained
quite unknown in his lifetime.' His engraving was patronised by famous
writers and artists of the time, notably Henry Fuseli, but usually only
for hack work, much of which has perished. The poems which have
fascinated critics all through the 20th century were hardly published,
let alone read in his lifetime. He printed the *Songs* himself, very expensively, and sold very few copies. *The Four Zoas*, which Ackroyd
describes as 'one of the most extraordinary documents of the decades
spanning the 18th and 19th centuries', wasn't published until 1889,
63 years after Blake's death. Again, most of Blake's contemporaries
dismissed him as 'mad'. As he got older, people referred to him more
and more as 'the mad visionary'. Even W H Auden a century and a
half later declared that 'Blake went dotty as he sang'. In fact, of course,
he was not mad at all. His close friend and colleague John Linell admitted he was often shocked by Blake but affirmed, 'I never saw anything the least like madness.' The reason for his 'madness' was familiar:
he swam against the stream and refused to compromise what he said
and never painted for commercial fortune.

The hostility of polite society which prescribed him mad ended
when he died. In old age he was, as ever, penniless and, as one shocked
visitor put it, 'dirty'. There were six people, including his wife, at his
funeral and he was buried in a common grave. But death changed the
open hostility to Blake into a grudging patronage which still prevails.
Schoolchildren are taught to learn by rote the famous poem 'Tiger,
Tiger'. They chant happily:

In what distant deeps or skies
Burnt the fire of thine eyes?

But which of them connects the poem, written late in 1792, to the
French Revolution, or to the press references after the September
massacres in Paris to 'tribunals of tigers' or to the eyes of Jean-Paul
Marat gleaming 'like those of a tiger cat?' And which of those Tory
matrons who round off their party conference every year with a spir-
ited rendering of Blake's poem 'Jerusalem' have the remotest idea
what Blake meant when he cried out for 'arrows of desire'? How many
of them have any idea, either, how determined was the commitment
in his pledge, 'I will not cease from mental fight'?

Determined, filled with contempt for the rich and sympathy with
the exploited and the poor, an eloquent and passionate prophet of liberation of every kind, sane to his friends and family, mad to the outside world, dogged by poverty and calumny all through his 70 years,
his poems and his art ignored in his life and patronised after it—
Blake seems to fit exactly into the pattern of other revolutionary
poets of the time, most notably Shelley, who lived in London not far
from Blake but never met him, and died aged 29 when Blake was 65.
Can we happily place Blake alongside Shelley in the line of British
poets and writers who emerged out of the French Enlightenment of
the late 18th century and filled the gap between the revolutions of
1789 and 1848?

No, we cannot. Here is the paradox about Blake, which is firmly
tackled in different ways by both these books. Blake shared with Shelley all the qualities mentioned above. Yet there was a great gulf fixed
between them. Shelley revered the Enlightenment, hailed the great
contribution to democracy of Rousseau, the anti-clericalism of D'Hol-
bach, the secular encyclopedias of Diderot. Above all, he worshipped
at the shrine of 'reason's mighty lore'. He was a rationalist, bitterly opposed to religion of every kind. He believed in open political activity to change the world. He wrote political pamphlets, tried to form
political associations, subscribed to the campaigns to release the victims of oppression.

Blake was none of these things and did none of them. Though he
knew the circle round Thomas Paine, Holcroft, Horne Tooke and
Mary Wollstonecraft, he did not associate with them. The story,
made into a BBC play, that he advised Paine to flee from London is,

Peter Ackroyd assures us, almost certainly apocryphal. This is how Peter Ackroyd explains the difference between Blake and the Painites:

> In many respects he was utterly unlike them. If points of religion had been brought up, for example, there would have been manifest differences. His friend in later life, Tatham, adds substance to the suggestion: 'In one of their conversations, Paine said that religion was a law and a tie to all able minds. Blake on the other hand said what he was always asserting: that the religion of Jesus was the perfect law of Liberty.' Paine also dismissed Isaiah as 'one continual incoherent rant' and Blake celebrated the glory of that prophet. Blake could hardly have been an enthusiast for the works of Joseph Priestley, whose materialism and predestinarianism were utterly opposed to everything Blake considered holy. Nor can he have been very impressed by Mary Wollstonecraft's belief in the 'law of reason' and 'rational religion'.

Blake came from an entirely different tradition, a tradition which execrated the 'reason' which inspired Paine, Mary Wollstonecraft, Priestley and Shelley. As we have seen, he attended the newly formed New Church of Jerusalem which propagated the views of the Swedish mystic Emmanuel Swedenborg. This was a Christian sect whose origins, like so many of its kind, derived from the eternal argument between the paid professionals of the Christian church established and maintained by ruling class robbers, and ordinary believers who want to keep their faith secure from the grasp of governments, monarchs, landowners and priests. Almost all these sects, therefore, practised and preached political disengagement as an essential feature of their faith. The Swedenborgians were specially insistent on this. They abominated the ridiculous tenets of the Trinity, with all the obeisance to God and God's representatives on earth which it entails, and replaced it with a 'divine presence' in all human beings. Part of the proof of that divine presence was a devotion to sectarian secrecy which kept the believers apart from the real world. They were seen as cranks, of course, and therefore as suspect revolutionaries. When a drunken Birmingham mob, bribed by the authorities, sacked and burned the house of the rationalist Joseph Priestley, they headed for the Swedenborgian's church to do the same. The church's pastor, appropriately named Proud, rushed out to head off the crowd, explaining that he and his church had nothing to do with temporal matters such as the French Revolution or Joseph Priestley, and brandishing gold coins which he pressed into the mob leaders' hands. This worked perfectly, and the crowd went away.

Ackroyd and Thompson prove that Blake was no uncritical Swedenborgian. He criticised the New Church again and again. But his ideas were sharply hostile to those of the rational Enlightenment. Where did they come from? EP Thompson strives to find a 'vector' which carried Blake's ideas to him from the 17th century. He fastens on a sect which grew up around John Reeve and Ludowich Muggleton after the defeat of the Levellers in 1649. This Muggletonian sect, as it became known, was 'antinomian', that is, 'against the law'. Its followers argued that the only real law was the law of the divine spirit inside each individual. The Muggletonians were subversive because they defied the law, but they blunted their subversiveness by keeping themselves to themselves in strict sectarian isolation.

Half Edward Thompson's book rather apologetically struggles and strains to establish this 'missing vector' between the Muggletonians and Blake. With one rather doubtful exception he can't find a single credible connection. But he does provide an argument for some form of thread between Blake and the antinomian sectarians who sprung up during the Commonwealth and survived right up to his time (they only died out recently. Thompson himself met the last of the Muggletonians— in Tunbridge Wells!).

The Muggletonians and Blake, Thompson argues, were suspicious of reason. Of course, the 'reason' and 'common sense' they disliked were the 'reason' and 'common sense' of upper class intellectuals who told ordinary people what to think. But this spilled over into a suspicion of the 'reason' and 'common sense' of people like Thomas Paine whose purpose was exactly the opposite: to assault and expose the rhetoric and arguments of the rulers, and to agitate among the ruled for action to change the world. In this sense, as Thompson grudgingly concludes, antinomian sects like the Muggletonians found themselves in opposition to the intellectual forces which led to the French Revolution.

If William Blake was suspicious of its intellectual origins, however, he was most definitely not opposed to the revolution. For a short time he even walked the streets wearing the cap of liberty. The second half of Thompson's book, which is much more exciting than the first, argues that for this short time there took place in Blake 'a conjunction between the old antinomian tradition and Jacobinism'.

Thompson's close study of poems like 'London', 'The Human Abstract' and 'The Garden of Love' reveals a 'burning indictment of the acquisitive ethic' which goes far beyond the bounds of Muggletonian mysticism and takes Blake close to the revolutionaries.

This is all fascinating, especially from a historian of the stamp of E P Thompson, whose *The Making of the English Working Class* (1973) is a classic for any socialist who wants to understand this period. But in trying to force the two traditions together, the rationalist revolutionary and the spiritualist antinomian, Thompson seems to abandon many of the lessons he himself spelt out in his monumental history. He writes:

> If Blake found congenial the Painite denunciation of the repressive institutions of State and Church, it did not follow that humanity's redemption from this state could be effected by a political reorganisation of these institutions alone. There must be some utopian leap, some human re-birth, from Mystery to renewed imaginative life.

This is not just an account of Paine's view. It seems to be Thompson's view too, for he repeats the phrase 'utopian leap' in the final paragraph of his book and concludes:

> To create the New Jerusalem something must be brought in from outside the rationalist system, and that something could be found only in the non-rational image of Jesus, in the affirmatives of Mercy, Pity, Peace and Love.

No conclusion of that kind can be found in *The Making of the English Working Class*, which starts with the founding of the London Corresponding Society, a working class organisation with 'members unlimited' which fought precisely and exclusively for parliamentary reform: that is, for the 'political reorganisation of the institutions of State and Church'. The Society backed up the more feeble Society for Constitutional Information. *The Making of the English Working Class* goes on to chronicle all the attempts by the new 'reformers from below' to challenge and change the unrepresentative and repressive monarchy, parliament, press, church, landowners and employers who ruled Britain. There was no call from any of these reformers for a 'utopian leap', perhaps because no practical political leap, by definition, can be utopian. 'Comrades, we shall now proceed to accomplish a utopian leap' is not a practical slogan. The whole concept is an abstraction. The chief consequence of relying on an abstraction is political quietism. If you wait and hope for a utopian leap, there is nothing you can do about it. You can only wait and hope.

Blake joined the New Church of the boring and ridiculous Swedenborgians, but he did not join the London Corresponding Society, or even the Society for Constitutional Information. He showed no interest in any of the agitations for parliamentary reform or against the gagging acts and repressive legislation at the end of the 1790s. When the Luddite leaders were hanged in 1813, there was no donation for their families from Blake (as there was from Shelley). When the leaders of the Pentridge uprising (1817) were executed or the Manchester yeomanry mowed down the parliamentary reformers at Peterloo (1819) there was no protest from Blake (as there was on both occasions from Shelley). Thompson compares Blake unfavourably to William Godwin, who is deservedly denounced for spouting his polite philosophy from the sidelines. But at least Godwin risked his neck by publicly supporting his friends on trial for treason in 1794, which is more than Blake managed to do. Indeed, on more than one occasion, when the authorities threatened persecution, Blake specifically adapted and softened his language to keep himself clear of the prosecutors. If there was, as Thompson argues, a brief moment where his antinomianism merged with a Jacobin sense of outrage, the moment soon passed, and he hurried back to his splendid isolation.

Peter Ackroyd quotes back at Blake a comment from his hero Milton:

> I cannot praise a fugitive and cloister'd virtue, unexercis'd and unbreath'd, that never sallies out and sees her adversary, but slinks out of the race, where that immortal garland is to be fought for, not without dust and heat.

Blake, Ackroyd continues, 'eschewed the "heat" of any public voice or role, but, as a result, it is as if he were another Milton raging in a darkened room'. I find all this illuminating because I confess that the bulk of Blake's longer poems have always mystified and often irritated me. I do not mean only that the poems seem constantly to dissolve into imagery or metaphor. A lot of Shelley's poetry does that too. But the imagery in Blake is too abstract, too unrelated, too much founded on utopian leaps. E P Thompson recognises this vagueness, but comes round to it. In one sense he almost revels in Blake's isolation and his assaults on what Thompson (I think wrongly) calls 'ideology'. Perhaps at the end of his life Thompson found in Blake some solace for his own political loneliness. Peter Ackroyd, a Blake enthusiast to the last, is more circumspect:

> His poetry is often one of declaration and assertion, just as his art resides upon the pictorial plane; much of his creative activity takes place on the immediate surface and there are occasions when an image, or a verse, seems to have no concerted or established sense—with the proviso of course that this indeterminacy, this missing signification, is often part of a work's power. It is like the oblique character of the man himself who, according to one interlocutor, made assertions without bothering with argument or debate; his work shares that same denotative brilliance, but sometimes at the expense of bewildering those who encounter it.

I enrol myself in the ranks of the bewildered. But I will not end there, because both these books have led me back to Blake and dug up treasures previously buried in mysticism and symbolism. The whole point of the poets who flourished in revolutionary times and who did not bow the knee to God or King or Law is that they have something significant to say to future revolutionaries. Blake should be read precisely because he was a maverick, a pain in the neck not just to the rulers but also to those who more formally and more rationally opposed the rulers. Whatever his religious origins and however haughty his disengagement, he believed perhaps more passionately than all his contemporaries in human emancipation, and he lived his life accordingly. In particular, he needs to be read by any socialist who imagines that in a society where labour is emancipated everyone will be the same and want the same.

Is there anyone attempting to work in the tradition of William Blake today? Well, there is Leon Rosselson, a veteran London singer so full of wonderful tunes and emancipating poems that he is ignored by polite society as systematically as Blake was. His latest CD, *Intruders*, is full of both; and I commend it heartily as I commend both these books, especially Peter Ackroyd's. The CD ends with a tune I find myself humming almost everywhere. The chorus is pure Blake, incorporating on the one hand the isolated, individualistic Blake who preferred abstract divinity to politics, and, on the other, the revolutionary Blake who saw perhaps more clearly than anyone else the fantastic, kaleidoscopic potential of human liberation:

> For all things are holy, the poet once said,
> And all that is different is part of the dance.
> And the web of life's colours needs each single thread
> For the dance to continue unbroken.

First published as a review of Blake *by Peter Ackroyd (Sinclair-Stevenson 1995) and* Witness Against the Beast: William Blake and the Moral Law *by E P Thompson (Cambridge University Press 1993).*

Red verse in Horsham

In 1892 the playwright and critic Bernard Shaw was invited to Horsham to take part in a lunch to celebrate the first centenary of the birth of the poet Shelley.

Unhappily for important people in this market town, Shelley is probably the only famous person ever to have been born in Horsham, so they had to make the best of it. In 1892 they had their lunch and opened a public library.

Shaw mocked them mercilessly.

> On all sides there went up the cry: 'We want our great Shelley, our darling Shelley, our best noblest highest of poets. We will not have it said that he was a Leveller, an atheist, a foe to marriage, an advocate of incest.'

Shaw got the 5.19 back to London and went to another Shelley celebration meeting in the East End, composed almost entirely of working people which, he reported, 'beat Horsham hollow'.

A hundred and four years later the chief executive of Horsham District Council (controlled by the Liberals, with a Tory opposition and no Labour representation at all) rings me up.

Would I come and speak at the opening of a huge sculpture commissioned by the council and paid for by Sainsbury's to celebrate the second centenary of Shelley's birth?

I went through the usual preliminaries—was he sure he had the right member of the Foot family? Did he realise (a) Shelley's politics, and (b) mine?

Yes, yes, yes, he said—my name had been put forward by someone from the Workers Educational Association.

Huge sculpture

OK, so I went. It was a cold November evening. The magnificent sculpture of a fountain is by Angela Connor, who said enough to me to make it clear she and I were the only socialists on the platform.

I and the secretary of the Fountain Society were the only speakers and were both very glad (because of the cold) to stick to our five minute limit.

On the train down I wondered whether the district council had taken leave of its senses, and reckoned that there would be (at most) half a dozen people shivering in misery.

In fact there were more than 1,000 people crowded round the fountain.

After the short ceremony, as the huge fountain started rather falteringly to spurt its jets into the air, most of them stayed, cheerfully chatting and shuffling their feet to keep out the cold.

I simply could not, cannot understand it, unless it is that people are interested in the place where they live, and especially in the giants of history who have lived there in the past, and on whose shoulders we try to light up the present.

Egalitarian democracy

Anyway, I said that Shelley was by any reckoning among the five greatest poets who had ever written in English; that his control of language, rhyme and rhythm was as unsurpassed as his intellect was all-embracing.

Why had so little of what he wrote been published in his lifetime? Because he was a Leveller, an atheist, a feminist and a republican— but above all a revolutionary who wanted the whole social order overturned and replaced by an egalitarian democracy.

When I said that Shelley had to contend all his short life with a Tory government, three times re-elected, which finally drowned in its own sleaze, I thought I heard people laughing.

The Lessing legend

When they are dead, heroes and heroines cannot let you down. When they are contemporary, still writing and thinking, they can cause the most frightful disillusionment. I still remember my indignation when, more than 20 years ago, I read the last chapter of E P Thompson's book on the Black Acts of the 18th century, *Whigs and Hunters*. The chapter, which subscribed to the idea of an eternal and consistent rule of law independent of economic circumstances, seemed to me an appalling betrayal of the Marxist clarity of Thompson's great history book, *The Making of the English Working Class*.

I recall something very similar much later when I started, but could not finish, Doris Lessing's novel *The Good Terrorist*, published at the height of Thatcherism during the Great Miners' Strike. This novel seemed to me nothing more nor less than reactionary propaganda. How could such a ferocious assault on left wing commitment have been mounted by such a committed left winger? Doris Lessing's early Martha Quest novels are full of life and energy, and a passion to change the world. She became a Communist in the most unlikely circumstances—in Rhodesia during the war—and, against all the odds, lived her life according to her principles.

The Golden Notebook, which was started in the late 1950s and published in 1962, is one of the great novels of our time. Its central theme is the condescension of women, and the relationship of that condescension to the subordination of the majority of the human race. *The Golden Notebook* is often described as a 'women's book', and of course it is. But it is a man's book too.

The novel hardly ever pontificates but, more than anything else I have ever read, it grapples with a secular sexual morality which makes it compulsive and compulsory reading for men. After taking part in a debate with Islamicists not long ago at a London college, I was rebuked by one of the women in the audience (they sat separately from the men, and wore veils). 'If there is no God,' she asked, 'how

Socialist Review February 1998

would we know what was right and wrong?' I was tempted to reply (but didn't) that for a bit of an answer to this impossible question *The Golden Notebook* is a million times better than any religious work.

The novel throbs with a passion for liberation: liberation from masculine patronising, from puritanical commandments and enforced stereotypical nuclear families, from baptisms and weddings and all other superstitious ceremonials. Her demand for women's liberation had nothing of the feminine exclusivity of the separatist women's liberationists of the 1980s. When she wrote *The Golden Notebook* Doris Lessing's socialist commitment, however damaged by the behaviour of male socialists or by Stalinism, was still strong. The point in exposing the absurd ways in which men, including socialist men, treated women was to move forward to a new society in which both sexes could freely take part.

The sections in the book entitled 'The Red Notebook' cover the central character's membership of and disillusionment with the Communist Party before and after the 20th Congress of 1956, in which Nikita Khruschev denounced the crimes of Joseph Stalin, his predecessor as general secretary of the Russian Communist Party.

The congress led to mass defection from Communist parties all over the world. Among those who left the British CP were Edward Thompson and Doris Lessing who, at 37, was in her prime. Two passages from *The Golden Notebook* stand out in my memory. The first is a report by a member of a British teachers' delegation to Russia in the early 1950s when Stalin was still alive. At the end of his stay, the teacher reports, he was summoned to meet the general secretary, a plain simple man in a plain simple office smoking a pipe, asking plain simple questions about the state of affairs in Britain, and nodding wisely as the earnest teacher spilled out his plain simple opinions. The story was the most ludicrous fantasy. But the fantasy was shared, *The Golden Notebook* argues, by almost every such delegate in those times. When I read the passage I remembered the great Clydeside revolutionary Harry McShane telling me in some embarrassment about his visit to Russia as part of a delegation in 1931: 'I sat listening to the trams outside, and revelling in the fact that these were our trams, the people's trams.' It took Harry more than 20 years to discover that they had been 'just trams after all, trams like everywhere else'.

The point about the fantasy was not simply that iconoclastic socialists demeaned themselves by dreaming up such fantasy and pretending it was true. There was another side to it—the great yearning among socialists for a place and time where rulers have no airs or graces and are, because of the democratic nature of the society they represent, quite normal, secular people whose only aim in government is to run the society as fairly as they can. This yearning comes out more clearly in another remarkable passage when the writer of 'The Red Notebook' recalls her stint as a literary adviser to a Communist newspaper. She publishes an advertisement asking readers to send in their own fictional work. She is astounded by the flood of original material which pours into the offices and the accompanying letters in which the authors, almost all working class people, give vent to their literary ambitions, some political, some romantic, some crude, but all throbbing with desire for a world where such expression is natural and free.

The shock of the revelations at the 20th Congress runs through the novel. The Communists in it are angry and disillusioned at the way they have been hoaxed. But the rational arguments which inspired these people are there too. I did not read *The Golden Notebook* until 25 years after it was written, and for a time could not believe that its author was also responsible for *The Good Terrorist*. The shock of the comparison sent me scurrying back to find a book by Doris Lessing which corresponded as a turning point, as Edward Thompson's *Whigs and Hunters* had done. I think I found it, at least to some extent, in her 1973 novel *The Summer Before the Dark*, where a liberated woman starts to revel in the sentimental domesticity which Doris Lessing rejected and mocked in her early novels and lifestyle. After that I was inclined to assume that hers was yet another dreary example of older people abandoning the ideas and zest of their youth and settling for the safe, comfortable and reactionary condescension they once exposed.

Such was the prejudice with which I embarked on her new autobiography, especially this second volume which covers the crucial period of her membership of the British Communist Party, the 20th Congress and the writing of *The Golden Notebook*.

'And now,' she writes on page 52, 'I have to record what was probably the most neurotic act of my life. I decided to join the Communist Party. And this at a time when my "doubts" had become something like a steady, private torment... To spell out the paradox. All over Europe, and to a much lesser extent the United States, it was the most sensitive, compassionate, socially concerned people who became Communists… These decent, kind people supported the worst, the most brutal tyranny of our time.'

Why? Her answer nowhere reflects that sympathy and concern for former Communists which is so central to *The Golden Notebook*. Her only answer is 'belief'. She explains:

> This [Communism] was a religious set of mind, identical with that of passionate religious True Believers…we inherited the mental framework of Christianity.

This is demonstrable drivel. Pretty well everyone who joined the party at that time or any other were non-believers, secularists, humanists, people who rejected and argued passionately against religious superstition and a substitute for independent thought.

No one joined the party from 'belief'. They joined because they were disgusted with the state of capitalist society, because they believed that capitalism had led the world into two world wars and would probably lead to a third, because they hated inequality and impoverishment, because they were convinced that the world economy could and should be run on egalitarian lines, and above all because they realised that they could only win a new world by combining their resources with others to fight against the old one. They joined, in short, for rational reasons.

The fact that they supported a regime every bit as murderous and tyrannous as anything thrown up by private capitalism must, therefore, be explicable in rational terms. Chief among these was the fact that Stalinist Russia pretended to be socialist, that its economy seemed to be based on planning, not free enterprise, and that its foreign policy appeared to be implacably opposed to that of the free market US.

The facts, now accepted by almost everyone, that Russia was not socialist, that its planning was bureaucratic in the interests of its own ruling class and that its foreign policy was as imperialist as that of the US were stubbornly resisted by the Stalinists. The refusal to accept these facts, and a party structure founded on Stalin's Russia where all ideas and inspiration came from the top down and not in the other direction, led to an intellectual tyranny, an abject acceptance of everything which emerged from the Kremlin and its Communist parties, and an atmosphere of collective lying which understandably still shocks Doris Lessing even though (or perhaps because) she was part of it.

'I have come to think,' she concludes, 'that there is something in the nature of Communism that breeds lies, makes people lie and twist facts.' She does not, cannot, even begin to justify that sentence. Communism is about the democratic control of the economy, need before greed, public interest before private interest, the pooling and conserving rather than the atomisation and waste of human and natural resources. How can such a concept by its nature 'make people lie'? It was not Communism nor socialism, but the betrayal of both, which led to people lying in and about Stalinist Russia. Once the essence of socialism, democratic control from below, was jettisoned, everything else, including straight talk and honest accounting, was jettisoned too.

The crushing disillusionment which overwhelmed so many Communists in the mid-1950s sent them scurrying in many different directions. Perhaps the most interesting part of this book are the letters which Doris Lessing wrote to Edward Thompson in 1956 when he, with John Saville, started the *New Reasoner*, a journal for former Communists who wanted to stay active socialists. Dorothy Thompson sent the letters to Doris after Edward's recent death, so we know what she said to him, but not what he said to her. We can only guess from her responses that he was trying to persuade her to stay a committed and campaigning socialist. 'I know I am a socialist, and I believe in the necessity for revolution when the moment is opportune', she replied on 21 February 1957, and then at once argued the exact opposite:

> But I don't want to make any more concepts. For myself, I mean. I want to let myself simmer into some sort of knowledge, but I don't know what it is... I haven't got any moral fervour left. No one who feels responsible for the bloodbaths and cynicism of the last 30 years can feel morally indignant about the bloody-mindedness of capitalism. I can't, anyway.

Doris Lessing, of course, was not at all responsible for a single bloodbath. She had plenty of moral fervour left—she had not even started on *The Golden Notebook*, after all. Her acceptance of the blame for Stalin's crimes in such absurd terms is the measure not just of the depth of her disillusionment, but of the abandonment of the socialist zeal which started her off in the first place. The socialist baby was thrown out with the Stalinist bathwater. Like thousands of other former Communists she placed the blame not on the intellectual and political failures of the actual party they joined, but on the very idea of joining a socialist party at all. She identified the chief cause of the failure of the Stalinist parties as the most essential element of socialist commitment, cooperating with others to establish a cooperative world.

Once the principle of collective activity, discussion and thought is abandoned, there is nothing left but individual initiative and whim. These desperate letters in 1957 and 1958 contain more clues than anything else about the decline in the power of Doris Lessing's writing. The abandonment of the ideas of her youth took a long time to complete. If anything, her initial doubts and disillusionment contributed to the wonders of *The Golden Notebook*. The real decline followed later, taking her, 'simmering' on her own, into all sorts of absurdities, weird cult religions, extra sensory perception, even a campaign to install nuclear shelters at the bottom of every garden. Again and again in this autobiography she reproaches herself for her Communist past, denounces all organised socialists as 'bigots and fanatics', lumps Trotsky in with Stalin, and rejoices grotesquely (and quite inaccurately) that 'by the time I had finished *The Golden Notebook*, I had written my way out of the package'.

Can her autobiography then be chucked aside as yet another apology for the existing order from a former socialist who has grown into a petulant reactionary? No, it most certainly cannot. As I look back on the marks I made on this book I am surprised not at all by the number of 'Oh no's and other exclamations of irritation, but by continuous surprised delight at the flashes of the old Lessing intuition and fury. It is almost as though, as she forces herself to remember her socialist youth, as she summons up what kept her active and militant for so long, her former commitment comes back to inspire her.

I single out, just for tasters, a wonderful analysis of Brecht's *Mother Courage*; a furious denunciation of the prevailing fashion for putting people in prison for not paying fines; a comparison of the mood at Thatcher's Tory conference with the Nuremberg rallies; bitter and eloquent assaults on the McCarthyite witch hunts in the US, on means testing, on 'academic polemical writing'; a warm memory of the camaraderie of CND's Aldermaston marches; and even an expression that 'somewhere out there is still an honesty and integrity— or so I believe—and a slight shift in our political fortunes would bring that [1945] face of Britain forward. At least, I hope so.'

She has been all round the houses but she has not gone down the drain. There is a lot of the old fire and passion left, and her story, as easy as ever to read, puts flesh and bones on the fictional characters in *The Golden Notebook*. We organised socialists may have a lot to say to her, but she has some advice for us too. In October 1956, at the height of the crisis of Stalinism, she wrote to Edward Thompson:

> Unless a communist party is a body of individuals each jealously guarding his or her independence of judgement, it must degenerate into a body of yes men.

And yes women too, of course, which Doris Lessing has never been.

First published as a review of Walking in the Shade, Volume Two of My Autobiography 1949-1962 *by Doris Lessing (Harper Collins 1998).*

Signed zeal delivered

George Orwell started an imaginary BBC interview with Jonathan Swift in 1942 by describing his 1738 edition of Swift's works. The edition is 'not easy to read', he said, 'but when I open it...I almost have the feeling that I can hear Swift speaking to me.' Swift interrupted: 'I warn you to beware of all modern editions.' I remember that warning as 20 volumes containing everything Orwell ever wrote barge their way through the front door. I must find a new shelf. I am not going to disturb the one I have filled with Orwelliana over nearly 40 years, ever since I read the first five pages of *Homage to Catalonia* and got a glimpse of an egalitarian democracy organised from the bottom up. This wonderful new edition gives me the chance to read all the books again, and much more besides, confident that nothing has been cut out or even abridged. Swift's warning, I discover, is almost redundant. Except for a silly shifting of chapters in *Homage to Catalonia*, there is nothing to beware of in this modern edition.

When Orwell went to Spain in 1936 to fight the fascists he was already a confirmed campaigner against racialism and imperialism. His stint as a policeman in Burma made sure of that. 'Even those poor bloody fools at the club might be better company,' muses a character in his first novel, *Burmese Days*, 'if we weren't all of us living a lie the whole time: the lie that we're here to uplift our poor black brothers instead of rob them.' His research for his book about the northern working class, *The Road to Wigan Pier*, turned him against capitalism as well. In Barcelona, he realised that he was taking part in a revolution that could put a stop to racialism, imperialism and capitalism once and for all. He had exposed what was wrong with the world. In Spain, he felt for the first time the power to change it. The little book he wrote on his return—in my view, his best—sparkles with the enthusiasm of that experience.

He learnt two lessons in Spain that stayed with him for the rest of his short life. The first was that the essence of socialism is equality;

Observer 23 August 1998

the second was that the socialist spirit of the Spanish Revolution was smashed by the Communist Party, and that the Russian government that organised this counter-revolution was not socialist, as it claimed, but the opposite. Russia under Stalin was a class society; 'a planned state capitalism with the grab motive left intact'; a bureaucratic tyranny that while it broke the spirit of the Spanish revolution was staging the disgusting show trials to wipe out the leaders of the Bolshevik revolution. George Orwell was one of the very first socialists to attack Stalinism.

Not long after *Homage to Catalonia* was published, he wrote:

> I do not believe that a man with £50,000 a year and a man with 15 shillings a week either can or will cooperate. The nature of their relationship is, quite simply, that one is robbing the other... It would seem, therefore, that if the problems of Western capitalism are to be solved, it will have to be through a third alternative, a movement which is generally revolutionary, willing to make drastic changes and to use violence if necessary, but which does not lose touch, as communism and fascism have done, with the essential values of democracy.

For nearly two years Orwell searched around for this alternative movement. He joined the Independent Labour Party and signed a manifesto pledging resistance to war. As late as January 1939 he was urging the art critic Herbert Read that it was 'necessary for those who intend to oppose the coming war to start organising for illegal anti-war activities'. It was no good trying to 'fight fascism in the name of democracy', he told a friend, because of 'what we know as democracy in time of difficulty turns immediately to fascism'. The only way to win was 'for the workers to keep the power in their own hands'.

When no recognisable anti-war movement arose, however, and Britain declared war against Hitler's Germany, Orwell did a smart about-turn. He denounced his recent view that fascism could not be fought in the name of capitalist democracy. He offered to sign up, but was refused because of the bullet wound in the throat he got in Spain. He joined the BBC and drafted weekly war reports which favourably, sometimes rather too favourably, measured the Allies' progress.

In *The Lion and the Unicorn*, an essay he published in 1941, he wrote of 'the overwhelming strength of patriotism, national loyalty'. But, even while he was peddling 'jingoistic muck' on the radio, he never lost sight of his socialist inspiration. *The Lion and the Unicorn* ends with the prediction, which he later ruefully admitted was not fulfilled, that the war against Hitler could not be won without a revolution, or at least without 'an irreversible shift of power'.

Nor did he lose sight of the other great lesson from Spain: the reactionary nature of Russian foreign policy and the subservience of all the Communist parties to it. After the collapse of the Stalin-Hitler pact, which Orwell denounced mercilessly, Russia became an ally in the war. Criticism of the Stalin regime was universally unpopular, especially on the left, but Orwell, who in 1943 became literary editor of the left-wing weekly *Tribune*, never stopped campaigning against the Russian corruption of British socialist theory and practice. He marvelled at the almost total obeisance to Stalinism among the intelligentsia. Gollancz, Faber & Faber (in the shape of Orwell's friend T S Eliot) and Jonathan Cape all turned down the manuscript of *Animal Farm*, his scintillating 1944 satire on Stalinism. Only *Tribune* (run at the time by Aneurin Bevan MP) and the *Observer*, edited by David Astor, protected Orwell's right to say what he thought—and not just about Russia. Orwell was opposed to the execution of former Nazi traitors and to the Zionist experiment in Palestine, and was allowed to say so.

Once again, however, his opposition to the Stalin regime did not push him to the right. His articles after the war are full of complaint about the return of class privileges and the failure of the Labour government to deal with them. He was shocked by the continued appointment of Tories to key diplomatic posts, by the failure to abolish the House of Lords and by the pandering to the royal family. He mused again that 'economic inequality makes democracy impossible'.

Throughout 1947, 1948 and 1949 he was almost permanently bedridden with tuberculosis. His writing became increasingly gloomy and pessimistic. The tone of *1984*, his famous satire published in 1949, a few months before his death, reflects that pessimism. His illness, his fury with the Communists and his disillusionment with the Labour government help to explain his recently publicised decision to send his glamorous friend Celia Kirwan, who was working for the IRD, an arm of British intelligence, the names of people he thought were 'crypto-Communist'. The editors of these volumes put up a stout defence of this decision, though there can never be a defence for a writer who sneaks to the state about potential dissidents.

The Kirwan episode gave rise to further charges that Orwell's anti-Communism paved the way for the subsequent McCarthyite witch-hunts in the United States. Orwell answered the accusation as early as September 1946, and his response is published in these volumes for the first time. 'In five years time it may be as dangerous to praise Stalin as it was to attack him two years ago. But I should not regard this as an advance. Nothing is gained by teaching a parrot a new word.' In spite of his unsavoury grassing to the IRD, Orwell's life and work indicates that he would have been as hostile to McCarthyite persecution as he was to Communists.

I have tried to trace from this gigantic maze the theme of Orwell's political development which interests me most, but the joys of this literary feast stretch far beyond what I have covered. The 11 volumes of letters, reviews and diaries give full rein to the extraordinary range of Orwell's interests: cooking, tea-making, boys' weeklies, snob schools, dirty postcards, Trotskyist pamphlets. He says somewhere he had 900 books, but he seems to have read seven or eight times that many. His old favourites come up again and again: Dickens, Gissing, Conrad, Trollope, Dostoevsky. They mingle with the contemporary writers who, like Orwell, rejected Stalinism without ever ingratiating themselves with the authorities: C L R James, Richard Wright, Arthur Koestler.

All this is presented in the context of his personal life, the tragic death of his wife and comrade Eileen, his enjoyment of his adopted baby son who survived her, his diffident attempts at seduction by post, his patience with his illness. Above all, the volumes sing with Orwell's irresistible writing style. Prose, he said, should be like a window pane, so you can see right through it. Every letter, every broadcast, even every diary entry is written clearly, sprinkled everywhere with wit, surprise and hope.

First published as a review of The Complete Works of George Orwell *edited by Peter Davison (Secker & Warburg 1998).*

McCann

Wandering through scrubland in Derry in the week after the police riot on 5 October 1968 I was introduced to Eamonn McCann, a young man in a rage. He had come from a meeting in which Nationalist councillors had swamped the energetic and effective Derry Housing Action Committee. The Nationalist grandees, he fumed, were 'middle class, middle aged and middle of the road'. They had, once again, strangled the breath out of the people they pretended to represent. I listened in stunned admiration, and observed that the young man's eyes, as they flashed with fury, seemed to twinkle at the same time with merriment.

Most young firebrands lose their early passions and mellow into respectable and respectful citizens. In the 30 years since that dramatic October, Eamonn McCann's indignation has not subsided an inch. He is as outraged now as he ever was by the condition of the working people in the North of Ireland, and in his native Derry. He refuses to accept that these people remain divided forever by ancient religious shibboleths which have no relevance to their real lives.

Though his obsessional knowledge of the Bible and the intricacies of Christian religion border on the macabre, he sees his fellow countrymen and women not as Protestants and Catholics but as human beings whose aspirations for a fulfilled life are frustrated, as they are everywhere else in the world, by much more relevant divisions: divisions between rich and poor, between employers and workers, between the few with their many mansions and the many with their rotten housing, stunted education and dead end jobs.

This unusual approach gives Eamonn a refreshingly sharp insight into political developments in the North. He is entirely free of the sectarianism which suffocates almost all the political analysis and dialogue in that most political of territories. Above all, his writing style never loses that most elusive but vital quality: clarity. So many political commentators, including socialist ones, insult their readers—and lose them—in jargon, obfuscation and swank.

'Introduction' in *McCann: War and Peace in Northern Ireland* 1998

Even at the peak of his indignation, Eamonn never loses the capacity to explain, and to amuse and entertain at the same time. His book *War and an Irish Town* remains by far the clearest account of the origin of what later became known as 'the Troubles'. His analysis of the 1972 Bloody Sunday massacre in Derry—a masterpiece of informed and passionate investigative journalism—helped to persuade the Irish and British governments to set up a full-scale inquiry. In recent months, the BBC, casting around desperately for an analysis of events which is not stained with sectarianism, have repeatedly fallen back on the 'extremist' Eamonn McCann to help their viewers out of the maze.

Hot Press has done the Irish people a profound service by publishing Eamonn McCann's political column on the North of Ireland over the last 16 years—and an even greater service by bringing the best of these columns together in this collection. I can guarantee the reader that when finishing reading this book—and it is impossible to start it without finishing it—he or she will have learned far more about the politics of Northern Ireland than could have been gleaned from a thousand sermons or their political equivalent.

First published as an introduction to McCann: War and Peace in Northern Ireland *by Eamonn McCann (Hot Press 1998).*

Laureate equals Tory at

I was amazed to see the names of fine, independent-minded, even socialist poets like Tony Harrison, Andrew Motion and Benjamin Zephaniah bandied about as possible candidates for the post of Poet Laureate. Surely everyone knows by now that to be Poet Laureate you have to be a Tory, a royalist or a creep.

If anyone has any doubt about this, or imagines that the post is some sort of honour, I refer them to Byron's 'Don Juan', which starts with a glorious, and originally censored, dedication:

> Bob Southey! You're a poet, Poet Laureate
> And representative of all the race,
> Although 'tis true that you turned out a Tory at
> Last

Byron was seldom deflected by problems with rhyme, and he quite rightly judged 'Tory at' a perfectly apposite rhyme for 'laureate'.

He came up against the same problem not much later in the poem when he was still spitting at the renegade Southey's compliance with the Tory government and its hated foreign secretary Castlereagh.

He asked whether the great John Milton would have grovelled in the same way:

> Would HE adore a sultan? HE obey
> That intellectual eunuch, Castlereagh?

In a note, Byron suggested an alternative to these two lines, as follows:

> Would he subside into a hackney Laureate—
> A scribbling, self-sold, soul-hired, scorn'd Iscariot?

Guardian 17 November 1998

'I doubt', Byron added, 'if "Laureate" and "Iscariot" be good rhymes, but must say as Ben Johnson did to Sylvester who challenged him to rhyme with "I, John Sylvester, lay with your sister."

'Johnson answered: "I, Ben Johnson, lay with your wife". Sylvester answered: "That is not rhyme". "No", said Johnson, "but it's true".'

Was Karl Marx history's greatest optimist?

There were only 11 people huddled together in Highgate Cemetery for the burial of Karl Marx in March 1883. At the end of a short speech his friend and collaborator Frederick Engels described Marx as 'the best hated and most calumniated man of his times'.

That hate and calumny had a specially persistent quality. For most rebels, socialists and even revolutionaries, death brings relief from high-born abuse. Hated though they were by top people in their life-time, after their death men like Aneurin Bevan, Keir Hardie and even James Connolly were treated with sympathy and even appreci-ation. Detestation of Karl Marx, however, has persisted for over a hundred years. Again and again his works are denounced as poisonous, irrelevant or obscure. In a passage quoted by Francis Wheen the former Labour prime minister, Harold Wilson, who had spent much of his youth poring over dull footnotes about the British railway system, remarked that he had only got as far as page two of Marx's *Capital*. 'I felt that two sentences of the main text and a page of footnotes was too much,' he explained.

I am reviewing a book by a friend and colleague, and should beware of hyperbole and puff, so I can only say that this is a marvellous book which combines years of voracious reading with the stylish writing and polemical wit which Francis Wheen regularly showers on readers of the *Guardian*. His object, triumphantly achieved, is to rescue Marx from those interminable haters and calumniators. One by one he despatches the myths.

Was Marx bound by dogma, who repeated by rote what had mys-teriously become known as Marxism? Wheen wishes such critics, who include Tony Blair, would read the *Economic and Philosophical Manuscripts*, which Marx wrote when he was 26 in 1844 and which 'reveal the workings of a ceaselessly inquisitive, subtle and undogmatic

Guardian 9 October 1999

mind.' Was Marx a morose recluse, trapped in the library of the British Museum? From these pages he emerges as a devoted husband and father, never happier than telling fairy stores about wicked capitalists to his daughters or joining them in extempore home performances of William Shakespeare. Is there a direct line from Marx to the gulag? Wheen takes great pains to show the difference between the democratic society envisaged by Marx and Engels and the caricature of such a society sponsored by Stalin and his successors. Was Marx's writing really as dull as Harold Wilson pretended? On the contrary, he was an investigative journalist of the most extraordinary skill whose pamphlets and polemics have lasted far longer than refined works on the same subject. Who, for instance, has ever written a more perceptive and readable account of the Paris Commune? Who more accurately pilloried the ghastly Lord Palmerston ('If he can do nothing, he will devise anything. He does not interfere, he intermeddles'), or the dogged Whig careerist, Lord John Russell ('Placed by birth, connection and social accidents on a colossal pedestal, he always remained the same homunculus – a malignant and distorted dwarf on the top of a pyramid')?

It was not, however, his polemics which won for Marx the abiding hatred of the rich and powerful. In that graveside speech Frederick Engels got to the nub of the matter:

> Marx was, before all else, a revolutionary. His real mission in life was to contribute in one way or another to the overthrow of capitalist society. Fighting was his element.

By 1844, Marx was convinced that the essence of capitalism was the exploitation of labour, a process which enriched a minority at the expense of the human potential of the vast majority. The conviction filled him with an overpowering indignation, which became the driving force of his life.

Marx lived in conditions of appalling poverty and pain, but never deviated from his central purpose—to provide the workers with material which would make it easier for them to emancipate themselves. This wasn't simply a matter of investigating and writing. It also required organisation—first of the small Communist League; later of the International Working Men's Association. The opening declaration of the International, which Marx wrote, asserted that the emancipation of the working class could only be carried out by the working class itself. Marx was bitterly intolerant of colleagues who sought to liberate the workers from on high. Such colleagues have been patronised by historians, but Francis Wheen dispenses with them all: Michael Bakunin, in particular, is exposed as a charlatan, Frederick Lassalle as a creep to the Prussian monarchy, H M Hyndman, founder of the British Social Democratic Federation, as a plagiarist and bore. All three sought to free the workers from capitalism without unleashing the workers' ability to organise and to fight. When Eleanor Marx asked her father whom he admired most in human history, he called up the name of a slave warrior from far before capitalism: 'Spartacus'. Wheen's book ends with an interview in which the American journalist John Swinton asked Marx the simple question: 'What is?' and Marx replied just as simply: 'Struggle.'

Perhaps the most familiar criticism of Marx is that his predictions have been confounded. A hundred and fifty years after the *Communist Manifesto*, after all, capitalism is still alive and well. Francis Wheen concedes that 'Marx's optimism was misplaced'—he was always absurdly sanguine, as revolutionaries have to be—but his 'vision of the global market was uncannily prescient'. The fact that his predictions of the downfall of capitalism have not been vindicated in no way detracts from the originality or contemporary relevance of his historic analysis.

Francis Wheen has unearthed from Marx an aphorism I had not heard before: 'Social reforms are never carried out by the weakness of the strong but always by the strength of the weak.' Certainly. But excuse me. Can this be the same Francis Wheen who, only a few months ago, when the most powerful nations on earth launched a ferocious bombing war on a nation weaker than almost all of them, took up his stand, unequivocally, on the side of the bombers? Surely some mistake.

First published as a review of Karl Marx *by Francis Wheen (Fourth Estate 1999).*

Cops and robbers

Blind ship of death

Report on *Marchioness* that court never heard

Bowbelle's log of shame

1964: *Bowbelle* is launched.

January 1965: Crashes into MV *Catford*, near Greenwich.

November 1965: Crashes into steamer *De Baif* near Dagenham.

August 1966: Runs aground at Orchards Wharf.

April 1967: Crashes into MV *Jo Tor* on the Thames.

January 1971: Crashes into the MV *Bradfield* off Margaret Ness.

May 1974: Hits tug *Lord Ritchie* and some pontoons.

May 1982: Collides with scaffolding under Cannon Street railway bridge.

June 1983: Crashes into the pleasure craft *Pride of Greenwich* under Charing Cross Bridge.

November 1987: Crashes into sister dredger *Bowsprite*.

February 1988: Hits Southwark Bridge.

June 1989: Smashes into the *Arco Sheldt* at Newhaven docks.

20 August 1989: Sinks the *Marchioness*, killing 51 people.

Today I expose what an MP calls 'the long sequence of deliberate evasions' by the government over the 1989 *Marchioness* pleasure boat disaster, which killed 51 people.

Last month a London magistrate threw out a private prosecution against South Coast Shipping, the owners of the dredger *Bowbelle* which smashed into the *Marchioness* from behind and sank her.

A few days later the government:

■ Revealed for the first time that the *Bowbelle* had been banned from the Thames four months previously.

■ Published their own report by top lawyer John Hayes which sets out the dreadful record of collisions by the *Bowbelle*.

Daily Mirror 24 July 1992

Nigel Spearing, Labour MP for Newham, asks:

What explanation can there be other than a desire by the Department of Transport to limit information which would have been available to the court?

A spokesman for RMC Group plc, the giant construction materials company, which owns South Coast Shipping, told me:

Contrary to recent reports, there has been no ban on the *Bowbelle* using the Thames. In December 1990, however, as the continuing recession led to a reduced demand for building materials, the vessel was taken from the river and has since been sold to overseas interests. The company feels it cannot comment further.

But the Department of Transport insist the boat *was* banned.

A spokesman told me: 'In March this year, we told the operators that the *Bow Trader* and the *Bowbelle* were not allowed to operate on the Thames.'

'We didn't announce that at the time. There was no particular reason why we should.'

Ian Philpott, a London photographer who lost his girlfriend on the *Marchioness*, finds this 'quite incredible'. He tells me:

For three years we've been campaigning to get this dangerous boat off the river. When it's finally banned, the government wait four months before deigning to let us know.

Captain Eric Beetham, a consultant on shipping casualties, who was for 20 years a ship's master, gave evidence at the private prosecution. He thinks the banning of the *Bowbelle*, if it had been known to the court, would have made a 'substantial difference' to the case.

The Department of Transport insist that the timing of the publication of the Hayes report and the revelation that the *Bowbelle* was banned had nothing to do with the private prosecution.

But this latest outcry comes at the end of a long and shocking record of neglect—by the company and the government.

In its 25 years, the *Bowbelle* was involved in 12 accidents before it sank the *Marchioness* (see above). In June 1983, in a collision grimly similar to the *Marchioness* horror, it crashed into the pleasure craft *Pride of Greenwich* under Charing Cross Bridge.

The senior nautical surveyor concluded that the crash was caused by 'grossly inadequate visibility from the respective steering positions'.

New procedures were drawn up. The Hayes report concludes: 'The Department of Transport did not check that the procedures were followed.'

In November 1987, the *Bowbelle* crashed into its own sister dredger, the *Bowsprite*, in fog in the upper pool of the Thames. There was no lookout on the *Bowbelle*. An inquiry found that none of the measures agreed in 1983 had been followed. The department also took no action over the vanishing lookout.

Says Hayes: 'The absence of a lookout on the *Bowbelle* was a serious matter and should have been treated as such.'

In December 1988, the *Bowsprite* broke in two and sank off the Belgian coast. Seven of the ten crew were flung into the sea. Four of them drowned. Internal company minutes suggested that the *Bowsprite* had 'hit a sandbank' or 'a submerged object'.

The Marine Accident Investigation report does not mention a sandbank or a submerged object. It says the ship broke up in deep water because of 'structural failures'.

The Department of Transport ordered an immediate inspection of the three other dredgers in the 'Bow' family. The *Bowbelle* failed the inspection.

Later that month—December 1988, nine months before the *Marchioness* disaster—the Department of Transport placed a prohibition order on the *Bowbelle*. Within a few weeks, the repaired dredger was back plying its highly profitable trade.

South Coast Shipping profits for the first seven months of 1989 were £5,198,570—16 percent up on the previous year.

In June 1989, the *Bowbelle* smashed into the *Arco Sheldt*, which was moored at Newhaven docks.

On August 20, it crashed into the *Marchioness*, killing 51 people, and causing the most awful anguish and grief to hundreds of friends and families.

The decision not to hold a public inquiry was taken in Downing Street.

Fact to remember 1: A prominent director of RMC is Sir Neil Macfarlane MP, former Tory Minister of Sport.

Fact to remember 2: Between 1987 and 1990, RMC gave £152,000 to the Conservative Party.

Fact to remember 3: In July 1988, Mr John Camden, chairman of RMC, presented the *Bowbelle*'s firm South Coast Shipping with a much sought-after prize.

It was the ceremonial sword awarded every year to the winners of the keenly-contested RMC Trophy competiton.

For safety.

MI5 mischief

Nearly ten years ago, on 5 December 1986, Colin Wallace emerged from Lewes prison after serving more than six years of a ten year sentence for the manslaughter of his friend Jonathan Lewis. Tomorrow, he goes with his lawyers to the Court of Appeal where he hopes to prove what he has always ferociously maintained: that he had nothing to do with Lewis's death.

He was met outside the prison that bleak December morning by a group of about 60 journalists, all of them anxious to discuss the astonishing allegations which had circulated while he was in prison. In essence, these were that he had been an expert in black propaganda and dirty tricks for the British army and the intelligence services in his native Northern Ireland.

His work had brought him quick promotion. In 1974, aged 30, he was the youngest senior information officer in the Ministry of Defence, and the youngest ever to have been recommended for the MBE. His central claim was that this glittering career was suddenly and cruelly cut short by the army and intelligence officers he had served. He had, he said, been sacked from the army in 1975 because he refused to co-operate with MI5 chiefs who wanted him to join in a dirty tricks campaign against recently elected Labour ministers, supporters of Edward Heath in the Conservative Party and all Liberals.

For at least a year, until he found work as a council information officer in Arundel, West Sussex, he claimed, all his attempts to get another job had been mysteriously thwarted.

Few of the journalists outside Lewes prison that morning believed a word of this fantastic story. It had been almost exclusively confined to *Lobster*, an occasional magazine which specialised in intelligence matters and was run on a shoestring from Hull by Robin Ramsey and Stephen Dorril.

Back in his Arundel home, where his wife Eileen had spent his time in prison trying to survive on 'potatoes', Wallace gave a long

Guardian 22 July 1996

interview to BBC Television, which was promptly shelved. York-shire Television, whose researcher had been to see Wallace in prison, decided against producing a programme about him.

Despite this almost universal incredulity, Wallace determined to go on telling his story. In that same year, 1986, two books were pub-lished which suggested that his allegations were not as absurd as they sounded. *Spycatcher*, by the former MI5 officer Peter Wright, ended with an allegation that rogue right wing elements in MI5 had ha-rassed the Wilson government from 1974 to 1976. John Stalker's ex-traordinary story alleged that he, a deputy chief constable appointed to inquire into killings by the Royal Ulster Constabulary, had been summarily taken off his inquiry and subjected to a campaign of dis-graceful dirty tricks and smears.

When I first visited Wallace for the *Daily Mirror* in May 1987, I, like many other journalists, was put off by his slickness. His prompt answers to every question, coupled with his past career as a professional deceiver of journalists, made him a dubious source.

My doubts were reinforced when I returned to London and rang the Ministry of Defence press office. Was it true, I asked, that Wal-lace had worked in Northern Ireland under a secret job description which involved 'psychological operations'? Did those operations in-clude inventing stories which would damage the IRA, and planting them on gullible journalists? Back came the weary and scornful replies: no, no. Wallace was a mere information officer. The suggestion that he'd taken part in psychological operations or worked with the SAS was ridiculous fantasy.

For the first time, I heard the phrase which was to run through of-ficial responses on this subject for the next three years. Wallace was a fantasist, a Walter Mitty. I phoned him testily and challenged him with the ministry's denial. At once, he came to London with a letter from his former boss at the Northern Ireland army information de-partment, Peter Broderick, setting out Wallace's secret job description, which did involve psychological operations. At that point, I started to realise that if there were any Walter Mittys about, they were prob-ably lurking in the Ministry of Defence.

Wallace's persistence, reinforced by his habit of meticulously keep-ing documents, started slowly to convince others. When Ken Liv-ingstone was elected to parliament for Brent East in the 1987 general election, he devoted his maiden speech to the allegations of Wallace and Fred Holroyd, a former army intelligence officer in Northern Ireland who had the same sort of grievance against the intelligence services which he believed had got rid of him, and selflessly supported Wallace during his last three years in prison.

Through 1988 and 1989, others of Wallace's allegations began to get a hearing in the media and in parliament. He had, he said, taken part in a black propaganda campaign called 'Clockwork Orange', which started as an anti-terrorist offensive but ended as an effort to spread the smear that senior Labour ministers were part of a Communist/Republican plot to subvert Crown and state. He had kept his 'Clockwork Orange' notes which forensic tests proved had been written in 1974.

While in the army, he had, he said, been approached twice by Belfast citizens worried about allegations of child abuse at Kincora, one of the city's residential homes for boys in care. His questions about Kincora and his insistence to his MI5 controller that he would no longer take part in any propaganda offensive against his elected ministers combined, he argued, to bring about his dismissal on the extraordinary charge that he had leaked to a journalist an entirely false 'classified' document which he himself had concocted.

Interminable questions about these claims from Ken Livingstone and Tam Dalyell led to interminable and increasingly irritable denials. The government tone was set by Brian Mawhinney, then Parliamentary Under-Secretary of State for Northern Ireland, now chairman of the Tory party, who replied to Ken Livingstone's maiden speech on 7 July 1987 as follows: 'I reject his conspiracy theories, and remind him that the allegations made by Messrs Wallace and Holroyd over the years about the conduct of the security forces in Northern Ireland have been fully and carefully investigated since they left the province in 1979. No evidence has been discovered to substantiate any of these allegations.'

Roger Freeman, then Parliamentary Under-Secretary at the Ministry of Defence, now cabinet minister in charge of government information, wrote to Ken Livingstone and Tam Dalyell on 1 August 1988: 'Mr Wallace has directly and through various intermediaries written to or petitioned all the departments concerned in this case, and I am satisfied that due consideration, in the light of course of earlier correspondence, has been paid to all the replies given and nothing of any substance was ever raised to cast doubt on the outcome of previous investigations.'

The allegations continued, and so did the denials. For a time, it looked as though the stalemate would continue for ever and that Wallace's strange story would never be properly tested. Then, suddenly, on 30 January 1990, the whole scene changed. Something happened in the Ministry of Defence to provoke a further search of papers about the Wallace case. The resulting discoveries forced a volte-face of quite extraordinary proportions.

The junior minister who was obliged to somersault in public was the under-secretary at defence, Archibald Hamilton MP. In a long answer to a planted written question, he dealt with Wallace's allegations about a secret project called 'Clockwork Orange', which his fellow ministers had systematically denounced as the product of Wallace's feverish imagination.

'Two documents have been found,' he admitted, 'dating from 1975 which contain brief references to a proposed project with that title... the documents show that Mr Wallace was involved in that project. The documents also state that the project was not cleared.'

What about the secret job description which had been equally vigorously denied? Hamilton conceded:

> The papers which have now come to light indicate that, when the case was made to establish Mr Wallace's post, it was proposed that its duties should include responsibilities for providing unattributable briefings to the press.

These duties, moreover, 'may have included disinformation'.

The two central government denials were now reversed. On the same day, Prime Minister Margaret Thatcher wrote to senior Tory back-bencher Terrence Higgins about questions he'd asked about the Wallace case. 'I regret to say,' she wrote, 'that a re-examination of departmental papers has brought to light information which shows that there were a number of statements in my letters...which were incorrect.'

It was Apology Day all round. Hamilton wrote to Ken Livingstone 'to clarify and where necessary to correct' answers to previous questions which were wholly false. For instance, the Ministry of Defence had contemptuously denied Wallace's allegation that he had organised a mock raid on Aldergrove airport, or that his department had forged CIA cards. Both allegations, Hamilton now admitted, were entirely true.

The government set up an inquiry under a senior Ministry of Defence official, David Heyhoe, to find out why these papers had lain hidden for so long. Heyhoe reported on 14 May 1990. He had discovered that an official in the division of the Ministry of Defence responsible for Northern Ireland had by accident come across a file marked 'Clockwork Orange'. As a result, 'other papers' had been found.

The fact that the papers were not available to ministers when answering questions about Wallace meant, Heyhoe recorded in a sentence of classical civil service obscurantism, that ministry staff had 'to deal with a personal case on as basis of incomplete records and a total discontinuity of collective memory'.

A second inquiry was set up into the treatment of Colin Wallace. This was undertaken in private by David Calcutt QC, Master of Magdalene College Cambridge. The short Calcutt report, published on 13 September 1990, was even more extraordinary than Heyhoe's. Although he'd been instructed by the then defence secretary Tom King only to publish his conclusions, Calcutt reported:

> I nevertheless take the view that a bare expression of my conclusions, without more, would possibly be open to misinterpretation, and that some reasoning, however brief, is needed.

There then came the following devastating passage:

> After wide reading and consultation I have reached the clear conclusion that the hearing which took place before the Civil Service Appeal Board on 17 October 1975 was unsatisfactory in two material respects.
>
> First I am satisfied that shortly before the hearing took place representatives of the Ministry of Defence were in private communication with the chairman of the hearing with regard to Mr Wallace's appeal. Such communications should not have happened; and I believe that what occurred affected the outcome of the appeal. Secondly, I am satisfied that the full range of Mr Wallace's work was not made plain to the Appeal Board. In my view, the Board needed to know the full range of his work if it was to adjudicate justly on his appeal...
>
> In my view neither dismissal nor resignation was within the range of penalties which would have been reasonable for the isolated incident which gave rise to the disciplinary proceedings... To this extent

I am of the opinion that an injustice was done to Mr Wallace, and so
I advise.

David Calcutt concluded that Wallace was entitled to compensation and recommended a sum of £30,000. The ministry's cheque for
that amount was delivered to the Wallace home in Arundel that
same afternoon by despatch rider.

Thus, within four years of his release from prison, the substance of
Colin Wallace's remarkable allegations had been confirmed by the authorities which had mocked them. The decisive judgement of the
Master of Magdalene had, in a few sentences, disposed of a decade of
official denials and prevarications. All sorts of questions still pro-
truded. Who from the Ministry of Defence had nobbled the appeals
tribunal? What did they tell the tribunal chairman, Sir Leslie Williams,
about Wallace which had such an impact on the tribunal's decision
effectively to uphold Wallace's dismissal? Why had so many vital official papers been overlooked?

The Commons Defence Select Committee decided to find out.
Their questions to the Ministry of Defence were systematically side-
tracked and obstructed on the grounds that Wallace's job had been
'sensitive'. In a pathetic report two years later the committee complained that they could not get the information they needed to answer
the questions, and abandoned their inquiry high and dry.

Wallace's allegations that he had been obstructed in his demands
for an inquiry into the most revolting abuse at the Kincora boys home
continued to be denied by ministers. But a book published earlier
this year on the Kincora affair by the BBC correspondent Chris Moore
revealed that William McGrath, the chief abuser of boys' in care at
Kincora had, for at least 15 years before his imprisonment in 1981,
been an MI5 agent. Moore produced substantial proof to show that
the security services had obstructed all inquiries into Kincora to protect their agent there.

Colin Wallace was, of course, delighted by the vindication of his allegations. Soon after leaving prison he'd got a junior post at the British
Airports Authority at Gatwick, which required him to rise every morning at 5am and get home late at night. He buckled down. Once again,
his capacity for hard work and his cheerful demeanour commended him
to his workmates, and earned him quick promotion. By 1992, he was a
senior manager at BAA's management training centre at Pease Pottage.
He continued to complain about his treatment by the authorities.

Suddenly, one afternoon in March 1992, he was told he was redundant. There was no criticism of his work, nor any other rational explanation. He was 49, unemployed again, hunting for work and refusing as ever to claim a penny in benefit. For six months, he and Eileen were back on the potatoes. Eventually, he and some former army colleagues started their own management training firm. He now works, as usual far away from home, near Tunbridge Wells.

Wallace's main story about his victimisation in Northern Ireland has been officially confirmed. Throughout, he has continued to campaign to establish his innocence of the killing of Jonathan Lewis. Three years ago his lawyer, Jim Nichol, submitted a petition to the Home Office calling for the Lewis case to be reopened. Nearly two years later, in January last year, the home secretary referred the case to the Court of Appeal.

Tomorrow morning, with the new Lord Chief Justice presiding, Michael Mansfield QC will start to review the evidence.

Note: At the appeal hearing, Colin Wallace's conviction was quashed.

Stagg hunting

Three whole pages of the *Mail on Sunday* on 20 October (and two more on 27 October) were devoted to reviving 'the case against Colin Stagg the jury never heard'.

This 'case'—that Colin Stagg stabbed Rachel Nickell to death on Wimbledon Common in front of her young son—was angrily chucked out two years ago by Mr Justice Ognall. A young woman police officer befriended Stagg and offered him sexual excitement if he told her he'd done the murder. She told Stagg that the only time she'd had an orgasm was when a man had told her about the sacrificial knifing of a blonde woman, and begged him to tell her something similar.

Stagg did not confess and the judge ruled that, even if he had, a confession made under such obvious entrapment would have been inadmissible as evidence. The prosecution team at once threw in the towel. Without Stagg's conversations with his blackmailing 'girlfriend', there was no case against him. The *Mail on Sunday*, however, knew better. It listed what it called 'an account of evidence gathered by the police about what was alleged to have happened' on Wimbledon Common on 15 July 1992.

There was no approach to Stagg or his defence lawyers before the article was published. There was no room for any of the 55 defence witnesses who had challenged the prosecution case at every point. There was no attempt at independent analysis of the evidence—just a series of statements gathered by the police for the prosecution.

The identification: the main witness, Jane Harriman, saw a man she thought looked suspicious on Wimbledon Common on the morning of the murder. The *Mail* reported that she picked out Stagg from an identity parade. The *Mail* did not report that her two boys, aged 13 and 11, both of whom saw the man, did not pick Stagg out from the parade. The *Mail* paraded another eyewitness, Amanda Phelan, who saw a man on the common washing his hands in a drainage ditch. The *Mail* suggests that this man was the murderer but does not report that Mrs Phelan did not pick out Colin Stagg either, nor that Mrs Phelan was not even called by the prosecution to give evidence at the committal hearing.

The black bag: Mrs Harriman was quite certain that the man she saw was carrying a black PVC bag with straps.

Prodigious efforts were made by the police to establish that Stagg ever had such a bag. But he hadn't. The *Mail on Sunday* got round this by saying Mrs Harriman described the bag on her suspect as a bum bag. She said nothing of the kind. This was a *Mail* invention to fit in with the evidence of another witness that Stagg was wearing a bum bag on the morning of the murder.

The victim's son: The *Mail* made much of how 'detectives were impressed' with the 'recall' of the victim's three year old son, Alex. The suggestion was that Alex's description of the man who murdered his mother fitted Colin Stagg. Nowhere did the *Mail* reveal what it knew perfectly well: that Alex had named another man, not Stagg, as the murderer.

The butcher and the newsagent: The *Mail* made great play with the statements of a butcher (Pat Heanan) and a newsagent (Yadnesh Patel) that Stagg had come into their shops that morning and mentioned that a young woman had been murdered on the Common. How could he have known that so soon? asked the *Mail* triumphantly. The answer is simple. Soon after the body was found, the Common was surrounded by hundreds of police who told anyone who asked that a young woman had been murdered. The first statements of Heanan and Patel quoted by the *Mail* were followed up by others from both of them which were much more equivocal about the timings, and not damaging to Stagg. Heanan and Patel were considered such weak witnesses they were not even called to give evidence at the committal proceedings. That fact, and their additional statements, were not reported by the *Mail*.

The blood: Early police reports just after the murder said that the murderer would be 'saturated in blood'. No one saw any blood on Stagg nor was there the smallest speck of blood found in his flat or on his clothes or belongings. By the time police pathologist Richard Shepperd gave evidence at the committal proceedings, he suggested that the attacker might have had very little blood on him. This evidence coincided neatly with that of the key prosecution witness, the 'psychological profiler' Paul Britton. Britton drew up a 'profile' of the killer: a local man who would have attacked his victim from behind and from the side, and thus kept out of the reach of her blood.

Shepperd originally told magistrates on oath that he had never seen Paul Britton's profile of the murderer. Whoops! The prosecution immediately disclosed a record of a conference at which Shepperd had been told in detail about Britton's profile. Shepperd had to change his story. This was so embarrassing for the prosecution that its two barristers, Nigel Sweeney QC and William Boyce, had to withdraw from the case so they could be witnesses for the defence.

The entrapment: The hearings before the stipendiary magistrate at Wimbledon, whose transcripts were available to the Mail, exposed the bankruptcy of the prosecution case. There was no forensic evidence of any kind to implicate Stagg. After his arrest, he answered every question. The policy took 520 pages of notes and still had got nothing but denials. The prosecution's only hope was 'Lizzie James', the fake girlfriend offering her body for a confession.

Naturally, Stagg, who was quickly hooked on his lovely new 'girlfriend', did his best to impress her. He noticed that she was happy when he talked about the Nickell murder, so he did so. The Mail make much of Stagg's description to 'Lizzie' of Rachel Nickell 'with her hands crossed as if in prayer beneath her head'. How, asks the Mail triumphantly, could Stagg have known that unless he was the murderer?

The defence team exposed what Mr Justice Ognall called 'a discrepancy' in this argument. 'The hands of the victim,' said the judge, 'are not palm to palm at all. The arms are in fact crossed at the wrist so that the hands barely touch'. Here was proof not of a confession but of an invention by Stagg to impress 'Lizzie's' insatiable desire for information about the murder which he hadn't got.

The entire press mocked Stagg's attempt on the day after the Mail story to make money out of any refutation he might give them. There was no reference to the obscene scramble for Stagg's exclusive story after his acquittal—a story for which Stagg was paid £40,000 by the News of the World. Nor could the Mail find space for the condition the News of the World laid down before paying the money: that Stagg take a lie detector test. He passed.

The case against Stagg was a disgrace even the legal establishment wants to forget. The police responsible were replaced by a new team which has been trying to follow up the many genuine leads abandoned by their predecessors. Asked why the story had been re-vived, Stagg's barrister James Sturman replied: 'This was the *Mail on Sunday* trying to titillate Middle England.'

'Thick as shite and still wrong'

*Jimmy Robinson, one of the Bridgewater Four,
on the men who kept him inside*

Let us start with the torture. The crucial figure in the long, awful story of the persecution of the Bridgewater Four was Pat Molloy. He was born in Ireland and became a skilful, gentle carpenter. He was a close friend of Jimmy Robinson. The two men engaged in periodic burglaries to finance their alcoholism.

When Jimmy Robinson grew tired of his dependency on small burglaries, he bought a gun and told Pat he was going to do 'a big one'—to get lots of money from one big raid. Molloy immediately refused to take part in any such project. When, on 30 November 1978, Robinson and the Hickey cousins, Michael and Vincent, set off on a mad-cap armed raid at a Worcestershire farmhouse near Romsley, Molloy would have nothing to do with it.

On Friday 8 December Molloy was arrested at a friend's house. He was told he was wanted for a meat robbery he'd done with Robinson in Tamworth the previous September. He had been arrested often before, but this time he was astonished by the police behaviour. A blanket was thrown over his head, he was frog-marched into a car and told he was going to Tamworth. But he was taken to Wombourne police station, Staffordshire, headquarters of the investigation into the murder at Yew Tree Farm, near Wordsley, of newspaper boy Carl Bridgewater.

The crime, obviously committed by a burglar whom the boy had innocently interrupted when delivering his paper, had shocked the nation. After ten weeks of frantic investigation, the Staffordshire detectives were desperate for leads. The coincidence between the armed raid on the Romsley farmhouse and the armed raid on Yew Tree Farm

Observer 1 March 1997

convinced them that the Romsley raiders, driven in a car that was traced to Vincent Hickey, were likely suspects for the Bridgewater murder.

When Vincent Hickey gave himself up on 4 December and, in the pathetic hope that he might get bail for the Romsley robbery, suggested he knew something about the murder—and when he named his cousin Michael, Robinson and Molloy—the police were convinced they were on the trail of the killers. All through that Friday and Saturday, 8 and 9 December 1978, Molloy was subjected to the full force of the regional crime squad's crack team of 'interrogators', led by Detective Constable John Perkins.

Perkins boasted he could break any suspect. His chief weapon, he explained, was his enormous fist, which he would hold up proudly to demonstrate its efficacy. Perkins and his mates told Molloy they knew he had been at the farm when the boy was murdered. Pathetically and obsequiously, Molloy repeated that he did not know what they were talking about. On Sunday 10 December Perkins and his mates got tanked up with beer at a local pub. In the party was Perkins's close mate, a car dealer, Mike Chamberlain. He later revealed on television that, after several pints, DC Perkins had held up the famous fist triumphantly and announced: 'Right boys. He'll crack today.' And back the officers went into the police station to confront the terrified Irishman.

Molloy did indeed 'crack' that evening. He signed a typed confession that he had been at Yew Tree Farm with Robinson and the Hickeys when the boy was shot. The victorious police officers desperately tried to get from Molloy some corroboration for his confession. They even took him to Yew Tree Farm, which he plainly did not recognise. As they questioned him further, his story contradicted itself and appeared to disintegrate. All this time—ten long days in a cell he knew not where—Molloy was held incommunicado. He was not allowed a lawyer. His family and friends did not know where he was, and if they had they would have been refused access to him.

On 18 December, he was at last allowed to see a Tamworth lawyer recommended by the police, John Wiggall. Immediately, Molloy insisted his confession was false, that he had made it partly out of revenge for being named by Vincent Hickey, and partly out of fear of further oppressive treatment. He said he had been with Robinson and his girlfriend, Carol Bradbury, in her Weoley Castle flat on the night of the murder, had never been to Yew Tree Farm or the area around it, and had nothing to do with the killing of the newspaper boy.

In the months that followed, Wiggall and the barristers he instructed were in a quandary. Molloy insisted he was not guilty, but had signed a statement saying he was. They were for some reason unimpressed by the fact that Carol Bradbury and her young daughter, Tracey, backed up Molloy's alibi. In those days, the very notion that a false confession to such a monstrous crime could be made under duress was unheard of, impossible to credit. The lawyers thought that, if Molloy stuck to what he said was the truth, he was likely to go down for murder. So they advised him not to tell the truth; not to contest his confession; to say nothing at the trial and allow his barrister to plead that, if the jury believed he was at the farm, then he was only there as a burglar who knew nothing about the murder.

Reluctantly, Molloy agreed to this strategy. He shrank at the back of the dock during the entire trial without ever getting the chance to say what he knew had happened. The unchallenged confession naming the other three was placed in the hands of the jury. The ridiculous legal fiction of the time pretended that the jury could not take the confession into account against the three men it named. This was obvious nonsense, as the foreman of the jury has since made plain. There was, effectively, no substantial evidence against any of the other three. Chiefly because they were named in Molloy's confession, they were convicted of murder and sent down for life.

Molloy's lawyers' stratagem—don't tell the court the truth and you might not go down for life—had to this extent succeeded. Molloy was convicted only of manslaughter and got 12 years. He would have been free in eight. The problem persisted, however. He had not been at the farm, and neither had the other three.

Molloy, who had committed no robberies, should never have gone to prison at all. Those who knew him might have imagined he would count his lucky stars and serve his eight years quietly. Instead, as he was hauled off to prison from the trial, he was overcome by remorse at what he had done to Robinson and the Hickeys and by indignation at the treatment he had received. He fired off a volley of statements to his lawyers which he insisted should form the basis of his appeal. He had not been at the farm. He had confessed for two reasons. First, he had been tortured:

I was questioned and insulted and called a thick Irish Mick. I was struck on the face several times, which broke my teeth, that was by Perkins, while he repeatedly asked me to sign a statement saying I was at the farm upstairs robbing it... The bearded one [Perkins] rushed back in and struck me a severe blow to the stomach and said he would be back in the morning for my signature. I was disturbed by the night staff every half hour. The meals I received were liberally dosed with salt and I was refused a drink. In the end I had to cup my hands in the lave basin and flush the toilet to get a drink of water.

He was terrified of further beatings.

Yet there was another emotion that convinced him to sign his statement: rage. As he put it all those years ago:

Perkins showed me a statement signed by Vince saying he was the driver, and me and Jim was at Yew Tree Farm with him. I was very upset about this because I knew me and Jim were not at Yew Tree Farm.

He had been shown a statement signed by Vince. Yet Vincent Hickey had signed no statement.

Ann Whelan first wrote to me at the *Daily Mirror* in February 1980, insisting that her son, Michael Hickey, was innocent of the Bridgewater murder. It was an outstanding letter, passionate and determined. But I was not convinced. The case against the men buttressed as it was by the unchallenged confession of Pat Molloy, seemed unanswerable. As 1980 went on, my initial doubts were dispelled by two developments.

The first was the release of papers by the Director of Public Prosecutions about Hubert Spencer, an ambulanceman based at Corbett Hospital in Stourbridge, who was in prison awaiting trial for the murder by shooting of his friend, Hubert Wilkes, who farmed the fields around Yew Tree Farm.

In the weeks after Carl's shooting, Spencer had been closely questioned by the murder squad. He was the only man in all the West Midlands who wore a uniform and drove a blue Vauxhall Viva. One of the best witnesses who had come forward said he saw a man in uniform driving a blue Vauxhall Viva into the farm entrance about an hour and a half before the boy's murder. Moreover, Spencer knew Carl Bridgewater. He coveted the antiques at Yew Tree Farm and had a record of petty burglary. He had access to shotguns. Spencer's murder of Wilkes was, and still is, completely inexplicable on any ordinary grounds. The two men were friends. The shooting had taken place over Christmas drinks, six weeks after the Bridgewater Four had been convicted at Stafford.

The coincidences seemed quite impossible to avoid. Certainly, if you ignored the Molloy confession, the evidence against Spencer was far stronger than that against the four. So, what about that confession? What convinced me more than anything else was Molloy's account of 'what happened at Wombourne'. It seemed very credible that a desperate and ruthless police squad, no doubt genuinely believing Molloy was part of the murder gang, should have resorted to beating and bullying to get their confession. The Spencer coincidences and Molloy's courageous and determined stand after he was convicted completely changed my mind and drove me into an alliance with Ann Whelan, which has lasted 17 years and produced innumerable articles and a book, most of which was written in her house.

She knew her son was innocent. Therefore she knew the other three were innocent. She worked hard to reconcile the four so their appeal would be concerted. She visited and sympathised with Pat Molloy. She made friends with his son Nick, who told her that when, as a small child, he and his mother visited his father in Liverpool jail soon after his confession, he had lifted his shirt to reveal his torso covered in weals and bruises—the work, no doubt, of the gallant DC Perkins. She went to see Molloy in the early summer of 1981, a few days before he suddenly died of a heart attack. Undeterred, she visited witness after witness.

Every time she uncovered some discrepancy, she would tell the authorities, and a new police inquiry would be set up. These would result, inevitably, in a Home Office statement announcing no further action. In all the years until now, the Manchester police, twice, the Cheshire, Warwickshire and Merseyside forces have all been engaged in these secret and fruitless inquiries.

In the freezing winter of 1983-84 Michael spent 90 days on the roof of Gartree prison, the longest prison protest in all history—an experience from which he has never fully recovered. Still the new evidence trickled out, still the police investigated, still there was no further action. William Whitelaw, home secretary in 1981, refused to reopen the case. So did home secretary Leon Brittan in 1984: he refused me permission even to meet the men in prison—despite a letter from the editor of the *Daily Mirror* putting the case for such a visit. David Mellor, Minister of State at the Home Office, announced that he and his colleagues were 'quite comfortable' with the Bridgewater verdict.

While all the new evidence that we could find pointed away from the men's guilt, the authorities became more and more determined to uphold it. Nor was Ann assisted very much by the media, especially the newspapers in the West Midlands, which denounced her as a busybody and a perverter of the course of justice.

A breakthrough came in 1986, when Ann went to Barnsley to see Brian Sinton, a petty crook who had told the trial that Michael Hickey had confessed to the murder while sharing a shower with him at Winson Green prison. This was by far the strongest evidence against Michael.

When Sinton came to see me and repeated his denunciation of his own evidence, the case against Michael was destroyed. Yet it took another year, and an hour-long documentary by Thames Television, to convince the home secretary, Douglas Hurd, to refer the case to the Court of Appeal.

It is, I think, not coincidental that Hurd, who plainly doubted the men's guilt, was not a Queen's Counsel. Anyone with a blind faith in British justice should study the proceedings in November 1988 to March 1989 of the hearing before Lord Justice Russell, a prosecutor of the Birmingham Six, Mr Justice Leonard, a defence lawyer in the original trial of the Guildford Four, and Mr Justice Potts. Every shred of the voluminous new evidence produced at the trial favoured the men's case. Sinton stuck doggedly to his assertion that he had lied in the original trial. Mervyn Ritter, who had told the court Robinson had confessed to him in prison, was exposed as an inveterate and pathological liar who would do anything for the authorities. The men's assertion, ridiculed at the trial, that they had been at a garage in Birmingham on the afternoon of the trial, was established to the satisfaction of the prosecution. Yet the judges seemed driven by their fantastic obsession that Ann Whelan had either bullied, bribed or badgered witnesses into changing their story.

For a time at the hearing it looked as though she and I and Jim Nichol, her lawyer, were the guilty parties. We had interfered with the course of justice by daring to suggest that their immaculate system had made a grotesque error. Such a concept was unthinkable to them.

The Birmingham Six, the Guildford Four, the Tottenham Three, Stefan Kizsko, Judy Ward, and many others later to be cleared, were still in prison.

On 17 March 1989 we sat listening all day to the judges droning through their interminable verdict. Mervyn Ritter, the pathological liar, was described by Mr Justice Leonard as a 'witness of truth'. Though there was no remaining credible evidence against him, Michael was still guilty. A new principle of English law was established—that a man is guilty if his cousin is. There was some evidence (his original verbal remarks about the murder) against Vincent. Vincent and Michael both agreed they were together on the afternoon of the murder. Therefore, though there was no substantial evidence against him, Michael was obviously guilty.

This is not fantasy. It is the only credible conclusion from the judgment. Jimmy Robinson and Vincent Hickey stormed out of the dock hurling abuse at the judges, and the three's wrongful imprisonment was renewed. Most people would have been knocked out forever by this judgement. But not Ann Whelan or Jim Nichol.

Their attention turned to the confession of Pat Molloy, who was not an appellant at the 1988-89 hearings. Linguistic experts asserted that the words of the confession could not have been Molloy's. Eric Shepherd, a Home Office forensic scientist, asserted that the police account of the confession was rubbish. Home secretary Kenneth Clarke QC, in a shockingly lazy statement, refused to reopen the case in 1993. Two and a half years later, home secretary Michael Howard QC said he was 'not minded' to do so either.

But events were moving against the Home Office. A judicial review forced the home secretary to release the reasons for Clarke's squalid decision in 1993. Howard, if he persisted with his refusal, faced a further hammering in another judicial review. A powerful campaign for justice for the Bridgewater Four had been building up. A BBC drama documentary, *Bad Company,* had been watched by millions. Susan Wooldridge, who played Ann Whelan in the drama, and George Irving, who played Jimmy Robinson, became relentless campaigners for the characters they had played.

The campaign committee met monthly, then fortnightly, published a newsletter, alerted people all over the country to every development. Jill Morell, who recognised the official obstruction from her campaign to free John McCarthy, wrote a powerful pamphlet.

Last year, Howard finally conceded. Announcing a 'fine line' between the arguments, he sent the case back to the Court of Appeal, and thus unleashed another huge roomful of undisclosed documents into the eager hands of Jim Nichol. There are those who describe what happened in the last two weeks as a stroke of luck for the defence. It was not. It was the result of Ann Whelan's persistence—her certainty that she was right and would eventually be proved so—and Jim Nichol's meticulous determination. Once the veil of secrecy that protected the Home Office and police files was torn asunder, the fact that the case was a frame-up and a cover-up from first to last was bound to come out.

In the event, forensic tests have proved that what Pat Molloy said all those years ago was absolutely true. He had been shown a statement from Vincent Hickey even though Vincent had not made one. It was forged, together with Vincent's signature, by the enterprising DC Perkins. It was as bogus as poor Pat Molloy's confession. The Crown threw in its hand, and the men, their lives wrecked, walked free.

A lot more of this shocking story will come out at the hearings in April. For the moment, we can leave the last word to Jimmy Robinson, whose eternal good humour and rich vocabulary has continued to pierce the gloom. Soon after the verdict, and before he was sentenced in November 1979, he wrote to Carol Bradbury:

> The judge might bow me down but he'll never break me because I know that for all his wisdom and for all the power of his legal system behind him, he's wrong, terribly wrong and somewhere, as happens very occasionally, the legal system and procedure has gone wrong, drastically wrong. Not much to hang a hope on you might think, and I don't either, but just knowing I'm innocent and being done for nothing gives me a perverse kind of gloating feeling that for all their high-sounding words and legal jargon, and the smug and clever arguments they've trotted out, they're as thick as shite and still wrong.

Secret policemen's balls-up

The answer to the question asked in the last two *Eyes*—How many of the policemen blamed for the wrongful conviction of the Bridgewater Four will come to court to explain themselves?—is now available. None.

The Crown lawyers admit that officers from the former No 4 Regional Crime Squad in the West Midlands forged a confession by one of the Bridgewater Four to extract a confession from another. None of these officers appeared in the men's final appeal, which has just finished; and nor was any explanation for their absence given to the court by the Crown QCs Jeremy Roberts and William Coker.

Roberts and Coker spent several days trying to confine responsibility for the appalling miscarriage of justice to this small group of officers. They insisted that the Staffordshire police, prosecution lawyers and all the judges had behaved impeccably. This view got a terrible hammering during the last week of the appeal.

Representing Pat Molloy, whose confession was the linchpin of the prosecution, Michael Mansfield QC exposed the role in extracting the confession not just of the regional crime squad officers—but the big chiefs of the Staffordshire police, too.

During the interminable and oppressive interrogation of Pat Molloy the then DCI Weslea Watson had told the frightened suspect: 'Vincent Hickey has said that one of you [Molloy or Robinson] pulled the trigger.' That statement was completely false.

Watson also asked Molloy: 'Did you fire the gun? Well, you know it's been suggested by someone.' That statement was completely false. The officer who headed the inquiry DCS Bob Stewart, told Molloy: 'We have been told you were the one who fired the shotgun.' That statement was completely false.

Mr Mansfield went on to show how another set of Staffordshire officers had reported a conversation with Molloy in a car which cannot have taken place at the time stated.

Private Eye 30 May 1997

Recently disclosed documents show that one of the officers was somewhere else at the time. Staffordshire officers of all ranks, said Mr Mansfield, were responsible for the 'ring of deceit' which extracted a false confession from Molloy.

Edward Fitzgerald QC, counsel for Michael Hickey, accused two other Staffordshire officers, Clive Williams and Clive Massey, of providing suspect evidence. Michael, then 16, was arrested in December 1978, but on 22 December the Director of Public Prosecutions sent a memo to the police saying there was no evidence to charge the boy. That very afternoon, while Michael was having his fingerprints taken, Clive Williams, then a detective sergeant, burst in to the room and asked Michael about Carl Bridgewater. He asked: 'Was the newspaper boy smiling when the gun went off?' To which Michael replied: 'No he wasn't.'

Although in countless interviews Michael utterly denied having had anything to do with the murder, this short exchange (which Michael anyway denied) was produced by the prosecution as serious evidence of a confession. At the trial, Williams's record of the conversation showed that he had formally cautioned Michael—'You are not obliged to say anything but what you say may be given in evidence, remember that'. This caution made the conversation admissible evidence.

A draft report made up by the officers for their seniors at the time, which has only recently been disclosed, does not include the caution. Mr Fitzgerald alleged that the caution may have been deliberately inserted into the record later to legitimise the conversation as evidence. The Crown accepted this, but neither of the officers appeared to explain themselves. Yet if the DPP had not had evidence of this conversation Michael would never have been charged.

The appellants' complaints climbed up higher. Patrick O'Connor QC for James Robinson sharply criticised the second prosecution QC at the 1979 trial, Igor Judge. Molloy's confession could not in law be regarded as evidence against any of the other three men. Yet Mr O'Connor detailed 17 separate occasions where Igor Judge QC dragged the Molloy confession into his cross-examination of Robinson. Robinson was asked, for instance, why Pat Molloy put him at the farm with his gun on the afternoon of the murder. Robinson, of course, who had not been on the farm and knew Pat Molloy hadn't been there either, had no reply. Judge's cross-examination, said Mr O'Connor, broke rules which had been established since 1925 and was 'plainly improper'. Yet the judge, Mr Justice Drake, had never objected to it and even joined in. Igor Judge is now a lord justice, only slightly junior to Lord Justice Roch who presided over this month's Bridgewater appeal.

Mr Mansfield pointed out at the end of the appeal that 'those representing Robinson' had not objected either. 'They might have missed one inadmissible question,' he said, 'but how could they miss 17?' Mr O'Connor criticised Jimmy Robinson's barrister on a wide range of matters.

Mr Mansfield and Mr O'Connor had better be careful that they do not repeat such criticism outside the protection of the court. For Mr Douglas Draycott QC, who represented Robinson at the Bridgewater murder trial, is not a man to ignore an assault on his reputation. Last November the case of Satpal Ram, an Asian who had been attacked in a restaurant by a racist gang, had killed one of his assailants and been convicted of murder, came to the Court of Appeal. John Silverman, the BBC's home affairs correspondent, reported on the *Today* programme that one of the grounds of the appeal was the alleged incompetence of the appellant's trial barrister, Douglas Draycott QC. The appeal and all its grounds were rejected. Draycott, advised by the brilliant and indefatigable lawyers for the Police Federation, Russell Jones and Walker, sued the BBC for libel. The case was settled out of court. The BBC broadcast an apology and paid Mr Draycott £17,500.

The Stephen Lawrence case

Something like the real story is beginning to seep out at the public inquiry into the 1993 racist murder of Stephen Lawrence.

Within hours of the murder, the police were inundated with information that the murderers were a racist gang of five youths, including David Norris, son of Clifford Norris, a notorious gangster and arms dealer in south London who is now in prison.

Clifford Norris's name did not emerge in the early days of the inquiry. When it did, Edmund Lawson QC, counsel to the inquiry, waxed very sensitive at the suggestion that he was suppressing information.

On 19 May he made a long statement defending himself from such criticism:

> If anything should come to our notice to suggest that there was any connection between Clifford Norris and any police officer, we would procure ['ensure', shurely? Ed] that that information was disclosed. Thus far it has not come to our notice, despite our looking at a great many documents, but if it did, it would be disclosed.

Whoops! Mr Lawson had plainly forgotten about a police complaints report against a Scotland Yard flying squad officer who had very close connections to Clifford Norris. Scotland Yard tells the *Eye* that this report was disclosed to the inquiry on 12 May, a full week before Mr Lawson's assurances on 19 May. By 20 May, however, he had found the report and was publicly grovelling.

'As you are aware, sir,' he told the inquiry chairman Sir William Macpherson, 'the report is now available to the inquiry, and it is right to say that it was previously available to the inquiry, and the fault for it not being drawn to your attention unequivocally is mine. I am afraid I overlooked it and I apologise to you and others in that respect. There is a report available which deals in some detail with the investigation carried out in the Metropolitan Police into the reports received from Customs and Excise and the outcome of that investigation.'

Private Eye 12 June 1998

Reluctantly the police agreed to hand over the report on condition that the flying squad officer's name be kept quiet. He was to be known as Officer XX. This further backward step into obfuscation by an important public inquiry is quite unjustified—and apparently unenforceable. Unless the *Eye* is given a credible reason for it, we intend in future issues to name the officer.

In the late 1980s Customs and Excise officers carried out a long investigation into Clifford Norris. They were surprised on three occasions to find their suspect hobnobbing in pubs with Detective Sergeant XX. The detail of the report's disclosures were spelled out on 3 June during the questioning of Detective Chief Superintendant William Illsley, a senior officer in overall charge of the Lawrence murder investigation by Rajiv Menon, barrister for Duwayne Brookes, Stephen Lawrence's friend and the only eyewitness to the murder.

Q: They thought, customs, that XX was warning Clifford Norris that he was a suspect because after the meetings he kind of vanished and because of some of the suspicious things that XX was doing during those meetings. He was observed making notes, he used a calculator, and on one occasion he was carrying a carrier bag which contained a number of oblong slabs or packages, and on one occasion Clifford Norris handed a carrier bag to him. All this aroused the suspicions of the customs officers. They reported to the police.
Mr Illsley: Yes
Q: An internal inquiry was set up. When XX was interviewed as part of that inquiry he said that various meetings with Clifford Norris in public houses was by pure chance and that, although unauthorised by any senior officer, he was meeting Mr Norris for the purpose of cultivating him as an informer. The police inquiry concluded that there was more to the relationship between XX and Clifford Norris than XX was prepared to admit?
A: Yes, sir.
Q: Yet for reasons best known to that internal inquiry they chose not to discipline him but simply to give him 'words of advice'.
A: Yes.

DS XX was disciplined over another matter—pretending he was attending a trial at the Old Bailey when he wasn't. He was demoted from sergeant to constable. But the importance of the new evidence was that it proved that at least one officer in the area had been mysteriously connected with the gangland criminal, Norris.

For a time the inquiry was told that DC XX had nothing to do with the Lawrence murder. But soon two more pieces of information emerged which linked the demoted officer very firmly to the murder investigation.

The first link was to DCS Ian Crampton, the officer who took charge of the Lawrence murder investigation immediately after the teenager was stabbed. It was Crampton's crass decision to engage after the murder in a policy of delay; and not to arrest young Norris or his four fellow suspects.

Crampton agreed that XX had worked under him at Bexleyheath police station in the 1980s when Crampton was the detective chief superintendent in charge of the station. When XX was hauled up in front of a disciplinary inquiry for his pub meetings with Norris and his fibs about the Old Bailey, DCS Crampton wrote him a warm reference.

> One of the officers serving under my command is DS XX... I found him to be reliable and honest and at no time had I any reason to question or suspect his integrity. His outlook, general vitality and experience made him an asset to the CIF office.

No doubt this generous reference helped the detective sergeant get off so lightly on such serious disciplinary charges. DCS Crampton told the inquiry that when he wrote the reference he had no idea that XX's disciplinary hearing had anything to do with Clifford Norris.

The second link between XX and the Lawrence murder emerged almost by chance during the cross-examination of Sergeant Peter Flook, an officer, now retired, who originally put much of the blame for the failure of the police investigation on the Lawrence family and their lawyer, but at the inquiry apologised for many of his more imaginative allegations.

Stephen Kamlish, a barrister for the Lawrence family, observed that there was 'an established link' between DC XX and the 'escorting of Duwayne Brookes'. It was soon agreed that DC XX had been appointed as an official police escort of the witness Duwayne Brookes while Mr Brookes was giving evidence in the Lawrences' 1996 private prosecution at the Old Bailey of three notorious south London racists for the Lawrence murder. On the day Mr Brookes gave evidence he was escorted by XX from the court to a hotel.

In cross-examination by Rajiv Menon on 3 June, DCS William Illsley was asked:

Can you think of a less appropriate officer in the Metropolitan Police to protect Duwayne Brookes during the all-important period when he was giving evidence at the Old Bailey... Would you have expected an officer such as XX, given that he had this particular association in the past, if he is chosen for this kind of specialist duty, to declare that connection with Clifford Norris so that somebody more appropriate could be selected for the job?

Mr Illsley replied: 'Absolutely, sir. Yes.'

Q: First he should never have been chosen. Secondly, the officer himself should have declared his known association with the father of the suspect and withdrawn from duty?
A: Absolutely, sir. Yes.

Grant withheld

After the exciting riot scenes involving the five suspects for the murder of Stephen Lawrence, the inquiry settled down to a routine day in which a senior police officer convincingly refuted the crucial evidence of two of his colleagues.

The controversy concerned a man so central to the Stephen Lawrence story that he has not been called to give evidence. He has been known throughout the inquiry by the pseudonym 'James Grant'. He is a young white skinhead who walked into Eltham police station at about 6pm on Friday 23 April 1993, the day after Stephen was stabbed to death.

Interviewed by Detective Constable Christopher Budgen, he said he could name at least two of Stephen's murderers, James Acourt and David Norris, both of whom, he said, had stabbed Stephen. (The fact that Stephen had been stabbed twice was not then publicly known.)

Grant indicated that his source of information was extremely close to the gang which attacked Stephen, and that he knew of two other sources. One (who became known as Witness B) had been on the top of a bus when he had seen the five men—two of whom he could identify—running away from the scene of the murder. The other—Witness K—visited the Acourts' home soon after the murder and saw the boys changing their clothes and wiping a knife.

Not surprisingly DC Budgen was very excited by this information. He asked Grant to wait while he rushed upstairs to tell his superior officer, Detective Inspector Bullock. Mr Bullock told Budgen to put the information into the system. Asked to explain this rather casual approach, Budgen gave the inquiry an interesting glimpse into the strange ways of Scotland Yard detectives. 'I felt,' he said, 'that Mr Bullock did not like me and therefore would not have taken a lot of interest in what I had to say.' The constable went downstairs again, told Grant to keep in touch and sent him on his way.

Private Eye 10 July 1998

The following day a new officer—Detective Sergeant John Davidson, who had 25 years experience—was brought in to take charge of the informant Grant. (DC Budgen was taken off the inquiry a week later.) Davidson had a number of meetings with Grant in which more and more vital information about the suspects was disclosed. All the information about these meetings has gone missing.

Mr Davidson told the inquiry that he had written it all down on a 'docket'. He went on: 'I believe the docket went missing, sir. I know it went missing because I know the docket was in my hand. I don't know where it went.'

Q: You say that all the dockets written by you in each of the meetings, and there are quite a number of them, half a dozen meetings or more, have been isolated?
A: Yes, sir.
Q: And not a single docket has come to light, and you say that is not your responsibility, you handed them in?
A: Yes, sir.

Mr Davidson went on to say that he had seen Witness B, the man on the bus, and had dismissed him as a 'Walter Mitty', and that he could not remember whether he even spoke to Witness K, the man who visited the Acourts' house on the evening of the murder. He also insisted, as did DC Budgen, that James Grant had not named his source.

This was refuted by Grant himself when he spoke to Kent police, who were investigating the police handling of the original murder inquiry. Grant insisted to the Kent officers that he had given police the name of his source—who was never interviewed. Michael Mansfield, the Lawrences' barrister, suggested: 'You really did not want this informant's material to be followed up.' Davidson replied: 'I don't like your suggestion, sir.'

Without the contemporary documents it is hard to decide who is right. So what did happen to those 'dockets'?

Davidson and Budgen both insisted that on 27 April 1993—five days after the murder—they had gone to Greenwich police station to 'register' James Grant as an informant. Once a police informant is registered, no one can interview him without the permission of the informant's controller—a very senior offer; and everything the informant says is widely circulated to senior officers throughout the division.

Until last week, on Thursday 2 July, no one doubted that Grant had indeed been registered.

The main evidence on that day came from Detective Chief Inspector Les Owen, who at the time of the murder was the controller of informants at Greenwich police station. Davidson and Budgen had testified that they had registered Grant with Mr Owen. Davidson said he saw Owen personally—Budgen that he had left the vital docket on Owen's desk. Quietly but firmly Mr Owen totally rejected the two officers' evidence. Grant, he said, had not been registered with him, and could not have been without inevitable consequences which never happened. To his certain knowledge, Mr Owen insisted, he had never met either officer. No docket had been left on his desk. He agreed at once with Mansfield's suggestion that the two officers' story was 'completely wrong'. When Mansfield suggested that the officers had pretended they had registered Grant as a 'smokescreen' to cover up his information, Mr Owen could not comment.

If Grant was not registered as an informant, the entire edifice of the official police explanation as to how such vital information was dealt with so disastrously falls apart. The matter should be resolved. But the inquiry team has broken off for two weeks. The idea that the glaring contradiction between the evidence of Sergeant Davidson and that of DCI Owen should be sorted out by further investigation—or by calling 'James Grant', who has indicated that he is quite happy to give evidence—does not seem to have occurred to them.

Sleaze

What's in a name?

Not much backbone judging by Tories' squeals for help

What are we to make of the huge gang of wealthy Tory MPs snivelling, bawling and even leaking to the Labour left about their losses at Lloyd's of London, the world's biggest insurance market?

They demand that Lloyd's should be held responsible for its mistakes and corruption.

Hold on a minute. Only ten years ago Tory MPs took up weeks of House of Commons time to pass a law which handed over all controls of Lloyd's of London to one organisation: the Committee of Lloyd's of London.

Under that law, the Committee of Lloyd's has immunity from being sued for negligence or incompetence or anything else.

The private bill was keenly supported by 52 Tory MPs who were 'names' at Lloyd's. To be a name, you must have at least £100,000 in the bank when all your debts are paid.

When the bill was first moved, names were making pots of money. The didn't want any outside body poking its nose into Lloyd's. But the Speaker told the 52 MP names that they had a conflict of interest and could not vote.

That didn't stop them speaking. A powerful speech for the bill was made by the new MP for Hemel Hempstead, Nicholas Lyell, a name at Lloyd's. He is now Sir Nicholas and is Solicitor General.

Another new MP, Archie Hamilton (Epsom and Ewell), wished the bill and Lloyd's chairman Peter Green 'every good fortune'.

A great sob could be heard in the chamber as Mr Hamilton explained: I have no money, which may be one reason why I am not a member of Lloyd's. I admit to having received two very lavish lunches through the hospitality of the Committee of Lloyd's.'

Daily Mirror 21 February 1992

Ambitious

Mr Hamilton never looked back. Three years later he became a name at Lloyd's, and is now Minister for the Armed Forces.

Forty-two MPs, almost all Labour, voted against the bill's second reading, while 206 MPs, almost all Tories, voted for it.

The teller for the Ayes was an ambitious young banker called John Major.

In February 1982 the bill, in its later stages, ran into trouble for lack of time. Lloyds rushed buckets of champagne to the committee rooms to stiffen the MPs' resolve.

In a rare move, the Tories proposed that the debate should go on until it was finished, however long it took. Twenty one Tory names voted for the motion, including current ministers like Peter Brooke, Lord James Douglas-Hamilton, Tim Renton and Richard Needham.

So Lloyd's got its act of parliament and its immunity.

Soon afterwards, Mr Peter Cameron-Webb and Peter Dixon hopped across the Atlantic with £30 million of other people's money, which they had swindled from the Lloyd's market. (They've been living in luxury ever since and haven't been charged.)

Chairman Peter Green, the lavish luncher, got a knighthood. In 1986 he was found guilty on five charges of discreditable conduct, fined £30,000 and banned from the market.

Only three months ago, the present chairman of Lloyd's, David Co-leridge, was embarrassed when he had to admit on TV that he had been a member of an exclusive 'baby syndicate' of the type he now denounces.

Foul

Names today, even if they are Tory MPs, can't any longer rely on rivers of money pouring from Lloyd's into their pockets.

So rich Tory MPs, who once demanded 'self regulation' and immunity for Lloyd's, now cry 'Foul' and call for new laws to compensate them for the collapse of the market they so passionately protected.

Hush, minister

Will Aitken reveal the arms deal secrets?

Jonathan Aitken, the new Minister for Defence Procurement, is a lifelong campaigner against government secrecy.

But will he join my campaign to publish the suppressed report on the biggest arms deal of the century?

Two weeks ago I protested about the House of Commons Public Accounts Committee decision not to publish the National Audit Office report into the multi-billion pound sale of Tornado jets and other arms by British Aerospace to the feudal dictators of Saudi Arabia.

No one knows more about selling to the Saudis than Mr Aitken.

In the latest House of Commons register of interests, he declares his directorship in:

> Al Bilad (UK) Limited (subsidiary of foreign parent company which received payments from contracts with Saudi Arabian royal family interests and government agencies).

Until last month, when he went to the Ministry of Defence and resigned all his directorships, Mr Aitken was deputy chairman of Aitken Hume. A third of the shares in Aitken Hume are owned by one of the most powerful businessmen in the world, Mr Wafic Said.

Wafic Said was described recently in the House of Commons by former arms firm chairman Gerald James as:

> The British Aerospace agent in Saudi Arabia responsible for winning the Tornado and Al-Yamamah deals, and a close friend of Mark Thatcher.

How close? In October 1987 Mrs Thatcher, then British prime minister, flew into Dallas, Texas, to greet her son, Mark, who lives there.

Daily Mirror 1 May 1992

On 19 October a banquet was thrown in her honour in the sumptuous Verandah Club. The guest list included the brightest, best and richest in America.

Only eight men sat at the prime minister's table. One of them was Wafic Said.

Mr Said had helped Mrs Thatcher clinch the multi-billion pound Saudi-British Aerospace deal. It was signed by the Minister of Defence two days after the Texas banquet.

Jonathan Aitken, the minister now responsible for arms sales, may not be too keen to campaign to publish the report about a deal clinched by his former close business colleague.

But will he at least give us more facts about the shocking export, under the nose of what is now his ministry, of super-guns made in Britain for Saddam Hussein?

After all, the debonair minister was also a director of a subsidiary of Astra Holdings, a company at the centre of the super-gun scandal. He left Astra several months after that company reported to the Ministry of Defence that it was exporting propellant for super-guns to Iraq.

Barrels for the super-guns were made by Walter Somers, a subsidiary of Eagle Trust, and Forgemasters of Sheffield.

Can you guess the name of the then financial advisers to Eagle Trust?

Aitken Hume.

A director of Forgemaster Holdings in the mid-1980s, well before the superguns were ordered, was Mr S T Graham CBE. He later became a director of a company whose name may sound familiar.

Aitken Hume.

Dirty money

When the Bank of Credit and Commerce International was closed down on 5 July 1991, a million people throughout the world lost their deposits. Many of the losers were from the Third World; small businessmen who had struggled to make a living in countries other than their own, and who had been impressed by BCCI's multilingual staff and its often trumpeted concern for the starving millions.

No previous bank collapse has caused so much distress. Many of the shocked depositors believed for a short while that their tragedy was the result of an act of God, or at least of some financial misfortune, such as a stock exchange crash, which could not have been foreseen. But, as the months dragged on without a penny compensation, and as the articles and books and reports started to be published, the astonishing truth emerged. The BCCI scandal had nothing to do with misfortune. It was the result of systematic fraud, conducted by what the New York District Attorney called 'a corrupt and criminal organisation' over a period of nearly 20 years. The mastermind behind the fraud was Agha Hassan Abedi. Abedi had what is known inside banks as charisma and outside banks as a nice line in drivel. He 'inspired' his staff to work hard by writing them homilies about God and loyalty. 'It is in the medium of giving', he wrote, 'that life flows into life, and God's divinity in all its embracing fullness, shines and rains softly, smoothly and bliss-fully on His Creation.' That sort of thing impressed the entrepreneurs who made their names in the eighties. Anita Roddick, for instance, whose Body Shop is one of the few such enterprises which has not yet gone bust, proudly quoted a slice of Abedi gibberish in her modest account of her magnificent achievements. Abedi's blarney was always aimed upwards, at the great minds and hearts of world society, and, for that reason, was consistently successful.

His insights were few, but he made the most of them. First among them was the understanding that there was an awful lot of money

London Review of Books 17 November 1992

floating around in the Gulf sheikhdoms. From his native Pakistan, Abedi made a beeline for Abu Dhabi, the richest of those states, and wove his ridiculous spell round the billionaire Sheikh Zayed and the millionaire families who formed his court. In exchange for the millions necessary to start the bank which was his life's dream, Abedi could provide anything those families wanted. Senator Kerry's report reveals:

> The prostitution handled by BCCI was carried over from practices originally instituted by Abedi at the United Bank, when, working with a woman, Begum Ashgari Rahim, he cemented his relationship with the Al-Nahyan family of Abu Dhabi through providing them with Pakistani prostitutes... She first won the favours or attention of the ruling family by arranging to get virgin women from the villages from ages 16 to 20. Rahim would make payments to their families, take the teenaged girls into the cities and there taught them how to dress and how to act, including the correct mannerisms appropriate to their intended roles as short-term sexual companions for the sheikhs... There was substantial competition among clothiers and jewellers for her business.

This sort of thing worked wonders, and, before long, the Abu Dhabi sheikhs were putting up the money for the new bank. But Abedi was not satisfied with a nice little earner in the Middle East. He wanted to win to his divine mission the most important people in the Western world. The basic principle which drove him on was that important people make the important decisions, and even the most important people have their price. The price for Bert Lance, a close friend of President Carter and briefly a member of Carter's administration, was obvious. Poor Bert had got into trouble with his own bank at home in Georgia and owed about $3 million. Abedi lent him the three million. It was never repaid, of course, but the two men were firm friends for life. Another much more distinguished convert was Clark Clifford, the beautifully spoken lawyer who had been a friend of the Kennedys and defence secretary to Lyndon Johnson. When Abedi first met him Clifford was looking for a cause—especially if it had a few million dollars attached to it. Adams and Frantz describe in detail one deal in which Clifford and his partner Robert Altman, well known in Washington social circles since he was married to Wonderwoman, bought and sold shares through BCCI and ended up with $9.8 million in their pockets. Kerry reveals that Clifford's and

Altman's firm was paid some $45 million in legal fees by BCCI. That sort of money persuaded Clifford to help BCCI to take over the biggest bank in Washington, through a number of not so subtle devices, despite being told by US government regulators that they could do no such thing.

Then there was President Carter himself. After being beaten in the 1980 election by Ronald Reagan, Carter had an understandable yearning to be taken seriously, and Abedi took him very seriously indeed. The holy banker flew round and round the world with the ex-president so that both men could declare their shared faith in the importance of Third World development—and conduct a bit of business on the side. When the Carter Centre opened in Atlanta 'to study Third World issues', Abedi lobbed in a vital half-million dollars. Senator Kerry concludes: 'President Carter became closely associated for a decade with a bank that constituted organised crime. This outcome was not in the interest of the United States.' Another Third World enthusiast from Georgia was Andy Young, Carter's former ambassador at the UN. Mr Young, too, was swept off his feet by Agha Hassan Abedi, and, during his two terms as mayor of Atlanta, took a consultancy fee of $50,000 a year from BCCI. During that time he travelled widely on BCCI jets, as did so many other important people, especially from the Third World itself. In South Korea, in Nigeria, in Jamaica (which impoverished island was at one time almost entirely owned and controlled by BCCI), in Brazil (the Brazilian ambassador to the United States became one of BCCI's most important employees, especially when he teamed up with the enormously influential Kissinger Associates), in Peru (where at one stage BCCI managed to 'hide' all government funds in another country after slipping the requisite $3 million into the pockets of state bank officials), in Argentina, in Paraguay, in China, India and the Far East, top people of every kind flocked to Mr Abedi, captivated by his charisma, his reforming zeal, and his largesse.

Like that other charismatic zealot, Robert Maxwell, Abedi made a special fuss of prosecutors, attorneys general and ministers of justice. So successful was he in this sphere that very few law offices bothered even to investigate the source of BCCI's funds. Much of this, it now turns out, was more likely than not to have been 'dirty money' from the sale of cocaine or, far more deadly, of armaments. Two of Abedi's favourite dictators in this field were Manuel Noriega, the drug smuggling president of Panama whose airline tickets on one BCCI-sponsored spree down the West Coast of the United States cost $30,000; and Saddam Hussein, who managed not to pay back a loan of $12 million on the grounds that he had a 'special relationship' with BCCI, in that it did not require him to make any special repayments.

All this generosity to important people had a purpose. It was to secure government funds for BCCI which would give a solid appearance to the bank's balance sheet and cut down the likelihood of investigation. Above all else, Abedi detested investigation—and not just because of all the money-laundering, drug-smuggling and arms traffic in which his bank was involved. The pillar on which he built his bank was the well-tried fraud known in the US after a former rogue called Ponzi. Simply put, Ponzi—and Abedi—borrowed money from one bank to pay back a loan from another. The device works perfectly well until someone rumbles it. That someone has to be paid off. Then others find out and they have to be paid off too. Suddenly, there are people all over the world being paid off in huge dollops of cash which the bank doesn't have—and the whole rotten edifice collapses.

British readers will be tut-tutting by now, remarking perhaps what nasty things can go on in what Margaret Thatcher's well-bred minister of state Alan Clark tastefully described as Bongo Bongo Land. They should read this, from Kochan and Whittington's little book:

> BCCI made hay out of the London connection. Arabs from the newly-enriched Gulf states came to the UK to enjoy the casinos, buy property, educate their children, shop and race their horses, and they banked in droves at the BCCI branches in their favoured prosperous locations—Marble Arch, Kensington, Mayfair and so on. Between 1973 and 1977, the number of BCCI branches in the United Kingdom grew from four to 45.

In fact, the centre of BCCI was good old Britain where everything is, to coin a phrase, safe as the Bank of England. Here was Abedi's favourite home, in leafy Harrow, his favourite place of business, his favourite famous friend, solid, dependable former prime minister James Callaghan, who developed for the cranky banker what he called 'a warm personal regard'—and his favourite regulator, the Bank of England. Abedi used to complain to his progressive friends that the Bank of England would never let BCCI into its 'club', but, in truth, he was delighted with the cooperative attitude of the Bank.

These two books about BCCI are rapidly-constructed and competent narratives by journalists (Adams and Frantz from the United States, Kochan and Whittington from Britain). Adams and Frantz give a thriller-like account of the 'sting' with which the US customs first brought BCCI officials to the Florida courts. But neither book can deal with the question which should most disturb British readers: why and how did a corrupt bank which was regulated by the Bank of England get away with it for so long? The question is dealt with directly by these two government reports. The Kerry report, which is as yet unavailable in Britain, is a magnificent document: a huge, toughly-written indictment not just of the corruption and filth in BCCI but of the breathtaking complacency of the authorities on both sides of the Atlantic.

Senator Kerry believes (though Senator Brown does not always agree) that his investigation was deliberately and continually impeded by the Bush administration. The close proximity of Bush to Irangate and now to Iraqgate makes that seem very likely. For British readers, however, the senator's report is at its most powerful when it deals with the Bank of England. These are Kerry's (very striking) conclusions: (1) The Bank had 'deep concerns' about BCCI from the late seventies but 'sought to avoid having to conduct the regulatory oversight' necessary. (2) In 1988 and 1989 the Bank 'learned of BCCI's involvement in the financing of terrorism and in drug money laundering' but 'declined to exercise the broader supervision which it had the ability to exercise'. (3) In the spring of 1990 the Bank knew of substantial loan losses and had evidence of fraud. The response was 'not to close BCCI down but to prop it up'. (4) In April 1990 the Bank 'relied on British secrecy and confidentiality laws to reduce the risk of BCCI's collapse. As a result innocent depositors and creditors who did business with BCCI after that date were denied vital information that could have protected them against losses.' (5) The Bank's decision in 1990 to permit BCCI to move its headquarters and records out of London 'had profound negative consequences all over the world. Essential witnesses and documents were handed over to Abu Dhabi, which has not given them up to investigators.' This was a costly and likely irretrievable error on the part of the Bank of England. Two further nails were hammered into what ought to be the Bank's coffin. First, the decision to close BCCI in July 1991 had nothing to do with the Bank's own judgment. The Bank of England was pushed into it by the US authorities, which, later that month, unleashed a huge fraud indictment against BCCI which is still in progress. Second, from April 1990, 'the Bank of England had...inadvertently become partner to a cover-up of BCCI's criminality'.

It is hard to imagine a more savage indictment of any authority, let alone one which purports to safeguard banking practices in the banking centre of the world. Kerry cannot contain his indignation, not so much at the dithering and incompetence of the Bank, though they were staggering, but at the secrecy laws and fetish for confidentiality which allowed the BCCI scandal to be covered up. He has overwhelming proof that arms traffickers and terrorists used BCCI, and that intelligence agencies on both sides of the Atlantic cooperated with the bank, sometimes to track down the wrong-doers, sometimes to collude with them. He reveals that the first people allowed into the BCCI London headquarters after the closure was announced were officers from MI5, who swiftly 'sealed' a large quantity of documents which have never been made available to the Kerry inquiry. He notes that British judges, sitting in secret, have intervened to resist the disclosure to his inquiry of documents and bank accounts which would shed a great deal of light on the success of BCCI in Britain, and the share in that success of intelligence spooks and armaments bandits.

Very little attention was paid in the British media when the Kerry report was published at the end of September. Price Waterhouse, BCCI's auditors, which also gets a terrible drubbing from the report, put out a baleful statement to the effect that it had not given evidence to Kerry (though Robert Bench, a partner in Price Waterhouse US, was a principal witness). When a report on the same subject by Lord Justice Bingham was published in October, editors and ministers seized it eagerly, searched it for any direct indictment of the Bank such as Kerry had delivered, but found nothing so forthright. Because Bingham did not call for anyone to resign or be disciplined, they concluded, everything and everyone could stay in place. Bingham's report is written in a quite different style from Kerry's. It shows no shock or outrage, as though bank frauds of this magnitude are really things which gentlemen ought to take in their stride. Well-bred British judges naturally shy away from the stridency of bumptious senators from Massachusetts. Was not Lord Justice Bingham, after all, at public school with one of the Price Waterhouse partners, Tim Hoult, who gave evidence to him?

The Bingham report, moreover, has large holes in it caused by the secrecy and confidentiality which Kerry denounces. A glorious example is Section F, headed 'The Intelligence Agencies'. The section starts: 'For security reasons, the involvement of the intelligence agencies is described in a separate appendix, Appendix 8.' Feverishly, the reader searches for Appendix 8. It is not there! Back then to Section F. After the reference to Appendix 8, there is a demure asterisk corresponding to another asterisk at the bottom of the page. Published there, for all to see, are three words: 'not being published'. Not being published! Why? The allegation is that terrorists and arms traffickers used British banks to conduct their illegal trade—and that the intelligence services were involved. In the United States, elected senators were allowed to pursue that allegation, find it partly proved and publish their findings. In Britain, such disclosure, in an inquiry set up by an elected parliament, is out of the question. But wait. Anyone who concludes that the Bingham report is a straight cover-up for the Bank is making a big mistake.

Despite its moderate tone and its reluctance to condemn out loud, the report is a long catalogue of carelessness on the part of the Bank, the auditors and other agencies responsible. Again and again, Bingham produces evidence of reports to the Bank of strange goings-on at BCCI, all of which were cynically ignored. Bingham reports that he finds the Bank's reaction 'hard to understand'; that he is 'puzzled'; that he 'cannot accept' the official explanation. Perhaps the summit of his laid-back approach is reached, appropriately enough, in an addendum when he discusses what the Bank told the Treasury about BCCI:

> When, on 4 April 1990, BCCI was described as 'in many ways remarkably successful', the Treasury could scarcely have deduced that a loss of $49 million for 1988 was going to be followed by one of $498 million for 1989. When on 5 April 1991, the Bank was reported to be happy about the financial position of BCCI, the Treasury could scarcely have appreciated that the Bank was technically insolvent. This picture of BCCI which the Bank gave the Treasury during this period was in my opinion misleading, both in what was said and more particularly in what was not.

The Bank, in short, was lying. It was lying directly to cover up the real state of affairs at BCCI. But Bingham's very next sentence is:

'The Bank had no intention to mislead.' This is so preposterous that, for a time, I took it as an editing mistake where the word 'no' had been wrongly inserted. Obviously, the Bank intended to mislead. That was its policy—to keep things quiet in the hope that they could be sorted out in secret. The whole thrust of the Bingham report is to provide the facts to incriminate the Bank and then to flounce away from incrimination.

Enormous relief swept over the British government when it read Bingham. The Chancellor of the Exchequer, Norman Lamont, who was educated at Cambridge and trained at Rothschild's, told the House of Commons he had every faith in Robin Leigh-Pemberton, governor of the Bank of England, a personal friend of the prime minister who appointed him, Margaret Thatcher. When the House of Commons debated the Bingham report on 6 November, Lamont didn't even bother to speak. His place was taken by his economic secretary, Anthony Nelson, who was educated at Cambridge and trained at Rothschild's. Nelson made a speech of monumental complacency to the effect that there was always a rotten apple in the barrel and the government was resolutely determined to leave no stone unturned or avenue unexplored to ensure that nothing of the kind ever happened again.

As is plain from the Kerry report (which only one MP who spoke, Peter Hain, appeared to have read), BCCI was not just a rotten apple in the barrel. The barrel has been stinking for at least half a century. In the 1960s we had the Bank of Sark affair (£100 million stolen) and Bernie Cornfeld, who with Robert Vesco, swiped hundreds of millions of dollars from investors in a 'mutual fund' modestly called the Fund of Funds. Cornfeld pioneered the dual use of the offshore trust and the Luxembourg bank which Abedi made into an art form. In the 1970s and 1980s the banking world was shaken by the gigantic fraud set up by Roberto Calvi and Michele Sindona of the Banco Ambrosiano and the Franklin Bank. Like Abedi, Calvi and Sindona felt they were on the side of God—and had not a little help in their endeavours from the Vatican. Abedi's techniques were also used, almost to the letter, by Michael Hand in the intricate drug and money laundering operation at the Australian Nugan Hand Bank. Perhaps the best example comes once again from dear safe old Britain. When the Johnson Matthey Bank went bust in 1985, the Bank of England was so terrified of the consequences that it quickly formed a 'lifeboat'—ie, had a whip-round among the clearing banks to bail out the depositors. Then a committee was set up to leave no stone unturned or avenue unexplored to ensure that nothing of the kind would ever happen again. It was called the 'Leigh-Pemberton Committee' after the governor of the Bank of England—the man who presided over the BCCI disaster, which followed almost immediately.

The problem is not that that a few crooks escaped the net. It is that the net itself welcomes, encourages and bankrolls the crooks. The free-enterprise fanaticism which has swept the intellectual and political world in the last 12 years—free enterprise policed by free entrepreneurs—was followed, inevitably, by the most untrammelled corruption; and the loving way in which Abedi and his crooks were cosseted and caressed by famous banks, famous politicians and famous lawyers shows just how firmly-rooted that corruption is.

First published as a review of A Full Service Bank: How BCCI Stole Millions Around the World *by James Ring Adams and Douglas Frantz (Simon & Schuster);* Bankrupt: The BCCI Fraud *by Nick Kochan and Bob Whittington (Gollancz);* The BCCI Affair: A Report to the Senate Committee on Foreign Relations *by Senators John Kerry and Hank Brown (US Senate Foreign Relations Committee);* Inquiry into the Supervision of the Bank of Credit and Commerce International *by Lord Justice Bingham (HMSO).*

Swindlers list

There was an embarrassing splurge of publicity when it was announced that about half a million people had been swindled in a multi-billion pound pension scam. But no one listed the politicians responsible: the Rt Hon Norman Fowler, chairman of the Tory party; the Rt Hon Anthony Newton, leader of the House of Commons; and the Rt Hon John Major, prime minister.

Soon after the huge Tory victory in 1983, a group of ardent Thatcherites, based at the Centre for Policy Studies and the new 'independent' University of Buckingham, began a campaign to 'free' the pensions industry.

Prominent campaigners were Nigel Vinson, deputy chairman of Barclays Bank and for many years a director of the Centre for Policy Studies, and Philip Chappell, a director of Morgan Grenfell merchant bank.

A wunch of bankers

In pamphlets and papers and even a book, the bankers campaigned for 'portable pensions for all'. They declared it a fundamental individual freedom to own a personal pension free from the welfare state and free from the mushrooming pension schemes based in the workplace, which they denounced as 'collectivist' and 'crypto-socialist'. They wanted everyone to be free to buy their own pensions from an insurance company, a building society, or a bank.

Their campaign was eagerly supported by Margaret Thatcher, who passed on her enthusiasm to her devoted secretary of state for social services, Norman Fowler. Soon after the 1983 election, he set up a 'retirement' study group. Its members were chosen from a typically wide range. Alongside Fowler and his minister of state, Barney Heyhoe, sat Professor Alan Peacock, vice-chancellor of the University of Buckingham; Mark Weinberg, the new chairman of Allied

Private Eye 25 February 1994

Dunbar Assurance, a large life assurance group, and Marshall Field, general manager of Phoenix Assurance.

The group took evidence from the Centre for Policy Studies, which recommended an immediate and drastic switch to private pensions, and the National Association of Pension Funds (NAPF), which was worried about the possible break-up of workplace schemes.

Derek Bandey, a pensions specialist who was chairman of the NAPF's parliamentary committee, tells the *Eye*:

> I kept warning the government that there is more freedom and more security in a fund managed by elected trustees than in private pensions managed by a bank or an insurance company.

When Fowler ignored these warnings and announced proposals for a new law to 'free pensions', the NAPF was thoroughly alarmed. In September 1985 it declared:

> It would be obdurate and short sighted of the government to disregard the strength of feeling about the very real disruption that must follow if the proposal are implemented... We regret that the stability necessary to provide for the long term retirement needs of the working population is now to be destroyed.

Obdurate and shortsighted throughout, Fowler took no notice. When a Gallup poll he commissioned suggested that not many people would leave their workplace pension schemes, he decided to bribe them. His social security bill offered an 'incentive'—a 2 percent rebate on national insurance contributions—to people who left their schemes and bought private pensions. 'The individual', the secretary of state promised the Commons on 28 January 1986, 'will have a splendid deal.'

Derek Bandey was not impressed: 'I told them their new bill was a cowboys' charter.'

The new bill was the 1986 Social Security Act. To help get it through the Commons, Fowler had two new lieutenants: his minister of state Tony Newton and his parliamentary under-secretary, a former banker called John Major. From January to May 1986, these two took the bill through its standing committee. Again and again they brushed aside warnings about their cowboys' charter.

When Labour's Margaret Beckett said: 'We are concerned about the unscrupulous overselling of personal pensions' (4 February 1986),

Newton replied that people could always get advice from the bank managers. 'I must say,' he said, 'that people have more confidence in their bank managers than in their MPs' (6 February).

John Major ridiculed the warning of Labour MP Michael Meacher that 'many people will come out of the occupational schemes to their disadvantage' (11 February). When asked directly how many people would lose from new private pensions, Major replied: 'The concept of turning this into a one-way, risk-free option is entirely alien' (18 February).

He promised safeguards, but when specific ones were demanded, he turned them down. He turned down a statutory limit on commissions or administrative charges. Ill-briefed, bland, inflexible, he stuck doggedly to his leader's 'principle' that a 'person can own his own pension'.

Margaret Beckett snapped back angrily—and prophetically: 'I have this vision of some outraged pensioners of the future coming to Mr Major's successor claiming that they cannot afford to eat and being told: 'At least your pension is your own' (28 January).

Fowler and fouler

The bill had its third reading on 20 May 1986. Fowler trumpeted: 'We are opening up the provision of pensions not just to life assurance companies but to building societies, banks and unit trusts.'

The response from the City was electric. An army of hurriedly-trained salespeople, hungry for commission, swarmed round schools, pit villages and hospitals to flog private pensions. Miners, teachers and nurses were told they could opt out of their workplace pension schemes and pay less for a bigger pension.

The results were predictable. Between 1989 and 1992, at least half a million people transferred. In 1991 and 1992, as the recession bit, £5.5 billion worth of pension money went from relatively safe schemes to much riskier ones. For four years no one seemed to notice. Then, last year, the 'regulators' (the Securities and Investment Board) finally stirred. They commissioned a report on 735 representative transfers.

Published last December at the modest price of £60, the 24-page report disclosed that only 9 percent of these transfers showed 'substantial compliance with the main conduct of business requirements'.

The remaining 91 percent were judged either 'unsatisfactory' (54 percent), suspect' (8 percent) or both (29 percent). 'Suspect' was defined as 'showing evidence of an apparently perverse recommendation, positive evidence of miselling or of playing on emotive issues'—in a word, rip-off.

In a private speech to pension fund experts recently, Paul Trickett, head of the Mineworkers' Pension Scheme, revealed that in the five years to September 1993, the scheme had paid transfer values totalling £736 million, well over 90 percent of which went to personal pension plans. 'I would argue', he said 'that the basis on which many people have been encouraged to transfer has been questionable and on many occasions I have been forced to wonder whether the advice to transfer might not be linked to the generation of commission.'

He reckoned that £335 million had been swiped in commissions from the mineworkers' scheme alone. He named the top five beneficiaries of transfers from his scheme: the Trustee Saving Bank, privatised by Thatcher; Pearl Insurance; the Prudential; Britannic Assurance; and Legal and General, which raised its contribution to the Tory party in 1992 from £28,000 to £40,000.

Who else did well? Nigel Vinson got his peerage and Marshall Field his CBE in 1985, the year of their pensions triumph. Mark Weinberg and Professor Peacock were knighted in 1987. But the most startling promotion of all came to the ministers who made the swindle possible.

In 1990 Norman Fowler left the cabinet with his knighthood to spend more time with his wallet. A few months later, the young banker he groomed during those gruelling standing committee sessions on the 'freeing of pensions' was in 10 Downing Street. Sir Norman was called back from the City to renew the old partnership. The Great Pensions Triumvirate was completed when Newton was made Leader of the House. Prompt government action to repair the pensions damage is not expected.

Derek Bandey, now retired, tells the *Eye*: 'I can remember saying to ministers during the passage of the bill that this would be the greatest rip-off of all time. I take no comfort in having been proved right.'

Aitken's CD past

In the same year that Jonathan Aitken MP became a director of the arms company BMARC, the Official Receiver and the Department of Trade and Industry considered taking proceedings to disqualify him from all directorships.

Their concern arose from the MP's directorship of Beaverbrook Investments, and its purchase in 1986 of a company called Oasis Merchandising Services. Oasis was formed in 1985 by a Chichester businessman called Nigel Howick. Howick wanted to supplement his records business, called Stage One, by selling CDs and tapes in motorway outlets. He teamed up with a Gravesend salesman called Brian Smith. Smith tells the *Eye* that his side of the business prospered: 'Sales were improving and there were big customers ready to come in.' Then, in the autumn of 1986, Beaverbrook Investments took out a mortgage on all the assets of Oasis Merchandising, and a few weeks later bought the whole company.

A year later, in November 1987, Oasis was wound up by Beaverbrook, and receivers were called in. In January 1988 both companies were investigated very closely by the Official Receiver in Croydon, whose office on 24 March submitted what they called a 'fraudulent trading report' about Oasis. The assistant official receiver, a Mr C F Webb, described the allegations in the report as 'of a serious nature involving a public company which held a floating charge over the assets of the company which is the subject of this report'. He warned that 'a prominent Member of Parliament' was involved.

The Department of Trade, which is responsible for the Official Receiver, always insists that inquiries about companies are conducted without fear or favour of the importance of the individuals under investigation. But on this occasion something like panic seems to have gripped the department.

In April a 'draft submission' to ministers about the Oasis case was drafted by Graham Horne, the chief examiner of the DTI's prosecutions unit at Companies House. The draft was circulated in the department and amended. One official, Mr G J A Harp, thought the department had been too slow to report the matter to the politicians. He thought that ministers should have been warned 'within days of the winding up order'.

At once it was decided that Jonathan Aitken's involvement in the case was too hot to handle in the lower reaches, or by ordinary police (though Detective Chief Inspector Gale of the Metropolitan Police was kept informed).

In July, Edward Thompson, a senior solicitor at the DTI, attended an anxious meeting at the Serious Fraud Office, to which the case had been referred. The only reason for the referral appears to have been the status of Jonathan Aitken. The chief problem was the 'floating charge' on Oasis held by Beaverbrook Investments, which meant that Beaverbrook had first call on all the company's business and assets.

Was this fair to the other creditors? After examining the accounts and the reports of interviews with the main parties, the meeting at the SFO, chaired by Mr C W Dickson, decided that there wasn't enough evidence to support a charge of fraudulent trading. The meeting eagerly decided instead to consider taking disqualification proceedings against the directors of Beaverbrook.

Everyone at the meeting agreed that there was a case for a public examination of Jonathan Aitken, and urged the retention of a senior barrister for that purpose. No final decision was taken about possible criminal proceedings, and the inquiries in the department continued apace.

On 2 August, Mr Thompson warned his superiors that Jonathan Aitken was a very powerful businessman and would be likely to fight any disqualification proceedings very hard indeed. The Official Solicitor, then Mr Les Cramp, set in motion a 'disqualification report' for the DTI's disqualification unit.

At that stage, in mid-August 1988, almost everyone involved from the Official Receiver downwards took the view that disqualification proceedings against the directors of Beaverbrook Investments were appropriate.

But there, rather suddenly, the whole affair screeched to a stop.

On 18 July the *Eye* submitted a list of questions on this matter to the Department of Trade and Industry. In their reply on 21 July, the DTI confirmed:

(1) The Official Receiver's preliminary report 'concerning the

insolvent trading of the company' on 28 March 1988.

(2) The meeting on 28 July at the SFO, which was attended, say the DTI, by 'representatives of the Official Receiver, the Insolvency Service, departmental solicitors and the police.'

(3) The meeting's decision that there wasn't enough evidence for criminal proceedings, and to 'consider whether civil disqualification proceedings against the directors were appropriate'.

What happened then, was the *Eye*'s main question. The reply suddenly became vague. 'It has not yet been possible to trace all the case papers dating back to 1988. One particular resource problem faced by the Official Receiver at the time was some 300 boxes of papers belonging to the company had to be examined.'

The outcome was: 'No disqualification proceedings were commenced against any director.' Quite, but why? The DTI can't be sure. 'It appears,' they guess, 'that the Official Receiver was unable to satisfy himself as to the sufficiency of the evidence in support of unfit conduct on which to base proceedings.'

The *Eye* asked: 'Was Lord Young, then Secretary of State at the DTI and/or other ministers at the department informed about the proposed disqualification proceedings? If so, what was their reaction?'

For this the department reserved their most mealy-mouthed reply: 'There does not appear to have been, from the files recovered to date, any briefing of ministers.' If this is true, the panic-stricken reactions of DTI and senior Official Receiver officials from the outset of the inquiry—that ministers should immediately be informed—were scrupulously ignored.

Jonathan Aitken was not disqualified. He held on to his 40-odd directorships, including that of BMARC. In 1992 John Major brought him into the government as Minister of Defence Procurement; and in 1994 he was promoted to the cabinet as Chief Secretary to the Treasury, a post from which he has just resigned to make it easier for him to sue Granada Television and the *Guardian*.

Down in Gravesend, Brian Smith still can't understand why his firm was put into receivership. The firm's business, he said, had been sold on twice by receivers to its former competitors and appeared to be flourishing. 'I thought it was very successful,' he says. 'But you know what all these big people are like. They've got loads of money and it's only the people who do the work who in the end suffer, really.'

What can he mean?

Swindlers list: 2

For almost a year, five big banks and insurance companies have been trying to prevent six people they swindled from suing them in the courts. The six are victims of the biggest swindle in British history.

Between 1988 and 1994 a million people were hoodwinked by commission-hungry salespeople into buying pension policies incomparably worse than the ones they already had. The banks and insurance firms which employed the sales staff swiped at least £4 billion of ordinary people's money. The whole process was made possible by a 1988 law which was dreamed up in the Centre for Policy Studies and drummed through the Commons by Norman Fowler, former chairman of the Tory party, Tony Newton, now leader of the House, and John Major, prime minister.

The six who sued were two nurses, a school janitor, a legal aid administrator, an assembly line worker and a redundant miner. The miner was sold a complicated and comparatively worthless pension scheme by the merchant bank Hill Samuel despite the fact that he could not read. The companies involved were the Prudential, Gan Life (twice), Hill Samuel, TSB and Irish Life.

These companies have argued that they, the swindlers, were themselves better able than the courts to assess the cases and compensate the people they had swindled. But, this month, Judge Raymond Jack came down firmly on the side of the swindled six.

The judge observed that none of the six companies had met the first deadline set by the Securities and Investment Board for dealing with high priority cases—31 December 1995; that many of the cases were rapidly approaching their 'limitation' deadline, which could prevent the plaintiffs from suing; and that no offer had been made by the companies to pay for independent legal advice on the proper levels of compensation. The whole review was bogged down by computer problems. Swindled pensioners were growing old and dying.

Private Eye 26 January 1996

Yet no more than a tiny handful, less than a tenth of 1 percent, has had a penny compensation.

The companies argued that their reviews were being 'rigorously' supervised by the government appointed regulator, the Personal Investment Authority. The PIA is run by a board of 20 people. Ten of these are 'practitioner directors': David Berridge, chief executive of Scottish Equitable Life, which sells pensions; Danis Brown, partner of the independent Financial Advisory Centre, which advises firms which sell pensions; Lawrence Churchill, chief executive of National Westminster Life Assurance, which sells pensions; Allan Daffern, chief executive of Willis Corroon Financial Planning, which sells pensions; Ken Davy, chairman of DBS Financial Management, which sells pensions; Tony Gordon, of Redcliffe Associates plc, which sells pensions; Peter Gray, chairman of Tunbridge Wells Equitable Friendly Society, which sells pensions; David Mills, a general manager from the Midland Bank, which sells pensions; Michael Pickard, chairman of the Royal London Mutual Insurance Society, which sells pensions; and Jeremy Willoughby, director and company secretary of Gartmore plc which... You get the picture.

There is nothing odd about this, says the PIA spokesman. The whole point of 'practitioner directors' is that they are engaged in the activity they are regulating. They are 'balanced' by ten 'public interest directors' who are meant to be independent of that activity. But are they?

Joe Palmer, the chairman, is former chief executive of Legal and General, which sells pensions. Sir Terence Heiser is a director of Abbey National plc, whose subsidiaries...sell pensions. A PIA spokesman explained: 'The board was aware when it appointed Sir Terry of his non-executive directorship of Abbey National but was satisfied that he could still bring his considerable expertise to serve on the board.'

The other eight 'public interest directors' are three 'consumer consultants', a former Treasury solicitor, the chairman of the Police Complaints Authority, the political editor of the *Economist*, a former managing partner of the accountants Ernst & Young, and Professor David Llewellyn, Professor of Money (sic) and chairman of the University of Loughborough Banking Centre, funded by the Midland Bank. Among the 20 regulators there is not a single trade unionist (though trade unions represent tens of thousands of swindled pensioners); nor anyone who can remotely be described as a representative of the swin-dled million.

The problems of packing the PIA board with so many pensions ex-perts came to the surface in July 1994 with a stinging public rebuke for the life insurance and pensions arm of Barclays Bank. That same month Ken Bignall, vice-chairman and managing director of Bar-clays Financial Services, resigned from the board of the PIA.

Scottcha!!

The government's prompt reaction to the Scott report, which accused ministers of 'designedly' deceiving parliament and public, was designedly to deceive parliament and public.

The man chosen for the job was Ian Lang, President of the Board of Trade and a name at Lloyd's. Mr Lang boasted: 'The report confirms', and I quote, 'the government was not prepared to countenance the supply of lethal equipment to either Iran or Iraq.'

That depends, though, on what you mean by 'lethal'. Lathes and other machinery approved for export from Britain to Iraq in 1990 were, according to one Ministry of Defence expert quoted by Scott, 'sufficient to equip a factory designed to produce 500,000 155mm shells per annum' (D6.106). 'Non-lethal' defence-related equipment worth more than £300 million was exported from Britain to Iraq in the 1980s. Mr Lang was good enough to say that 'during the 1980s some evidence existed that certain other countries might have diverted arms to Iraq.'

Old Lang's lying

Then came the lie direct: 'As far as British goods were concerned, steps were taken to counter this.' In fact no steps at all were taken to counter it. Scott says:

> Government knowledge that Jordan was being used as a diversionary destination (for arms to Iraq) goes back at least to 1983 (E2.4).

> No special procedures were put in place in order to try and assess the likelihood of diversion to Iraq (E2.12).

> To be fair to Jordan, its use as a 'front' had been deliberately encouraged by the United Kingdom in the early 1980s for the purpose of arranging the sale to Iraq of 29 armoured recovery vehicles (2.16).

Private Eye 23 February 1996

In the period from 1984 to 1990, no special procedures were put in place in order to combat the use of Jordan as a diversionary route for British exports to Iraq... Even the apparent complicity of senior officers in the Jordanian armed forces in conspiracies to facilitate the export of military materials to Iraq did not move the Foreign Office to protest (E2.56).

How much lethal equipment went to Iraq through Jordan? Scott can't find out, but the trade in arms between Britain and Jordan in the 1980s was 3,000 percent higher than in the 1970s. Scott also reveals 'a fair probability' that 15,000 large artillery shells went to Iraq from Britain via Saudi Arabia (E6.6).

Lang's capacity for deception moved into even higher gear when he came to defend his colleague the Chief Secretary to the Treasury, William Waldegrave. 'My right honourable friend', he drooled, 'is absolved of the charge that he intended to mislead members of this House or anyone else.'

On the contrary, the Scott report again and again convicts Waldegrave of giving parliament and public information about the government's arms sales policy to Iraq which was untrue and which he knew to be untrue. In late 1988 and early 1989, three ministers of state—Waldegrave (FCO), Alan Clark (DTI) and Lord Trefgarne (MOD)—agreed to change one of three guidelines governing government policy on defence equipment sales to Iran and Iraq. The change was immediately put into effect by officials. It substantially increased defence sales to Iraq and cut defence sales to Iran, yet the three ministers agreed among themselves not to tell parliament, the public or even, apparently, their secretaries of state or the prime minister.

The new policy was rigorously pursued, while parliament and public were told the old policy was still in force. In four months in 1989, Waldegrave signed 26 letters to MPs declaring that the 'government have not changed their policy on defence sales to Iraq or Iran'. Scott commented: 'Mr Waldegrave knew, first hand, the facts that, in my opinion, rendered the "no change in policy" statement untrue.' In plain language, the minister was lying to parliament.

In numerous, interminable and (for us taxpayers) expensive submissions, Waldegrave protested to Scott that the guidelines had not been changed. Scott totally rejected this. 'To describe this revised formulation as no more than an interpretation of the old is, in my opinion... so plainly inapposite as to be incapable of being sustained by serious argument' (D3.123) and 'not even remotely tenable' (D3.90). Waldegrave's excuse for not telling the prime minister about the change was 'unconvincing...without substance' (D3.104). His suggestion that the policy had not changed because the prime minister had not approved the change was 'sophistry' (D3.125). The section on Waldegrave is a formidable indictment which, in ordinary times, no minister could survive.

Richard the faint-heart

Chief Secretary Waldegrave has survived so far only because Scott briefly indulged himself in the linguistic gymnastics for which he so freely criticises others. The most ridiculous example is in paragraph D3.124:

> I accept that Mr Waldegrave did not have any duplicitous intention and regarded the relaxed interpretation of guideline (iii) as being a justifiable use of the flexibility believed to be inherent in the guidelines. But that that was so underlines to my mind the duplicitous nature of the flexibility claimed for the guidelines.

These two sentences should be submitted for analysis to the most sophisticated language laboratory in the country. Before the results are published we can only guess what they mean: that Mr Waldegrave was not duplicitous in relaxing the interpretation of a guideline (iii) but was duplicitous in claiming that the guidelines were flexible. This absurd and meaningless formula has been seized on by the Chief Secretary to claim that the Scott report has 'cleared my name' when, over the course of more than 100 pages, the report does the opposite.

Mr Lang was even less successful in defending the Attorney General, Sir Nicholas Lyell, who is lambasted over and over again in the report for getting the law wrong on gagging orders—public interest immunity certificates—in criminal trials, and, above all, for not informing the prosecution or the judge in the Matrix Churchill trial that one minister, Michael Heseltine, wanted the relevant documents disclosed to the defence. No amount of assurances about Sir Nicholas's personal sincerity can get him off the hook on which Scott impales him.

If there was shred of principle left in the Major government, both ministers would have resigned at once, and the debate on the Scott report could have been relatively free of party controversy. But Major will cling to his discredited ministers until his own security is threatened, when he will finally let them go.

Some commentators have concluded from the few sentences which hail the alleged 'good faith' of the two ministers that the Scott report is a whitewash or that Scott was 'nobbled' (*Observer*, 18 February). They complement the government press, which has excitedly denounced the report as 'rubbish' (*Sun*), 'almost unreadable' (*Sunday Times*) and 'boring' (*Evening Standard*). In fact, for all his faintheartedness when it comes to criticising ministers and especially prime ministers, Scott has a lot to tell us about the way we are governed.

Plague of the market

The argument about BSE continues to be conducted at such a kindergarten level—'If you ban my beef, I won't play ball with you'—that everyone in high places ignores the question: how did we get into the mess in the first place?

There are lots of experts on European politics who can tell you how the balance of power is tipping in the commission, but haven't got a clue what caused BSE in Britain in the mid-1980s or how to put a stop to it.

The discussions in parliament are particularly ill-informed and irrelevant. MPs 'represent' their constituencies by chauvinistic clamour about jobs lost in closed abattoirs, redundant butchers, desolated dairy farms, etc.

It seems there is no one there to represent the fears of a population threatened by a terrifying, mystifying and murderous epidemic.

The Southwood Commission, which was set up soon after BSE started raging through British farms, concluded that it was all the fault of feeding meat to herbivorous cattle.

Real culprit

Though this process was introduced without a whisper of protest from Labour or Liberal parties, everyone now agrees it was disgraceful.

Yet no one has been brought to book for it.

The Southwood Commission, and the huge parliamentary select committee inquiry which followed it, concluded that, once the new regulations about animal feed and removing the spines and heads of cattle were introduced, BSE would quickly vanish.

Not so. Seven years after the regulations, BSE continues to rage through British herds. It follows either that the cause had nothing to do with the feed, or that the regulations have not been properly enforced, or that BSE can be passed on from one generation of cattle to the next.

Socialist Worker 29 June 1996

Once again, everyone accepts that in the first few years of the regulations they were scrupulously ignored at every stage.

The regulations have now been tightened up. But still the BSE plague rushes on.

If the disease is inherited, or if its cause lies somewhere else in the food chain—in the rendering industry for instance, whose monopoly producer, Prosper Mulder, contributed so generously to the Tory party—the grim fact remains that no one knows whether even a mass slaughter of cattle will stop the disease.

Tory mafia

At the end of the 20th century, in the oldest industrial country in the world, where scientists can devise rockets to hit others travelling many times faster than the speed of sound, no one has a clue about the extent of or solution to a relatively straightforward cattle disease.

All the proposed answers to the BSE crisis avoid the real culprit: free enterprise. Whatever the scientific cause of BSE, the political and economic cause was the grotesque notion that regulations and restrictions in the public interest, even when that public interest protects people's lives, are 'bad for business' and should therefore be curtailed.

This is the culture which led to the 'freeing' of wholly inappropriate and probably contaminated animal feed, to the lowering of temperatures and monopolisation in the rendering industry, and to the increasing confidence among the Tory mafia which runs farms, slaughterhouses and butchers that it can do what it likes.

If these farms and industries had been publicly owned and publicly controlled in the interests of the people who eat meat rather than the people who profit from it, the awful ravages of the BSE plague would have been impossible.

'Argies' with British guns

Remember the Scott inquiry? It may seem like a long time ago, but the report of the Lord Justice (now promoted to Vice-Chancellor) was published only seven months ago.

Many curious facts emerged from the Scott hearings about the way we are governed. But perhaps the strangest of all was that armaments which were ostensibly made to protect Britain and to defeat Britain's enemies were being sold hand over fist to a country which became Britain's enemy.

The contradiction was brilliantly exposed in the role of a single person: a Lieutenant-Colonel Richard Glazebrook. Glazebrook's job at the Ministry of Defence was to make sure that weapons and machinery were not sold to anyone who might use them against Britain.

Glazebrook constantly found himself in a minority of one in the Ministry of Defence committees which decided what should be sold.

These committees were entirely dominated by representatives of the arms companies 'regional marketing directors', as they were called—which used their majorities to call the tune.

Scott's recommendations were intended to make absolutely sure that this sort of thing never happened again.

Well, here we are, seven months later, and what is happening? A couple of excellent Channel 4 *Despatches* programmes reveal the astonishing fact that Argentinian warships are powered by British made engines whose spare parts have recently been made readily available.

Can this possibly be right? Is Britain equipping the hated navy of the 'Argies'—the same navy which surrounded the Falkland Islands in 1982, and whose *General Belgrano* was so heroically sunk with 300 dead more than 200 miles outside the 'exclusion zone'?

Total ban

Margaret Thatcher regarded her victory over Argentina as the high

Socialist Worker 7 November 1996

peak of her time in Downing Street. Immediately afterwards she slapped a total ban on every export to Argentina which could be regarded as military.

For years their ships had been bought from and powered by British shipbuilding and engineering.

The nastier the Argentinian dictatorship, the more readily the British government, including the Labour government of 1974-79, sold it warships, equipped them and repaired them.

Desperately, the Argentinian naval command set up factories across the Western hemisphere to make the spare parts required for the British engines—parts which were denied them by the patriotic fury of Mrs Thatcher and her acolytes.

Then, suddenly, the picture changed. In 1995, Rolls Royce, whose engines still power many Argentinian warships, approached the British department of trade.

The Argentinian navy, they whined, was begging for vital spare parts to keep the ancient engines going. Please, please could they break the rules and sell the parts?

The DTI agreed almost at once.

This was happening at the very time that Ian Lang, the President of the Board of Trade, was defending the government's record during the Scott inquiry and, in the process, jeering at the last Labour government for selling arms to Argentina!

As we sit back and enjoy what will certainly be another government embarrassment about this, we can reflect upon the real lesson: the extent of corporate power.

From time to time, capitalist greed for profit will be reined back in the interests of 'the country' or 'the military' or even by parliament.

But, in the end, the representatives of capitalism are more powerful than parliamentary democracy or patriotism, and will find a way to shrug off both so they can make profits.

Why this man is unfit to be mayor

The bookmakers have quoted Jeffrey Archer as 3/1 favourite to be London's mayor. But between any politician and the electorate, there is the matter of trust. And on this issue, Archer's record is lousy.

Lord Archer promised the other day that, if he gets elected mayor of London, he will never write another book. At last, it seemed, he had come up with a good reason to vote for him. But wait. Why should we believe him? For the most consistent characteristics of Jeffrey Archer's long and chequered political career are his devotion to fantasy and his parsimony with the truth.

Even his birth certificate wasn't accurate, though that was hardly his fault. His father, a bigamist, conman and forger, was absurdly described as 'a journalist'. Jeffrey later claimed by way of contrast that his father was a colonel in the Somerset Light Infantry, which he wasn't, and had won the Distinguished Conduct Medal, which he hadn't. (Jeffrey's claims for his forebears didn't stop there. He also claimed that his grandfather was Lord Mayor of Bristol, which he wasn't.)

In 1963, Jeffey Archer became one of the very few people to get into Oxford University without any A levels. The university was told he had three. He also claimed two years on an anatomy course in America which never existed. He said he had qualified at something called the International Federation of Physical Culture, which his lawyers once told me was 'a society in America'. But when Michael Crick researched his magnificent 1995 biography, *Jeffrey Archer: Stranger Than Fiction*, he discovered that the IFPC was a correspondence course run from a single room in Chancery Lane, London.

Did I say he got into Oxford? Well, yes, in a way. Archer went to the Oxford Department of Education, which was only loosely connected to the university. His course—a diploma in education—lasted only a year. Jeffrey managed to run for the university athletics club

Evening Standard 25 March 1998

and even to captain it when he was not a resident member of the university, as the club's rules insisted he had to be.

In 1966 he married Mary Weedon. She described herself on the marriage certificate as a 'research graduate', which she was. So did Jeffrey, but he wasn't.

After an undistinguished year at a charity called the National Birthday Trust, Archer was elected to the Greater London Council in the Tory landslide of 1967. He has claimed often since that he was the 'youngest-ever GLC councillor'. But he was two years older than his colleague Anthony Bradbury, who was elected in the same year. At once, he approached his colleagues on the GLC with an enticing offer. If they let him fill out their expense forms, he would keep 10 percent of the 'take'. Many agreed. Years later, when Michael Crick started asking former GLC councillors about this, he got an angry letter from Archer threatening instant legal action for libel if a single other councillor was asked a question about Archer's handling of their expenses. Crick coolly went on asking. He collected statements from 24 GLC councillors backing the 10 percent story, and published it in his book. From Archer, not a writ, nor a whisper.

While at the GLC, Archer got taken on as a fundraiser for the United Nations Association, where he systematically fiddled his expenses. His speciality was to claim for meals paid for by others and for journeys in other people's cars. Altogether, in his short time at the UNA, he made 69 false claims. When the claims were challenged, he was obliged to pay back about £150 of falsely-claimed money.

The late Humphry Berkeley, then UNA chairman, was outraged. When Archer was selected as Tory candidate at a by-election for the safe seat of Louth, Lincolnshire, Berkeley circulated the facts about the expense claims to the newspapers. He phoned me at *Private Eye* and read out some of the more fantastic claims. 'This man really shouldn't get into parliament,' I mumbled mildly. 'Parliament?' bellowed Berkeley, 'He should be in a remand home!' Confronted in a train by a reporter from the *Times* who had all the facts about the expense-fiddling, Archer blubbed and begged the journalist not to publish. When the journalist demurred, Archer threatened to sue.

When the story appeared in print, the Tory leaders told Archer he had to sue Berkeley or step down from the by-election. He sued. Years later, he dropped the action before it got to court. There was no apology. Archer paid all the costs.

But the suing had worked. Archer was elected MP for Louth. The blurbs on his books still claim he was 'the youngest member of the House of Commons when he won the by-election'. Not true, of course. Not nearly true. Archer was 29. Bernadette Devlin, who was elected an MP the same year, was 22.

All the gifts of providence were showered on the young MP for Louth—charm, good looks, a safe seat, a beautiful wife. The only thing missing was a fortune. All his life, as his novels testify, Archer has been fascinated by the process of getting rich quick on the stock exchange. In April 1972 he met Michael Altmann, a young executive at the First National Bank of Boston, who told him about a likely new share on the Toronto stock market. The enterprise was called Aquablast. It puffed something called the Wymann idler adjuster valve as a 'revolutionary anti-pollution device'.

Archer was tremendously excited and brought 50,000 shares. When a conman came to his house and promised that the Aquablast shares would soon quadruple in value, Archer rushed out, borrowed £170,000 and bought another 50,000 shares. The whole business, including the valve, was a ridiculous fraud, and in November 1975 most of the Aquablast directors ended up in a Toronto courtroom. The first witness for the prosecution was Jeffrey Archer. He was almost broke, and the disgrace had forced him to resign his seat in parliament.

Archer gave his evidence on 17 November. The following day, as the case broke for lunch, the Canadian federal policemen in charge of the prosecution case, George Wool and Larry Park, returned with prosecutor Doug Hunt to their offices. They took a call there from an officer in a Toronto police station who said he was holding a man called Archer on suspicion of shoplifting.

The man claimed he had been a prosecution witness in a fraud case. Wool confirmed that Archer had been a witness, and the man was released without charge.

Twelve years later, in the autumn of 1987, when I was working as an investigative reporter for the *Daily Mirror*, I was sent a document by a former employee of Simpsons, a store in downtown Toronto. The document, reproduced here for the first time, purported to be an unsigned statement from a man calling himself Jeffrey Archer and admitting to stealing three suits from the store, valued at $540, 'without paying and without permission'.

The document gave a number of details of the man Jeffrey Archer, including his address and home phone number in London, his height, age, even the colour of his eyes—all of which exactly fitted the former Tory MP for Louth.

My colleague Bryan Rostron and I had recently published a profile of Jeffrey Archer when Margaret Thatcher appointed him deputy chairman of the Tory party in 1985. We wrote to him, enclosing the document, asking if he was the man named in it, and if so, how he explained the story of the suits. Back came the remarkable reply: 'I can confirm that I was not involved in any such incident.'

Such a denial could not be taken lightly. Archer had just won a celebrated libel action against the *Daily Star*. The paper had wrongly suggested he had had sex with a prostitute who had identified him as her client (as had another of her clients) and to whom, after she telephoned him, Archer had proffered an envelope stuffed with thousands of pounds in £50 notes. The damages against the *Star* were hideous— half a million pounds. The *Daily Mirror* was obviously not going to publish a document suggesting Archer was a shoplifter when he had so vigorously denied even being involved in the incident. The suits story was dead.

Or was it? Eight years later, Michael Crick's book asserted blandly that the young Archer had indeed been arrested for taking the suits from Simpsons but had not intended to steal them. He had, Crick explained, got muddled up with the 'geography of the shop'. No doubt, no doubt. But Archer had told me he was 'not involved in any such incident'. Here was Crick saying he was. Both stories couldn't be true. One of them was false (and Archer never even complained about Crick's version).

His grim experience with Aquablast has not deterred Archer from dealing on the stock exchange. On 12 January 1994, Sir Peter Gibbings, chairman of Anglia Television, negotiated a secret merger with Clive Hollick of MAI. The next day Jeffrey Archer bought 25,000 Anglia shares for a Kurdish friend. When the news of the merger broke a few days later, Anglia's shares soared, and Archer sold the 25,000 at a profit of £80,000.

Lord Archer has always vehemently denied that he even discussed events at Anglia with his fragrant wife who was sitting on the Anglia board. But what did he think he was doing buying and selling shares in a company where his wife was a director? Even the most elementary rules about conflict of interest refer not just to actual cases of trading on inside information but to cases of apparent conflict.

In his campaign to be London's mayor, Jeffrey Archer likes to cast himself in the image of the charismatic mayor of New York, Rudy Giuliani. Last autumn Archer went to New York surrounded by fawning television crews and friendly hacks, and had himself filmed side by side with his hero Rudy.

What Lord Archer has probably not yet grasped is that Mayor Giuliani made his name as chief prosecutor of Manhattan, in which role he relentlessly prosecuted the great insider traders of Wall Street in the 1980s. If New Yorkers like their mayor, it is at least partly because he can spot a dissembling hustler from a very long distance.

Vaccine and not heard

Though hearings at the Phillips public inquiry into BSE have broken up for a few weeks, its officials are drawing up what may turn out to be their most controversial document. It is a draft factual account of government policy on vaccines prepared for injection into masses of people, almost all of which contain some material derived from beef.

The first hint that anyone in officialdom was worried about the impact of BSE on these vaccines came at a meeting of senior officials at the department of health on 17 March 1988.

The feeling of the meeting was summed up by the ministry of agriculture under-secretary Alistair Cruikshank as follows:

> There is probably no risk in drinking milk or eating flesh from animals affected by BSE, but that the position was much less clear in relation to brains, spleens and other organs. This raised questions about the safety of human vaccines prepared using bovine material.

The chief medical officer, Sir Donald Acheson, said he suspected there was no risk, but this could take '30 to 40 years to prove'. In the meantime, he warned, 'ministers would be very exposed, if, as seems inevitable, the press began to devote attention to the subject'.

The press showed no interest. But others were worried. A memo from Dr Hilary Pickles at the department of health on 21 June 1988 revealed:

> I understand the pharmaceutical industry are also concerned: they had been using bovine not sheep products in various processes because scrapie is endemic in British sheep...the highest risk would be from parenterals [for injection] prepared from brain [eg rabies vaccine].

The BSE scare led to the appointment of an expert committee of inquiry under Oxford zoology professor Sir Richard Southwood. On 30 August 1988 Sir Richard wrote to Acheson:

Private Eye 19 February 1999

The only outstanding practical matter that we need to address at the present time is the use of serum in pharmacological work. I heard...that Wellcome are now using serum from New Zealand.

Wellcome's initiative in getting its vaccine beef products from herds in New Zealand, which had not been fed on animal products as in Britain, was not yet insisted on by the government. Three times in 1988, Sir Richard Southwood wrote to the relevant statutory body, the Committee on Safety of Medicines, which is made up of top medical experts, many of whom are linked to the drug companies, asking for more urgent action on vaccines.

On 16 December 1988, a meeting of the Southwood committee considered that the response from the safety of medicines committee 'was somewhat complacent, particularly in relation to the problem of existing medicinal products'. On 26 January 1989, the Committee on Safety of Medicines wrote to Southwood that guidelines for the industry had been agreed. In future, bovine serum should only be taken from 'appropriately certified herds'.

The committee's letter went on: 'Many vaccines are stored for up to five years before being released and this will therefore have to be considered.'

The Southwood committee report was published the following month, February 1989.

The greatest risk in theory', it warned, 'would be from parenteral injection of material derived from bovine brain or lymphoid tissue. Medicinal products for injection which are prepared from bovine tissues...might also be capable of transmitting infections agents.

Prompted by the report, the Committee on Safety of Medicines sent 4,000 letters to drug companies asking for information about bovine products. Not all the information from these letters was passed on to the authorities. Sir Donald Acheson, chief medical officer, told the recent Phillips inquiry:

We were told that a number of things that we wanted to discuss were confidential in the commercial sense...and that they could not discuss them with us... They put up with me, but every now and again they would say, 'Sorry, we cannot share that with you.'

Nor was the information always accurate. A memo from the committee in September 1988 revealed: 'The computer list shows 33 product licences extant for preparations of bovine origin.' The memo categorically asserted: 'There are no licensed products derived from bovine brain.' At the recent inquiry, Sir Donald Acheson was asked:

Q: Would you have been concerned if there were licensed products from bovine brain?
A: Surely.
Q: I want you to look at an extract from the MCA questionnaire summary... One of the items is under a company number—we have 01234, because it is not right that the company should be identified here. Company name, a large company. The product name is Drug X. Animal specification is bovine and the animal ingredients include calf brain. Do you see that?
A: I do.
Q: If you had known about that at the time, would that have caused you concern?
A: It certainly would, unquestionably, which I did not.

After some delay, the Committee on Safety of Medicines guidelines ensured that the drug companies got their bovine materials from 'healthy herds' in Australia and New Zealand. But what happened to all those vaccines with bovine material from unhealthy British herds, which were stored up sometimes five years in advance? On 31 October 1990, the committee's BSE working group minutes recorded:

Vaccine stocks. Dr David Taylor declared a non-specific non personal interest in (company name deleted) and took part in the discussion. Dr Richard Kimberlin declared a specific personal interest and did not participate in the discussion but remained at the meeting.

The working group considered that the secretariat should explore with the company the possibility that the unabsorbed vaccines which had limited usage should be replaced with batches using bovine materials which complied with the guidelines, especially where the stock-out date extended beyond 1991. There may be some commercial loss to the licence holder but it is unlikely to be very large.

A list of the relevant vaccines was attached.

What happened then? What happened to the stored vaccines which, if injected into people, might carry the danger of infection? No one seems to know. The former Tory ministers who gave evidence to the Phillips inquiry didn't know. Asked about vaccines, they responded as follows:

William Waldegrave: 'I do not remember that as an issue.'
John Macgregor: 'I cannot remember, frankly...'
Tony Newton: 'I do not think I am in a position to help you.'
Edwina Currie: 'I have not refreshed my memory... Had the experts said: "We feel the vaccines being built up are not entirely free of risk, we are therefore going to recommend that they be destroyed and that replacement stocks are acquired, and that this may delay the onset of the [immunisation] campaign for weeks," we would have said: "Fine".'

Kenneth Clarke, who was secretary of state for health from 1988 to 1990:

> What one clearly got from all this was that they were advising us that we should continue with vaccine components and so on and the risk was so remote that [it] would not justify stopping it. I still believe that advice to have been correct.

The *Eye* asked the BSE inquiry, which has heard 300 witnesses, what information has come to light which reveals what happened to the stocks of vaccines with bovine serum from British cows manufactured before the BSE scare broke. A spokeswoman replied: 'We have no information which can answer any of those questions.'

The *Eye* put the same questions to the department of health. 'We outsourced the supplies of bovine material for vaccines away from Britain very early,' said a spokeswoman. In reply to the question 'When were the old stocks replaced?' the department sent a 16-page calendar of events, which reveals:

As late as July 1992: 'The group's previous concern about vaccine stocks in relation to a specific company [unnamed] were resolved by the company concerned producing a new batch with New Zealand foetal calf serum of assured quality.'

Not until November 1996: 'All currently licensed vaccines complied with the guidelines and did not contain any UK-sourced bovine material.'

Neither item, nor any other in the 16 pages, answered the question.

The Blair revolution

Late developer

For nearly a century, Labour MPs have been going to parliament to change the world, but have ended up changing only themselves. Tony Benn is unique. He went to parliament to change himself, but has ended up determined only to change the world. This extraordinary conversion has taken place not on the backbenches, where a young socialist's revolutionary determination is often toughened by being passed over for high office, but in high office itself. Indeed, the higher the office Tony Benn occupied, the more his eyes were opened to the horror of capitalist society, and to the impotence of socialists in high office to change it.

This unique journey from right to left adds enormously to the value of Tony Benn's *Diaries*. His contemporaries Dick Crossman and Barbara Castle have also published diaries. Others have written autobiographies. All are full of evidence of the impotence of office. Even Denis Healey in his recent popular autobiography admits that the notorious 'IMF cuts' in 1976 were probably based on a false prospectus presented to him by international bankers who knew they were deceiving him. But, in all these cases, the former secretaries of state have a basic belief in what they were doing. 'We tried to change the world' is their theme. 'We had a little bit of success, and would have done more if it hadn't been for bankers or, as Harold Wilson used to call his hidden enemies, "speculators".'

Only Tony Benn, even as he was signing papers in the red dispatch boxes, travelling round in chauffeur-driven limousines and dining at Lockets, began to realise that he was playing a lead part in a grim charade whose chief effect was to hypnotise and paralyse the people who voted Labour.

In his Foreword, Benn says he has included whole passages which embarrass him today. We have to trust him and his editors when they say that the editing of what he read into the tape evening after evening has not been influenced by what has happened since 1976. It does not seem as if it has. Perhaps the most remarkable aspect of this volume is the open and apparently unembarrassed way in which Tony Benn's conversion—from career politician to committed socialist—lumbers from contradiction to contradiction: here leaning backwards to his careerist past, here leaning forwards to his campaigning future, and here stuck in between, not knowing what to think or which way to turn.

The volume starts rather curiously with the final year of Labour in opposition, during which Tony Benn's ideas were increasingly winning the votes at Labour Party conferences and among the rank and file. There runs through all the diary entries of this period a tremendous confidence. At a CBI dinner in October 1973 he rounded on the gloomy industrialists, telling them:

> You're licked, pessimistic. There is more vitality on the union side than there is on the management side. We have got to have redistribution of power and establish a new social contract.

None of the guests, it seems, could manage a reply. Industrialists, bankers, rich Tories of every description felt that the day of doom was nigh. John Davies, Secretary of State for Industry in the Tory government and a former director general of the CBI, called his children round the hearth to tell them this was the last Christmas of its kind they would be enjoying together. Tony Benn, his planning agreements and his Social Contract were in the ascendant. The Tories lost the election of February 1974, and Tony Benn went straight to the Department of Industry as secretary of state. In April, his diary glowed with confidence:

> Sunday 28 April. As I look at it, I can see my way through now in breaking industry's resistance to my policies. I shall win over the managers and the small businessmen, and I shall get the nationalised industries to welcome the planning agreements; I shall isolate the big Tory companies, then show how much money they have been getting from the government, and if they don't want it, they don't have to have it.

Very quickly, however, he began to find that he and his government depended on quite a different kind of confidence. At another dinner with bankers and stock exchange officials the same April, he was told, sternly: 'We must restore confidence.' 'What is the price of restoring confidence?' countered Benn. 'Well,' replied the stock exchange chieftain, 'you have got to have better dividend distribution, otherwise equities will collapse.' The confidence which mattered could be measured only by the flow of dividends. Benn replied with some heat, but as the months went on, the same argument started to be used by his own colleagues in the Labour cabinet.

He reports Denis Healey, the Chancellor of the Exchequer, saying at a meeting of top ministers which had been called to water down the already weak proposals of his Industry Bill: 'The whole of our future depends on the confidence of businessmen.' Healey's policies were bent in every particular to building up that confidence. The climax comes at the end of the book, when, at a cabinet meeting on 7 December 1976, Healey proposed yet more cuts in public spending—he had already cut savagely, in 1975 and in the 1976 budget. Benn reports:

> Denis had a new paper to present and he was now asking for £1,199.25 million in 1977, which was nearly £200 million over the billion proposed by the IMF. Crosland pointed this out but Denis said that confidence had been undermined by leaks and therefore we'd have to make more cuts in public expenditure to prevent further loss of confidence.

Hospitals, schools, social security benefits, parks, swimming pools, public transport—all the things which had been at the centre of Labour's programme—now had to be cut, not even because the IMF said it made sense (which, it later appeared, it didn't) but because there were inaccurate leaks of what the IMF might have said.

All Tony Benn's own confidence had vanished by the end of 1974—even though in October Labour won another general election with an overall majority. He mused, to his top civil servant, just after the election: 'I've been in the department for seven months and I'm not aware of having done anything, made any progress at all.' The steady chip, chop at his precious Industry Bill, and the prime minister's continued insistence that he stop making public speeches which annoyed the City of London, drove him to reflect, as early as November 1975:

> I am afraid that somehow, without quite knowing how it happens, I will slip into the position that I occupied between 1964 and 1970 when I went along with a lot of policies which I knew to be wrong.

He could see perfectly well what was happening. His diary for the first few months of 1975—the end of the honeymoon period between the Labour government and what Prime Minister Wilson called their 'bailiffs'—is far more perceptive than Barbara Castle's (or even Denis Healey's—though he had the advantage of hindsight):

> The Tories now think that Wilson, Healey and Callaghan are doing their work so well that they don't want a coalition government. Better to let the Labour Party do their work for them.

This analysis led him to a startling prediction. On 11 May 1975 he wrote:

> A coalition has been born without being formally declared: it is broadly the Tories and Liberals throwing their weight behind Callaghan, I think. They won't touch Wilson. They'll get rid of him just as they got rid of Heath... I wouldn't be surprised to find a Callaghan government formed within the next couple of months.

He was out by only eight months. Wilson resigned in mysterious circumstances in March 1976. Callaghan was elected leader of the Labour Party and formed a government. From then on, the retreat which Benn had identified continued, through the grovelling to the IMF in 1976 to the coalition with the Liberals of 1977, and the long, weary stumble to defeat. Before the end of 1976, he identified what he called 'Thatcher's Private Argument':

> That the Labour government are doing to the trade union movement what the Tories could never do: that in doing it the government are getting profits up and holding prices down and therefore restoring the vitality of the capitalist mechanism; and that by doing so they will disillusion their own supporters and make it possible for the Tories to return.

He could see that was happening all right, but what was he doing about it? From early on, he started to think about resigning from the government in protest. All his most reliable friends—Dennis Skinner, Audrey Wise, Ken Coates, most of the activists in his Bristol constituency, even his son Stephen—advised him to do so. Benn's own belief, often expressed here, that the power and influence that mattered came from below, from the shop stewards and socialist trade unionists, led logically to a resignation and a return to the rank and file. But he did not resign. In the summer of 1975, as the Labour government collapsed under the biggest run on sterling ever, he humbly accepted his demotion to Secretary of State for Energy. He sat through the cuts of 1976, opposing them in cabinet, but necessarily keeping his mouth shut outside it. His reasons for this—chiefly that resignation would be seen as disloyal to the government—are unconvincing, even apologetic. Doubt, hesitation and pain replaced the glad confident morning. On one page, for instance, he reveals his ambition: 'If I want to do anything other than frolic around on the margins of politics, I must be leader and prime minister.' On the very next page, he is not so sure: 'If you set yourself that target, it is bound to begin the process of corruption.' As the book goes on, the balance seems to tip against his ambition, but he still remains in office, and there is another volume to come which must somehow explain how he stuck it out right until the bitter end—until the Tory victory over a punch-drunk labour movement which he had so accurately predicted. But even in 1975 his clinging to office was disturbing his sleep:

> Friday 10 October: I had a dream that Harold called me in and said: 'I want you to be Vice-Chamberlain of the Royal Household with a seat in the House of Lords in charge of boxing under the Minister of Sport.' He told me this in the great cabinet room, which was full of people. 'I'm afraid this doesn't mean a place in the cabinet for you,' he said. I replied, 'Harold I must think about it,' and Sir John Hunt said: 'Boxing is very important. We must preserve the quality and excellence of the Lonsdale Belt.'

The book is full of political treasures. There is a host of stories, for instance, to prove what is now established fact: that MI5 or sections of it were using their vast and secret powers against the government they were meant to be serving. Benn was constantly at the sharp end of this. He proved on more than one occasion that his home telephone was tapped—but he, a senior secretary of state in the cabinet, could do nothing about it. When he complained to the general secretary of the telephone engineers' union, Brian Stanley, Stanley said he thought his own phone was tapped too—by his own members. Jack Jones and Hugh Scanlon, the 'terrible twins' of the trade unions in the period which toppled the Heath government, became the leading spokesmen for wage restraint and cuts during the Labour government, and were rewarded by being blacklisted by MI5. Benn confirms that he wanted Jones on the National Enterprise Board but Jones was banned after hostile MI5 reports, which also, initially, knocked Hugh Scanlon off the Gas Council.

Tony Benn's household was the subject of repeated press inquiries, mostly at the dead of night, about his son Joshua being in hospital. At least five times in two years, the Benn family was shattered by this dreadful news, conveyed usually by a concerned reporter from the *Daily Mail*. Each time, the information was entirely false. Joshua was not in hospital. When, after one specially unnerving inquiry, Benn rang David English, *Daily Mail* editor and Thatcher knight, to protest, he was told that the editor was at home and could not be disturbed. Such double standards are the stuff of national newspaper editors. But where did the rumour originate? Perhaps from the same intelligence source which replied to Tony Benn when he complained about the sacking of a chiropodist in the civil service. 'The woman', said the reply, 'may be a fairly regular reader of the *Morning Star*, the newspaper of the Communist Party.' Of course, she may not have been, but even if not, 'she is known to have been interested in holidays arranged by the Young Communist League and in a sea trip to the Soviet Union.' To compound this scandal, 'there was a reliable report in 1974 that her father also reads the *Morning Star*.' The intelligence officer's report explained that 'we would prefer to err on the side of caution in this case.' The chiropodist remained sacked and there was nothing a secretary of state could do to reinstate her.

Benn has a sense of mischief which keeps his story rolling along. His sharp comments on his colleagues have stood the test of time. Of Tony Crosland: 'For him informality is a sort of substitute for radicalism.' Of Shirley Williams: 'The most reactionary politician I know.' Of Neil Kinnock: 'Not a substantial person. He is a media figure really.'

The central fascination of these diaries is the gradual transformation of the bright young dynamic dinner-partying careerist of the early 1960s into the powerful campaigner of the 1980s. It emerges in fits and starts, but its progress is persistent, almost dogged. It shines most clearly on the rare occasions when Benn discusses what he has read. One of the insidious ways in which reformers are broken when they become ministers is by the denial of time to read. Reading anything outside red boxes or blue books is frowned on by literary civil servants, who encourage their minister to concentrate on the job in hand. Benn's *Diaries* suggest that he started to read real books for the first time when he was a minister in the 1974-79 Labour government. As he declares his child-like zeal, say, for the Levellers or the Diggers in the English Revolution, he gives the strong impression that he had never heard of any of these people before he met and quarrelled with Sir Anthony Part at the Department of Industry. The civil service mandarins seem to have driven him back to a glorious time when the king had his head chopped off and all his civil service supporters fled for their lives. Even more remarkable is his sudden discovery at the age of 50 of the socialist theory which inspired the movement which put him in parliament in the first place. The whole book bears warm testimony to the closeness and affection of the Benn family, and it is, apparently, to Caroline Benn that we owe the most gratitude for her husband's conversion. At Christmas 1976 the secretary of state hung out his Christmas stocking (as he had done for the previous 50 years or so). In it the next morning he found a copy of the *Communist Manifesto*. He read it on Christmas Day, and it led him to this re-markable, and moving confession—the real key, I suspect, to his extraordinary political development:

> There is no doubt that in the years up to 1968 I was just a career politi-cian and in 1968 I began thinking about technology and participa-tion and all that. It wasn't particularly socialist and my Fabian tract of 1970 was almost anti-socialist, corporatist in character. Up to 1973 I shifted to the left and analysed the left. Then in 1974, at the Depart-ment of Industry, I learned it all again by struggle and by seeing it and thinking about it, and I have been driven further and further towards a real socialist position... I record this now while I am reading all the basic texts in order to try to understand what is going on.

I don't really care whether it is Sir Anthony Part or Caroline Benn or Marx that we have to thank for that, but British politics of the last ten years has been the richer for it.

First published as a review of Against the Tide: Diaries 1973-1976 *by Tony Benn (Hutchinson 1989).*

'Positive' surrender

The National Union of Mineworkers was polite enough to invite Labour's energy spokesman, Mr Frank Dobson, to speak at its conference in Scarborough last week.

The union, not surprisingly, is opposed to the government's plans to take the coal industry back to the dark days of the filthiest representatives of the ruling class, the coal owners.

The proposals are so hideous, the delegates must have mused, that even Mr Dobson, a man not best known for his amazing rhetoric, might be moved to some indignation. Perhaps he would read up a little on the history of the coal owners.

A reference to the mass evictions in Durham in the 1840s by the Marquess of Londonderry would have gone down well. So might a study of the comparative safety statistics in British mines under private and public ownership.

The very least the rank and file can have expected was a ferocious attack on the Tories and a declaration of unswerving support for the NUM's campaign against privatisation from the Labour Party, inside and outside parliament.

Well, here is the *Financial Times* report of what happened: 'Mr Dobson said he believed "the cards are stacked heavily against keeping coal in the public sector" and the NUM should draw up plans to protect the most vulnerable pits and maintain safety standards.'

This speech was not greeted with rapturous applause.

Perhaps the sceptical miners imagined themselves following Mr Dobson's advice. The first part of the Dobson plan had them 'drawing up plans to protect the most vulnerable pits'. Here is a possible plan for protecting a vulnerable pit. (1) Try to ensure that the pit does not close. (2) If it does close, try to ensure jobs for all the miners thrown out of work. (3) If that doesn't work, try to get decent redundancy pay. (4) If that doesn't work, burst into tears.

This would be a positive Dobson plan as opposed to a negative plan to try to stop privatisation and closures by refusing to dig coal until public ownership is guaranteed. According to Dobson, the 'cards' are 'stacked against' the success of any such plan, so the miners should settle for failure.

Rough guide

Dobson Plan 2 calls on miners to 'protect safety standards'. Here is a rough guide to such a plan. (1) Ask the new private management, which has taken over without a struggle or even a complaint, because the cards are stacked against struggles and complaints, to maintain safety standards. (2) If they don't, lower the standards a little. (3) If that doesn't work, lower the standards a lot. (4) If management still insist on cutting safety corners, burst into tears.

So desperate are the Labour leaders to surrender that it is becoming almost impossible for socialists to read or listen to them any longer.

I doubt whether there has been a time in the entire century when British Labour has been so abject, so obsequious to Tories, to employers, to the City, to the newspaper barons—to everyone in authority.

Before the election they were at least afraid to lose. Now it seems they positively want to lose. They take on the mantle of defeat with a cheerful enthusiasm which would astonish the most dedicated masochist.

Their only hint of eloquence is in their pleas to their followers to play their part in the disaster. Their slogan is written in scarlet across the flag they sing about every year: 'We lost. We're certain to lose again. So make sure you all lose as well.'

Tony Blurs the past

Hark to Tony Blair, in a radio interview on 17 July:

> The trade unions will have no special and privileged place in the next Labour government. They will have the same access to it as the other side of industry.

This is heralded in every single newspaper as an example of the 'new fairness' of the new Labour leadership. Out go 'special privileges' for the unions. In comes a new approach: everyone, whatever side they are on, will be treated equally. This sounds unanswerable.

Why should someone be discriminated against according to 'which side' of industry they are on? At last this ancient discrimination has been put to flight by the charming and equable Mr Blair.

Harold Wilson once likened government in Britain to a driver of a motor car whose job is to steer a difficult path along a road covered with hazards.

Blair's new formula presents government as a football referee, carefully enforcing the rules of a game where 22 players of roughly equal strength and ability fight for supremacy on the field.

From now on the referee will play fair between 'one side of industry' and 'the other'.

A rather different argument won the day 94 years ago when a handful of trade union delegates, socialists and former Liberals came together to form the Labour Party.

Their problem was this: one side of industry owned all the means of production, one side of industry determined the level of wages and of prices, and one side of industry decided whether people were hired or fired.

The level of investment in industry, what was made, how it was made and by whom, foreign policy, whether or not there should be wars with millions killed—all these matters were determined by a small wealthy minority.

Socialist Worker 30 July 1994

This minority had been represented in parliament for more than 200 years by two parties, Liberals (or Whigs) and Tories.

It was time, the delegates decided, to seek parliamentary representation for their side of industry—the people who did the work.

Blair and Co argue that a lot of water has flown under the bridge since those bad old days and that society has changed so much that the central principle behind the foundation of the Labour Party—parliamentary representation for trade unionists in particular and the working class in general—can now be chucked overboard.

But a small wealthy handful still own all the capital wealth and a grossly disproportionate slice of the income.

Their economic decisions still shut out the enormous majority of people affected by them.

All the statistics show the rich getting richer at the expense of the poor and of trade unionists whose organisations have been crippled and humiliated by a series of laws and open class offensives.

There are not 50 million people of roughly similar strength and ability running around the British field of life, demanding a fair referee.

There are a tiny handful—no more than one and a half million—who are economic and political giants determined to exploit the majority.

The need for parliamentary representation of the weak against the strong, the poor against the rich, trade unionists against employers, has never been more dramatically exposed by the statistics of society.

Those politicians who argue that the millionaires with their police forces, their judges and their armies, who vote Tory, should have 'equal access' to Labour ministers as the working people who vote Labour, are not just making an error of judgement.

They are preparing the ground for an assault on Labour voters more outrageous and contemptible than even Ramsay MacDonald ever imagined.

Mr Straight and Mr Good

'Happy are they', Hazlitt wrote, 'for whom the guiding star of their youth still shines from afar.' Judging from this hagiography, the Chancellor of the Exchequer must be very unhappy. The guiding star of his youth has entirely vanished from his firmament. In 1975 the young Gordon Brown compiled, edited and published a socialist manifesto entitled *Red Paper for Scotland*. At 24, he had just completed a three-year term as rector of Edinburgh University and chaired the University Court in the face of continuous opposition from some of the most powerful men in Scotland. The central political problem of the age, he wrote, was 'the sheer enormity of the gap between people's conditions of living and their legitimate aspirations'. This gap could easily be filled by the 'social forces of production', but those forces were held back by the so-called free market. It had become 'increasingly impossible to manage the economy both for private profit and the needs of society as a whole'. The solution had to be drastic: 'a massive and irreversible shift of power to working people' and 'a framework of free universal welfare services controlled by the people who use them'. This was a slightly altered version of Labour's Programme 1973, which called for FAIS, a 'fundamental and irreversible shift of power to working people and their families'. Brown argued that a Labour government should bring under public control (without compensation) the building, food, insurance and pensions industries, energy, land, shipbuilding, textiles, banking and all monopolies and multinationals. The undemocratic and divisive power of these organisations had to be challenged by the new Labour government since part of the problem was the 'accumulative [sic] failure' of previous Labour governments to deal with it.

When, in 1983, Brown, with the help of his friends in the Transport and General Workers Union, became Labour candidate for the safe seat of desperately impoverished Dunfermline East, he co-edited with Robin Cook another series of socialist essays, *The Great Divide*.

London Review of Books 19 February 1998

In his Introduction, he grappled with the familiar argument that the shocking conditions of the poor could only be improved in times of economic growth. 'The era of economic growth', he observed, 'is not only over but unlikely to return in the near future. New principles for social security in a low-growth economy are badly needed. The first prerequisite for eradicating poverty is the redistribution of income and wealth from rich to poor.'

Paul Routledge patronises the young Brown: 'As a panacea for all social ills this vision could hardly be faulted. As a political strategy it was lamentably deficient.' Similarly, Gordon Brown now dismisses the policies set out in *Red Paper* and the *Great Divide* as the excesses of youth. In fact, the remedies were carefully argued. Their urgency and their comprehensive scope were demanded, Brown insisted, by the grim facts of an increasingly divided society.

Move on four years to Labour's defeat in the 1987 general election and the subsequent policy review conducted by the shadow secretary for trade and industry, Bryan Gould. Who are the two young members of the Tribune Group passionately arguing against the inclusion in Labour's new programme of a modest measure, supported by the Tribune Group, to buy 2 percent shares in British Telecom and thus restore public control over a monstrous private monopoly? Gordon Brown and Tony Blair. To Gould's fury they stipulated that all mention of state ownership had to go. The 'Two Bs' did not get their way on that occasion, but they were already embarked on a journey in precisely the opposite direction from that laid down by *Red Paper* and *The Great Divide*. Who, for instance, are the two ambitious members of the Tribune Group sidling up to Roy Hattersley in 1988 and assuring him of their support in the race for Labour's deputy leadership against the candidate supported by Tribune Group, John Prescott? Right again. Gordon Brown and Tony Blair.

In *The Candidate*, the great American film about political compromise starring Robert Redford, a young welfare lawyer is persuaded against his instinct to go into politics to change the world. He starts by answering questions with independent judgement and in direct language. Yes, he is in favour of abortion on demand. Yes, he is in favour of increasing welfare benefits and much more public control of housing and the environment. Gradually, he is persuaded that if he wants the power to make changes, he must modify his language. The direct answers become indirect. Two sides to a question emerge where previously there was only one. The candidate abandons all specific measures but promises to 'house the homeless, and feed the foodless'. His campaign slogan is impeccably vague: 'There must be a better way.' By the time he wins the election, all the measures which he went into politics to promulgate have vanished from his agenda.

The career of Gordon Brown in the last ten years closely resembles that of 'the candidate'. The sharp, tough language of his youth has dissolved into cliche. 'Equality' has become 'fairness' or, worse, 'equality of opportunity'. The big plans for public control have turned into 'the big idea'. And the 'big idea', needless to say, is that 'people have big ideas'. The old Clause IV, a plainly expressed commitment to common ownership of the means of production, is replaced by an unctuous formula which promises everything and nothing at the same time. The shift of language disguises a U-turn in political direction. The demand for a publicly directed economy becomes a demand for a 'dynamic economy', in between which two words 'market' is suddenly inserted. From that clear demand for 'free universal welfare services' the word 'universal' is first dropped—and then ridiculed. Paul Routledge finds another perfect example. Speaking at the 1993 Labour Party conference in Brighton, Brown recalled his old fervour for FAIS, but changed the terms slightly to dispense with its meaning:

> Our aim is a fundamental and irreversible shift in favour of work and opportunity and against the privilege and abuse of power under Conservative governments.

It sounds the same as FAIS but is very different.

Routledge notes, too, how the buzzwords of the Brown/Blair language are all about change—'new', 'young', 'modern', 'relevant'. The words are used to describe policies which are old, ancient, irrelevant. It was Gordon Brown who announced proudly that the parameters of public spending for the vital first two years of the Labour government would be those set down by the Tories; that there would be no increases in income tax, not even on the 0.2 percent of the population who make more than £100,000 a year; and therefore no increase in public spending; no change on the rate capping which emasculated Labour local authorities; no change in the draconian Tory anti-union laws; no change in anything. The great irresponsible monopolies derided by Brown in his youth have become the great allies of New Labour. Brown's chief man in the Treasury is his friend and generous host Geoffrey Robinson, whose enormous wealth is stashed away in a tax haven. One millionaire in the government is not enough. As soon as New Labour was elected, its ministers scurried into the City to seek out millionaires to conduct the government's business: David Simon from BP, Martin Taylor from Barclays Bank, Peter Davis from the Pru, even that devoted Thatcherite Alan Sugar of Tottenham Hotspur. Past Labour governments had made some small effort to assert their democratic rights over unelected financial power. In the first weeks of the new Labour administration in 1964 there was a bitter wrangle between Harold Wilson and the governor of the Bank of England, Lord Cromer. Cromer demanded an immediate rise in interest rates. Wilson replied that he had fought an election on economic expansion and low interest rates, and was inclined to stick by his promise to the electorate. It took several 'spontaneous' flights of sterling to bring Wilson to heel. New Labour and Gordon Brown wanted none of that. They told the governor of the Bank of England, to his intense delight, that he and a group of unelected, unrepresentative financiers, including a former CIA agent, would have complete control of the level of interest rates. This surrender of a vital democratic power was greeted with prolonged hallelujahs by a millionaire press almost wholly converted to New Labour. In a perversion of language his hero couldn't have improved on, Routledge manages to describe this decision as an act of 'radical reform'.

The praise seems to have gone to Brown's head. At the 1997 Labour conference he took off into a flight of rhetoric worthy of Robert Redford's candidate:

> We have seen an outpouring of compassion from people's hearts. We have seen a glimpse of what Britain has it in itself to become. No more a nation divided against itself but a nation united. No longer fearful of the future but hopeful and confident.

And then, harking back perhaps to his childhood in the Kirkcaldy manse: 'No more the rich man in his castle, the poor man at his gate.' What about the many Scottish castles which are now homes for beneficiaries of Tory tax cuts, privatisations and sleaze? They know that under New Labour they are safe. As for the poor at the gates, they had better not be single parents or disabled, or the radical reformers will be after their benefits.

Who can explain this metamorphosis? Routledge gives it a try. 'What Labour offered in the past', he writes, 'was not appropriate for 1992 and beyond... The Thatcher years had made people more self-reliant and that "dimension" must be accommodated in Labour's approach.' As usual, there is no attempt to prove this. Who precisely was made 'more self-reliant' during the 'Thatcher years'? The rich certainly were. So, to begin with, were large sections of the middle classes. But all the surveys showed that people's self-confidence, and therefore self-reliance, suffered hugely as the power of their employers grew without check and the welfare safety-net was dismantled. They became more scared than self-reliant.

What of the second common explanation for New Labour's *volte-face*? Here is Brown: 'We are in power today and in a position to empower people because we had the courage to change and modernise our party.' This is the myth to which Blair, Brown and all the others cling and will continue to cling during the tempestuous and terrifying years ahead. They won the election, they boast, because they ditched Clause IV, because they distanced themselves from the trade unions, because they accepted all the privatisations they once promised to reverse.

Most of the evidence contradicts this view. The polls show quite clearly that public opinion moved against the Tories long before John Smith died in 1994—and that the reasons for this shift had far more to do with the rise in VAT on fuel, Norman Lamont's Exchange Rate Mechanism fiasco, and Michael Heseltine's pit closures than with any decision of a Labour Party Special Conference. The evidence suggests that large numbers of people who voted Tory in 1992 were persuaded very soon that they had made a hideous mistake. These people would have voted every bit as enthusiastically for Smith or Robin Cook or John Prescott or Margaret Beckett, as they did for Blair. The extent of last year's May landslide is itself proof of the extraordinary shift in popular opinion. The huge majority was not expected or sought by the New Labour leaders. They know that at least part of it reflected something much more fundamental than a change in Labour Party policy: a yearning for a more egalitarian and secure society where the freedom of the rich is not the only principle. To move towards this requires at least a little of the old FAIS that Gordon Brown was advocating in 1975.

This book has been interpreted as a manifesto for Brown against

Blair. It is nothing of the kind. It is proof that Brown and Blair worked together to bring about the emasculation of the Labour government as a force for change; and that as a result they are both extremely pleased with themselves. When Blair went on television to explain how and why his party had taken a million pounds from a Tory motor-racing tycoon and then personally intervened to reverse Labour's policy on tobacco advertising to accommodate the tycoon, he was full of apologies and smiles. Surely no one could accuse him of corruption, he bleated. After all, 'I'm a straight guy.' This book ends with Gordon Brown saying much the same and without the slightest hesitation: 'I'm a good guy.'

First published as a review of Gordon Brown: The Biography *by Paul Routledge (Simon & Schuster 1998).*

House of cards

At a time of what seemed like unrelieved gloom, the political scene at Christmas was suddenly bathed in bright light. All of a sudden, without warning, a central pillar of New Labour turned into dust and blew away.

Peter Mandelson is New Labour in essence. His book, *The Blair Revolution*, which he wrote with one of the founders of the late unlamented SDP, Roger Liddle, argued that a New Labour government could provide social justice without interfering with the free flow of capitalism. The book is full of familiar cliches about the irrelevance of public ownership, the importance of reducing the influence of trade unions and the need to get to grips with outdated universal benefits. On page 127, the authors address 'one of the greatest sources of unfairness'—'the different prospects of couples setting off in life with a flying financial start from their parents and grandparents and those who have no such backing'. This unfairness inspires Mandelson and Liddle to one of the more radical proposals. Poor couples looking for housing should, they say, get a £5,000 subsidy from the government to help them with their mortgage. Where will the money come from? Why, from the inheritance taxes the Tories were threatening to abolish.

The authors are quick to reassure conservative critics that the mortgage bonus would only be available to people whose families could not afford it. It would not have been available, for instance, to Peter Mandelson, who was racked by house hunting problems at almost exactly the same time as he was writing his insipid little book. He was living in a perfectly presentable des res in Clerkenwell, with a pleasant three storey retreat in his constituency, Hartlepool. He was not satisfied, however. He was upwardly mobile. His bad years, when John Smith, an old fashioned right wing social democrat, loathed Mandelson were over. He regarded him as 'all froth and public relations' and banished him from the inner circle to which he had been promoted by Neil Kinnock.

Socialist Review January 1999

Smith's death in 1994 and his replacement by Tony Blair brought Mandelson scurrying back into Labour's ruling clique. Blair made a beeline for the rich, and recognised Mandelson's supreme quality—flattery. Mandelson is, above all else, a courtier, who loves the company of the rich and knows how to flatter them. The rich are always inclined to interpret flattery as perspicacity. Before long, with Blair's seal of approval on his forehead, Mandelson was flattering his way into the richest boardrooms in the land. The military top brass loved him. He even made friends with the Prince of Wales and his mistress. But his favourites of all the rich and famous were the media barons.

He personally persuaded Tony Blair that Rupert Murdoch was a profound political thinker whose papers needed to be courted. Murdoch's daughter and most likely successor became a close friend of Mandelson. Clive (Lord) Hollick (*Express*, Anglia TV etc) worked with Mandelson in Labour's election unit at Millbank. John Birt, director general of the BBC, was Mandelson's old buddy at London Weekend Television. How could this high flying courtier hope to keep up with all these rich and powerful friends from a dowdy flat in run down Clerkenwell? Something much grander was needed.

His greedy eyes turned to Notting Hill where his friend, the millionaire writer Robert Harris, entertained so lavishly, and where the former SDP leader Sir Ian Wrigglesworth showed off all the fruits of political compromise. A lovely house next to Wrigglesworth's was for sale, for a little matter of half a million quid. Poor Peter could not begin to raise that much. His salary as a backbencher was a mere £40,000. His flat, already mortgaged, would be lucky to bring in a hundred grand. The Britannia Building Society would only lend him a maximum of £150,000. True, his mother lived in a handsome house in Hampstead Garden Suburb, but even Peter Mandelson could hardly set light to New Labour's great crusade by evicting his mother and selling her house. Even his own proposal—for a £5,000 housing 'start'—would not have helped him.

In desperation, Peter turned to the only really rich man he knew on the Labour back benches, Robert Maxwell's former business colleague and Labour MP for Coventry Geoffrey Robinson. Robinson happily lent his new young friend £373,000, happily rolled up the interest and happily forgot to insist when, or even if, the loan should be repaid. Hey presto! As soon as Labour won the election, Robinson, an archetypal mediocrity, soared into the government with the grand title, which was not meant to be satirical, of Paymaster General.

When the loan was exposed just before Christmas, the Tory press was bewildered. All hailed Mandelson as an employers' friend, an enemy of trade unions, an opponent of socialism and a moderniser. But few could resist a crack at the old enemy. The result was that Mandelson was assaulted for trivia. Acres of space were given over to phoney indignation about his cheating the mortgage company. But most sensible people cheat their mortgage company. Similarly, the Tory party in parliament wriggled and jiggled as they tried to spot a 'conflict of interest' between Mandelson as secretary of state at the DTI and a two-bit DTI inquiry into some of Robinson's business deals.

All of this missed the point, which was hit at once and in a single sentence by a constituent of Mandelson's who muttered, 'I wish I could find someone to lend me £370,000.' The point was the sheer scale of the money lent, and the ludicrous lifestyle of people who lend and borrow that kind of sum. The man who proclaims the 'fairness' and 'social justice' of New Labour, who suggests a £5,000 sub for young couples looking for a new home, is at the same time borrowing a sum equivalent to 15 years of the average worker's total earnings just to buy a house.

The huge hoax which is New Labour was suddenly and brilliantly exposed. Nothing works on the public mind more than such a blatant example of personal greed. The whole strategy of 'softening' Labour's image in order to win elections was exposed as a means to propel its soft image makers into the salons of the rich.

Like so many marvellous moments, however, the exquisite delight in the fall of Mandelson may be short lived. Many people who put some faith and trust in New Labour may be plunged into despair. 'They all do it', 'they are all as bad as one another', 'all politicians and politics are rotten to the core'—these are all common reactions which have in the past turned Labour voters back to the Tories, or pushed them even further to the right. On its own, triumphalist rejoicing at Mandelson's fall may irritate many Labour voters into rejecting politics altogether.

On the other hand, the sudden vulnerability of New Labour, as its great white hope lies bleeding on the wayside, opens out all sorts of opportunities for setting out a socialist alternative. The New Labour road is plainly blocked. The past failures of Old Labour are partly responsible for the blocking. A new road to socialism, from the bottom up, through the skills, energies and solidarity of the people who produce the wealth, is wide open.

That's not fair, Gordon

The Chancellor of the Exchequer has devised a new cliche to define the 'third way'. 'Britain', he told the Commons last Tuesday, 'must leave behind the sterile, century-long conflict between enterprise and fairness.' His aim, he said, is 'to pursue enterprise and fairness together'. And that is much easier than it sounds. For in Gordon Brown's world, 'enterprise' means more taxpayers' money for the rich and 'fairness' means less taxpayers' money for the poor.

Some weeks ago, an Incomes Data Services (IDS) report on the soaring pay of company directors investigated the growing fashion for 'incentive schemes'. The findings revealed a curious gap between the payment of incentives to company directors and anything that could be described as enterprise in their companies. Share options, for instance, are becoming 'more diverse', and most companies set ridiculously low performance targets to make sure the options can be cashed in. An enduring problem with share options is that payouts on them are restricted to a sum four times someone's annual salary. This explains the recent popularity of long-term investment plans which set no limit on cash payments. Here, again, the criteria for handouts to directors are vague. 'Few companies give the names of the comparators and fewer still give their relative performance,' says the IDS report.

Shocked by these revelations of easy money for fat cats, Gordon Brown strode down to the CBI conference and proudly handed over a whole new batch of easy money for fat cats. Under his new scheme, companies can now 'award' up to £1 million share options tax free. These new options are known as Enterprise Management Initiatives (EMIs). The Treasury explained:

> For example, a key employee is granted an option of over 100,000 shares, when the market value is £1 a share. The employee exercises the option three years later when the shares are worth £3 each, making a gain of £200,000. No income tax is payable on the £200,000.

Guardian 16 November 1999

How much will this largesse cost? According to the Inland Revenue: 'Over 2,200 companies will take up EMIs over the first three years, at a cost of around £45 million a year to the Exchequer.' Forty-five million a year extra for the £200,000 brigade! That is almost exactly what ministers reckon to 'save' the Exchequer with their new rules for Incapacity Benefit, which will leave some 300,000 disabled people worse off than they are now.

'The evil that men do lives after them; the good is oft interred with their bones.' I reflected on this (usually inaccurate) sentiment when reading the obituaries of Edmund Dell, a former Labour Treasury minister. The *Financial Times* set out the frightful details of Dell's formal career, his obsession with free enterprise, his directorship at Guinness Peat, his outrage at not being offered an honour. I rush to his rescue by recalling a publication 50 years ago which was not mentioned in the *FT* obituary. While a young lecturer at Oxford after the war, Dell became a Communist and was lucky enough to fall in with the greatest of English Civil War historians, Christopher Hill. Together the two men produced *The Good Old Cause*, a history of the civil war through the sayings and reminiscences of the people who took part in it. Exciting and informative throughout, *The Good Old Cause* marked the high point in the life and work of Edmund Dell.

Another civil war enthusiast turns out to be John Major. In his autobiography he selects a famous quote—'The poorest he that is in England hath a right to live as the greatest he'—and has the nerve to claim it inspired him in his first speech as prime minister to the Tory party. Major attributes the quote to 'Lt-Col William Rainborough speaking during the Putney Debates of 1649'. Er, no. The great man was William's brother Lt-Col Thomas Rainborough, who could not have said anything in 1649 because he was dead. The Putney Debates were in 1647, and if you are wondering how two such howlers could get into a single sentence of a bestseller published by Harper Collins, you should remember that the firm is now owned by Rupert Murdoch and that anyone with any standards there has probably been sacked for supporting a union.

Strange visit to a New Guinea hospital

I had managed only one speech against the war in Kosovo when I was carted off to hospital in the middle of the night with what I later discovered was an aortic aneurism. Hardly had the surgeons opened me up than my aorta, an artery which runs from heart to head, ruptured. Almost all such ruptures end in death, and for many weeks I lay in a coma. When I came round, expertly patched up but still without much prospect of recovery, I was plagued by hallucinations. Chief among these was the heroic speech I had made not about Kosovo but to the massed ranks of the women's liberation movement in South Australia, from whose congress, I was quite sure, I was returning when I fell ill.

It was only when I finally convinced myself (a) that I had never been to South Australia in my life, (b) that if ever I did go there I was most unlikely to be a key speaker at a women's liberation congress, and (c) that the hospital where I was lying was not, as I had thought, on a sandbank near New Guinea but in Homerton, east London, a quarter of an hour's drive from home, that I asked about the Kosovo war. When I heard that it was still raging, supported not only by the New Labour government but also by the *Guardian* and several left wing journalists whose opinion I had previously respected, I was finally brought to my senses by that faithful old pick me up for sick socialists, indignation. Could the government, I wondered fitfully, survive such a monstrous war? Indeed, could the government survive at all? The war seemed to be a symptom of the diseases which had struck down the previous two Labour governments: support for US imperialist adventures abroad and impotence in the face of corporate power at home.

The Kosovo catastrophe was proof of the first. The reversal, in the face of the most extravagant and impertinent opposition from US power monopolies, of the Blair government's attempts to encourage the coal industry by curbing the growth of gas, proof of the second.

Yet, for some reason, thanks at least in part to the abject performances of the Conservative Party, the government did survive. One of the few political conversations I had in hospital was with a physiotherapist and trade unionist who told me, to my horror (not expressed, of course: the relationship between physiotherapist and lame patient is far too delicate for open controversy), that, taken all in all, he 'quite liked' the government. Nor was this only because Prime Minister Blair and his jovial health secretary, Frank Dobson, had shrewdly chosen Homerton Hospital as an appropriate place for the announcement of the government's new health plans. Compared with their Tory predecessors, the New Labour lot seemed to my physiotherapist friend to be sensible, almost benign.

This approach seemed to last through the summer and early autumn —for the rest of my time in hospital. As I gradually got better, and even my legs began to show some sign of life, I kept wondering why the Blairite con-trick—'The class war is over, so we Ministers of the Crown can suck up to the millionaires and invite them to our dinner tables while somehow tossing the workers the crumbs they want'— was working.

It was only after my final release in early October, after six months in the diligent care of the National Health Service, that the same old spectre—impotence in office—arose in dramatic form once again to persecute ministers.

The main cause was the Paddington rail crash, a disaster so avoidable that it shocked the entire nation. There was an immediate and apparently universal outcry against the privatised companies who owned the wrecked trains. 'Nationalise the railways!' suddenly became an unlikely but highly popular demand. A furious counter-attack was launched by the supporters of irresponsible private property. The *Economist* devoted an entire leading article to proving that the Paddington rail crash had nothing to do with privatisation. The article conveniently overlooked powerful arguments set out in the *Economist* of 23 July. That article was headed 'The Rail Billionaires', and sub-headed: 'The privatisation of British Rail has proved a disastrous failure. Without big changes, things are going to get worse.' An example followed: 'Indeed, until last year, some of Railtrack's suppliers decided, in effect, which parts of the track needed renewal.

Naturally, they appeared concerned less with passenger safety than with their own profits. Because they are paid by the mile, they have understandably tended to choose sections that are easy to renew rather than those that involve the most work.' 'Naturally'. 'Understandably'. There is 'indeed' a link between the drive to profit under privatisation and shortcuts which threaten safety. The point is not whether the Paddington outrage can be linked directly to some technological development under privatisation. The point is that the trains which smashed into each other belonged to companies both of which were bought and sold in the marketplace and which in the process delivered up to their original directors unimaginable riches.

The original *Economist* article spelled out the full scandal of this enrichment, of which the buying and selling of the three ROSCOs— the rail operating stock companies—was the most preposterous. The ROSCOs were undersold by the Tory government to the tune of £700 million. When they were subsequently swallowed by the big new private transport monopolies, almost as much as this vast sum vanished into the pockets of a handful of third-rate rail directors, whose successors decided that £700 million was far too much to invest in ATP, the safety system which would have prevented the outrages at Paddington and, before that, at Southall. The coincidence of those figures appeared exclusively, as far as I could see, in *Private Eye*.

All the Tory privatisations gave rise to similar scandals, but the privatisation of the railways was by far the worst. It was announced by Cecil Parkinson at a Tory party conference where there was little else left to cheer the Tory faithful. During the entire period that the enabling legislation dragged its way through parliament, never more than 15 percent of the population indicated their support for it. On all sides, including some Tory benches, rail privatisation was denounced as the latest manifestation of the Tories' reckless greed.

Nowhere was this denunciation more unequivocal than in the leadership of the Labour Party. At first, it seemed as though the Labour leaders recognised their power. If they announced that the privatised railways would be taken back into public ownership, then the entire privatisation project was bound to fail. After all, who would buy shares in a newly-privatised industry which the Labour Party was pledged instantly to renationalise? Not a penny profit could be made out of such a situation, and since profit was and is the only possible motive for investing in the railways, Labour's pledge on renationalisation was crucial to the future of the industry. This understanding of their own power led to the formation among Labour's transport spokespeople of the Crystal Clear Faction. Their leader was big bluff burly John Prescott, the man who doesn't mince words. He told Labour's conference in 1993: 'Let me make it crystal clear that any privatisation of the railway system that does take place will, on the arrival of a Labour government, be quickly and effectively dealt with...and be returned to public ownership.'

Nothing could be more crystal clear than that, and by the following year it was time for a pledge. Frank Dobson, Labour's transport spokesman at the 1994 conference, assured his ecstatic audience that Labour's promise on this occasion was not narrowly confined to party members. 'Let me give this pledge not just to this conference but to the people of Britain. The next Labour government...will bring the railway system back into public ownership.' The following year (1995) Labour's conference spokesman was Michael Meacher, a fully paid up member of the Crystal Clear Faction. He concentrated on the speculators who were hovering over the battered corpse of the rail industry:

> If there are any investors listening who are thinking of buying into our rail system, I have a message for them. The railways depend on public subsidies to the tune of £1.8 billion a year. There is no guarantee that subsidy will continue. If you want to buy a pig in a poke in all those circumstances, then it is up to you, but don't come crying to me when it all ends in tears.

The message seemed clear but it came from Michael Meacher, and he was Old Labour, so perhaps it could be disregarded. But wait. Hark to the speech made at the same conference by the new Labour leader himself, Tony Blair: 'To anyone thinking of grabbing our railways, built up over the years, so they can make a quick profit as our network is broken up and sold off, I say this: there will be a publicly owned and publicly accountable railway system under a Labour government.'

For a time the message was repeated so firmly by so many Labour politicians that it was believed even in the big corporations. Brian Souter, chairman of the burgeoning bus company Stagecoach, told a Commons committee two years later that in 1995 nobody in the industry would touch rail privatisation 'with a bargepole'. The prospect of Labour doing what it said it would was enough to frighten off all but the small fry. When the ROSCOs were flogged off in January 1996, no big investor dared to bid even a fraction of what they were worth. Labour's bold talk had worked. No serious contender was 'thinking of grabbing our railways' or 'buying a pig in a poke'. If the Labour Party had stuck to its promises, the railways would never have been privatised.

Instead, at the very moment of victory, New Labour's nerve collapsed. By 1996, the Labour Party's last conference in opposition, all the crystal clear pledges to renationalise had vanished. In their place came a bromide assurance of a 'modern integrated transport system, built in partnership between public and private finance, and restoring a unified system of railways'. Against all the evidence to the contrary, the New Labour leaders had decided that renationalisation would be electorally unpopular and too expensive. So they dropped it. The corporate giants who had been frightened off by Labour's determination were suddenly enthused by Labour's vacillation. One by one, the ROSCOs and most of the operating companies, including Great Western and Thames, whose trains were involved in the Paddington crash, were snapped up by the new transport giants.

In government, New Labour ministers tolerated the profiteering as though they had never opposed it. No special levies were raised on the huge fortunes amassed by the new rail billionaires. No attempt was made to alter the subsidy or otherwise interfere with a speculator's inalienable right to make quick profits out of a subsidised industry. Challenged about this in March 1998, John Prescott delivered perhaps the most remarkable statement of Labour's impotence in office ever made by a serving minister: 'The privatised railway is producing windfall profits for a few people as a result of the contracts awarded by the last government. There is nothing I can do about that.' He was after all only secretary of state and deputy prime minister, and under his regime crystal clarity had dissolved into fudge.

In the shocked and embarrassed aftermath of the Paddington disaster, Prescott finally stripped Railtrack of its responsibility for safety, and at the time of writing, it seems as if he will survive, at least partly as a result of his own self-declared impotence. A better prospect emerged from the train drivers' union which threatened to strike if proper safety equipment was not installed immediately. At the same time, the workers at Ford Dagenham threatened to strike against constant harassment by racist foremen.

When postal workers in Scotland struck and won their case against an arrogant and arbitrary sacking, it seemed suddenly as if my coming out of hospital had inspired a wave of revolt. As I write, the wave seems slowly to be receding, leaving behind the familiar sullen resentment which Tony Blair wrongly interprets as support.

Birth of a notion

Perhaps the most important political meeting of the century took place 100 years ago less than a mile from the current offices of the *Guardian*. No one took the slightest notice. Most of the 129 people who turned up on 27 February 1900 at the Memorial Hall, Farringdon, were trade union delegates, responding rather grudgingly to a TUC resolution calling for a new organisation to elect labour MPs. One reason for the lack of enthusiasm was that many of the trade union delegates were already politically active—in the Liberal Party. They had argued for years that the Liberal Party, with its huge resources, was the only appropriate place for labour representatives to learn and practise their politics.

Most of the Farringdon meeting was taken up with arguments about whether the new labour organisation should consist entirely of socialists or of trade unionists. Both these propositions were rejected in favour of a compromise calling for 'working class opinion to be represented in the House of Commons by men sympathetic with the aims and demands of the labour movement'.

This was strengthened somewhat by an amendment from Keir Hardie demanding a 'distinct labour group in parliament who shall have their own whips and agree their own policy'. Hardie's argument was that the Liberal Party, stuffed with landowners, employers and business executives, would always be incapable of representing the interests of labour. His amendment was eventually passed unanimously, and a Labour Representation Committee emerged with powers to nominate its own candidates for election to parliament. In the general election which followed closely on the formation of the LRC, however, only two LRC men were elected—Keir Hardie, a socialist, and Richard Bell, a Liberal. Neither man could stand the other. The new Labour project was saved from disaster by the House of Lords, whose judges declared that the employers of the Taff Vale railway company in South Wales were entitled to damages from a rail union after a strike which the union had not even supported.

The great Liberal Party steadfastly refused even to denounce this perverse judgement; and it became obvious to the trade union leaders that, if they wanted to keep their traditional immunity from such legal action, they must press ahead with their independent party. In the 1906 general election, 29 LRC-nominated MPs were elected, and the Taff Vale judgment was swiftly reversed. Ramsay MacDonald, the energetic secretary of the new Labour Party, hailed the triumph to a cheering crowd at the Queens Hall:

> The cottage had to fight for the palace but the palace has always been neglecting to legislate in the interests of the cottage. The cottage has now said: 'I am going to fight for myself and I am going to work and legislate for myself, because my experience has been that if I don't, nobody will do it for me' [applause]. The great democracy of the country has been cajoled by primrose dames and bribed by candidates on both sides who have more money than political intelligence' [prolonged applause].

The enthusiasm was irresistible. The supporters of old labour's allegiance to the Liberal Party were routed. In 1908 the Labour Party conference passed a motion committing the party to the common ownership of the means of production, a commitment which in 1918 was written into the Labour Party constitution. In the general election that year, and again in 1931, the Liberals teamed up with the Tories to smash the rising Labour Party, which continued, irritatingly, to rise again independently, securing substantial parliamentary majorities in 1945, 1966, 1974 and 1997. In all this time, the Liberal Party and its successors were reduced to a ridiculous rump.

Now, after a century of independence, the leaders of the victorious Labour Party have come up with an exciting new idea: cooperation with the Liberals. The Labour Party constitution has been rewritten to wipe out all reference to public ownership. The private office of the prime minister has been stuffed with Liberals or masterminds of the disastrous and defunct SDP. At a secret meeting after the last election, the new Labour prime minister appeared to offer two cabinet seats to the Liberals, and was only dissuaded from doing so by the infuriating size of Labour's independent majority.

Among the top people at the meeting was Roy (Lord) Jenkins, hagiographer of former Liberal icons Asquith, Dilke and Gladstone, who ditched his elected Labour seat for an unelected position in Europe, and then ditched Labour altogether for the Liberals. Who could possibly be better qualified to preside over Blair's top people's committee to construct a new electoral system?

Any day now we can expect a millennial speech from the prime minister to the effect that the traditional battle between the cottage and the palace is an error of outdated imagination; and that the time has come to return to the days when the great democracy of the country can be cajoled by primrose dames and bribed by candidates who have more money than political intelligence.

Secrets and lies

Glamorising an atrocity

I was trying to concentrate on what Nigel Lawson was saying to Brian Walden last Sunday, but I kept being put off by the fact that both men were wearing poppies.

Not long ago, I was asked to go in for an interview on early morning television. I had to turn up at half past five in the morning.

Hardly had I arrived than I was whisked into 'make up', where I was puffed and prettied for a few moments. I was then handed a poppy and told to stick it in my lapel. 'We're all wearing poppies today,' a young woman said brightly. She was very upset when I replied that I was not wearing any poppy, then or at any other time.

She rushed out of the room and appeared soon afterwards with the producer of the programme. He explained that it was decided as a matter of policy that all interviewees that morning (I suppose it was 11 November) should wear poppies in their jackets.

I said I would not. He assumed I was objecting as a matter of fashion and assured me that a poppy would offset the colour of my jacket.

When I explained that I objected not to the style of the poppy (still less to the colour, which was fine) but to what it represented he was most insulted and stormed out of the room.

Slaughter

I went into the 'waiting area', where I made small talk to Cecil Parkinson and Jack Cunningham, who were both wearing poppies. After a few minutes the producer appeared with the news that there was 'no time' for my interview but it was time for me to leave.

How I feel about poppies, cenotaphs, remembrance days and armistice celebrations is wonderfully expressed in a film now in the cinemas—Tavernier's *Life and Nothing But*.

The film is about the hunt for years after the First World War to fit the thousands of 'missing persons' to real corpses.

Socialist Worker 11 November 1989

The whole atmosphere stinks with the obsession and glorification of death in what, with the possible exception of the Holocaust, was the most futile and disgusting slaughter of human beings in all human history.

At one stage two men appear to petition the commander. They point out that about 10 percent of the men called up in the war were killed in it. Their complaint is that in their village no one died.

Seventeen young men were called up, and 17 came back without even a lost limb to show for their heroism. In all the surrounding villages people were building war memorials, holding masses, probably even wearing poppies (I am not sure when that awful symbol was first thought of), but in their village they had only the living.

The two delegates begged the commander to alter the local government boundaries to 'take in' a farm from a neighbouring village. Two men from the farm had been killed in the war. The next village had plenty of dead to celebrate and would not miss a mangy two!

If the village could claim two dead, the morale of all the villagers would soar. Everyone could join in the mass worship of the dead.

It starts as a joke, but the earnestness of the two men soon cuts out any laughter. This was a deadly serious business, into which was thrown the entire effort of the French ruling class.

Their most crucial priority at that time was to glorify those who had died, not for their lives but for their deaths, to make of death on the battlefield a human achievement of which all the loved ones of the dead could feel proud.

In all the sorrow, and the celebration of sorrow, no one would ask questions—why did all this have to happen, and who is responsible?

Atrocity

The wretched clusters of people searching for their dead husbands, brothers and sons are acting partly out of grief and nostalgia, but increasingly to build up their own self respect in a deeply chauvinist age.

The only point which matters about the First World War and its sequels is that they must not be allowed to happen again. Honouring and worshipping those who died in them, praising them for their patriotic sacrifice and wearing poppies as symbols of their blood on the ground where they fell serves only to glamorise the atrocity and pave the way to the next one.

Oil's not well in East Timor

'The people of the tiny Indonesian province of East Timor are excited about events in the Gulf', the *Financial Times* reported last week. How can that be?

How could anyone possibly be excited about the Gulf? Well, *Financial Times* correspondent Claire Bolderson has the answer: 'If the world will rally to save the Kuwaitis from their aggressive next door neighbour, they say, surely it will do the same for them.'

This is logic. The United Nations says it has a duty to protect the integrity of every member state. If one state is attacked by another, the entire world community must join forces to see the aggressor off.

The logic is specially powerful in East Timor. The people of that sad country have hardly known a single day of independence.

It is the eastern half of a large island in the South Seas. A bloody deal was struck between the two imperial powers—Holland took the west, Portugal the east.

After a time the Dutch, who were rather quicker than the other imperialists to realise the game was up, handed over their half to an independent Indonesia, while the Portuguese clung to East Timor every bit as ruthlessly as they clung to their colonies in Africa: Guinea, Angola and Mozambique.

As in Africa, Portugal was eventually forced out of East Timor in 1975. There was nothing but chaos, civil war and conquest to follow.

The Indonesians invaded and the Timoreans fought with tremendous (and almost wholly unreported) courage and sacrifice.

In the terrible wars and famines which followed, probably a third of the population, nearly 200,000 people out of 600,000, were killed.

Terror

The Indonesian dictators followed up their slaughter with the most ghastly exploitation and the most revolting terror. This has been

Socialist Worker 17 November 1990

going on pretty well without a pause now for 15 years.

East Timor is a model of the kind of country which ought to be protected by the international community. If there really was a world government with a sense of duty to the underprivileged and the oppressed, East Timor would have been rescued long ago from the dragon which devours it.

Yet the issue of sending troops to beat back the aggressors and allow a new free country to develop from the ruins of East Timor has never even been discussed at the United Nations.

Now and then a resolution deploring the invasion and the atrocities of Indonesia is discussed, and usually traded in exchange for a 'helpful' vote from Indonesia about some other part of the world where big companies or states make profits.

No one, in short, has lifted a finger to help the wretched people of East Timor, who must imagine that no one has ever heard of their plight.

Now that aggression and oppression are suddenly unpopular at the United Nations (and now that American imperialism, Russian imperialism, Chinese, French and British imperialism have responded to the invasion of Kuwait with huge forces, and talk of widespread war) it is hardly surprising that the hopes of the people of East Timor begin to rise.

Monster

For if the world moves against a monster in Baghdad, might it not do so against a monster in Jakarta? There is after all nothing in logic to separate the two monsters.

The regime in Baghdad is hardly more savage than its counterpart in Jakarta. It can hardly be argued that the invasion of Kuwait by Iraq in 1990 was any more intolerable than the invasion of East Timor by Indonesia 15 years earlier.

By every measure possible, the barbarism in East Timor has been as bad, if not far worse, than anything yet experienced in Kuwait.

No wonder the East Timoreans are hopeful. But they have misread the reasons for the war in the Gulf. They have to do with the cheap supply of oil.

The Americans and their 'allies' (what romantic memories that word conjures up) want to get rid of Saddam because he is seen by them as a threat to the stability of the region and the price of oil.

The people of East Timor, as they hope and pray for a similar force to rescue their country, have only to ask one question to discover whether or not they will be 'rescued' by 'allies' across the sea.

Is there oil in East Timor? If yes, which is possible, it won't be long before the US cavalry comes over the hill. If no, the people of East Timor, as far as the 'allies' are concerned, can rot in hell.

Bankers, lawyers, politicians: 'They all knew he was a crook'

If I had not already been a socialist, the astonishing events at the *Daily Mirror* in the last few days would have quickly made me one.

They are calling the Maxwell robbery the greatest financial scandal of all time.

He robbed some £300 million from the workers at the *Mirror*, either from their company or from their pension fund.

All around there is a great 'tut-tutting'. Newspapers which only weeks ago were describing Maxwell as a 'swashbuckling buccaneer' now fall over one another to denounce him for what he was—a revolting crook.

Nowhere is the embarrassment greater than in the City.

The best stockbrokers (Smith New Court), the top bankers (Rothschild and Samuel Montagu), the biggest accountants (Coopers Lybrand), an endless list of the top solicitors in the land—not to mention the City editors of pretty well every national newspaper—all served Maxwell when he was at the peak of his powers.

All of them knew he was a crook.

In 1971 a distinguished lawyer and a distinguished accountant declared after a careful examination of Maxwell's relations with a company called Leasco that Maxwell was not fit to chair a public company.

Maxwell fitted the needs of his class

In the early 1980s Maxwell became chairman of one of the biggest public companies in the country, the British Printing Corporation.

In July 1984, on what we on the *Mirror* called Black Friday, he became chairman of the Mirror Group of Newspapers—which ran five national newspapers with a combined circulation of four million copies every weekday and six million every Sunday.

Socialist Worker 14 December 1991

How could this happen?

That is a question everyone in high society has been asking themselves anxiously over the past week.

Some say it is just carelessness. The editor of the *Independent* newspaper blames the 'arrogance' of the City slickers, who thought they could control Maxwell's excesses.

Every reason has been thought of except the right one—that Maxwell was a valuable standard bearer for his class when it was on the offensive in the 1980s

His brash, old fashioned style fitted the needs of the bosses of the Thatcher decade.

Behind him, the more genteel class warriors, though they knew perfectly well that he had broken the rules before and would probably break the rules again, pushed him eagerly into the firing line on the class battle front.

They hoped he would win at least a few battles against the age-old enemy—the workers.

In 1983, when the Reed Corporation announced it would sell the *Mirror* newspapers, it made what is known in the City of London as a 'solemn promise'. It appointed a chairman and announced the shares would be sold.

Unions on the *Mirror*, then strong and confident, approached Reed. They suggested they should borrow the money and buy the newspapers.

Reed sanctimoniously and politely refused but made a 'solemn promise' that it would not sell to a single owner. It wanted the shares split up in small parcels.

A few months later Reed kept that solemn promise by selling the papers to Robert Maxwell, who was not only a single owner but a man the City's own experts had dubbed unfit to run a public company.

Why? Because Maxwell had proved himself fit in one crucial respect.

In an aggressive cowboy manner much admired by the bankers he had smashed the unions at BPCC and turned the company into profit. Could he not do the same at the *Mirror*?

Yes, he could. From the moment he came into the building, Maxwell set himself the single task of breaking the trade unions.

Using the two methods which had proved so effective at BPCC, bullying and bribery, he humbled and broke—in quick succession—the NGA, SOGAT and the NUJ.

Resistance was pathetic. I remember one dreadful mass meeting in 1985, when the NUJ gave Maxwell more than 50 compulsory redundancies. A few of us pleaded with the meeting to resist—to stop the paper until the redundancies were withdrawn.

The meeting was swayed by a City solicitor who advised us that if we went on strike and lost we would lose all our rights and agreements, all redundancy money, all notice money—everything.

Here was the living proof that Maxwell's main ally was the Tory government and its anti-union laws which the *Mirror* newspapers ostensibly opposed.

When Murdoch broke his unions by sacking all his workers and moving to Wapping, Maxwell boasted that he had achieved his 'slimming' process by 'negotiations'. And so, in a way, he had.

His allies were the Tory laws and the bosses all over the country who responded to the new laws with a ferocious offensive.

What was the effect of these victories on the atmosphere in the *Mirror* and on the papers themselves?

Walking through those corridors day after day I was constantly struck by an extraordinary phenomenon.

Here were hundreds of able and dedicated men and women.

Here were excellent editors—all three editors I worked under at the *Mirror* were men of outstanding journalistic ability, sensitive and intelligent social democratically minded men who understood well the capabilities of the people who worked for them.

Here were reporters, sub-editors, layout artists, columnists, print workers, library workers, telephonists, secretaries and filing clerks all good at their job, keen to work well and able to produce an excellent newspaper.

Yet all lived in daily fear of one man who had no recognisable ability of any kind.

He could bully people, sack people, even—worst of all—charm people. But every single journalistic initiative made by Maxwell was a disaster.

In the year or so after taking over, he tried to edit the paper. He personally rewrote the copy of experienced columnists like Geoffrey Goodman.

He went on television to boast about his million pound bingo prizes, and when a fortunate old woman in Southend won the million he took her to Blackpool and paraded her down the Golden Mile.

Above all, he forced the paper to concentrate on what he regarded as the most important story in the universe—himself.

When he went to Bulgaria to dine with the Stalinist dictator Zhikov, he took with him one of the *Mirror*'s top reporters, who was obliged to write about the two oafs sharing a bottle of Stalinist beer.

When he attended a parachute display with Prince Charles, half the *Mirror* front page was devoted entirely to a picture of the two Highnesses.

His friends in the Tory government and in big business—notably Lord Young, Lord King, Ronson of Heron and Lord Forte—were lushed up with helpful items in the news pages.

All this was greeted with disgust by the *Mirror* readers, who abandoned the papers in droves. Never in the history of newspapers has so much circulation been lost than in the first few months of Maxwell's editorial regime.

Only in the nick of time, as the circulation went into freefall, was he finally persuaded to back off a little and appoint a new editor who struggled desperately to stop the rot.

The interference slowed, but the sackings went on.

All over the building there were horror stories. Maxwell personally sacked a SOGAT mother of the chapel, Angela Molloy, for putting a notice on the union board.

He sacked the City editor's secretary when she could not find a company report in a few seconds after his bullying phone call.

He sacked a deputy sports editor for the way he subbed some copy— though at the editor's insistence he was reinstated. Then the editor who reinstated him was sacked.

When John Diamond, a new columnist, opposed the Gulf War, Maxwell sacked him as well.

It is impossible to convey the deadening effect all this had on the life and abilities of the people who worked there, or the corresponding relief which greeted their release from it all.

Maxwell's fall, like his rise, was symbolic of the Tory government's fortunes.

Like them, he believed the capitalist boom of the 1980s would last forever. There was no limit, he believed, to the glory and power which his beloved market system would shower upon him.

In a sort of frenzy he started buying up everything which came up for sale in the United States, Portugal, Argentina, Israel.

He borrowed and borrowed from his most faithful supporter, the National Westminster Bank, which could never forget the way he smashed the unions at BPCC and saved the bank an embarrassing insolvency.

Up and up went the takeovers and the loans in an endless spiral of megalomania and greed.

No one stopped him—not a banker, not an adviser, not a regulator, not a government minister, not a policeman.

What did stop him was the fatal flaw in the market system which promoted him.

Suddenly the boom evaporated. The 'impossible' recession swept over him.

Interest rates climbed and the revenue from his new companies slumped.

Squeezed more and more tightly, he turned for final salvation to the huge sums piled up in the his workers' pension funds.

Long ago Tories and capitalists used to argue that pension funds were proof of the burgeoning economic power of the workers.

'With so much money in pension funds', it was said, 'millions of workers have a stake in the system.'

The argument overlooked the reality of control of the pension funds. The money was paid in by workers but controlled by a handful of capitalists and accountants who used it to lubricate the stock exchange.

The Tory government tightened this minority control still further.

They relaxed the trusteeship laws, made it possible for employers to take a 'pensions holiday'—that is, not to pay a penny into the funds—and take huge dollops out of the pension to invest as they thought fit. In all this the workers who paid the money had no say whatever.

Maxwell saw at once the value of these new laws to his form of piracy.

From the moment he took over in 1984, he paid not a penny into the pension fund. He blocked trade union recommendations for trustees and promoted his own trustees, carefully chosen for the 'loyalty'.

In the end, when he was desperate, he managed to swipe the vast bulk of the fund for his own private companies, assisted by the signature only of his son.

All this, the *Financial Times* insists, may not have been illegal.

For the Tory laws on pensions, like the Tory laws on unions, are devised to make the rich richer without the people whose labour and pensions they exploit having the slightest power to call a halt.

Maxwell adored Margaret Thatcher, and Thatcher repaid the compliment.

When Julia Langdon joined the *Mirror* political staff from the *Guardian*, Thatcher applauded her decision. 'A dose of Maxwell will do you good,' she trumpeted.

But Maxwell was not a Tory—he supported the Labour Party.

Into his plush inner circle came a clutch of right wing Labour Party supporters, most of them ennobled as Maxwell hoped to be.

There was Lord Donoughue, the biographer of Herbert Morrison, Lord Williams—a City slicker and deputy leader of the Labour peers—former Attorney General Sam Silkin and former Solicitor General Peter Archer.

While Maxwell behaved like a Tory, while he broke the unions like a Tory, while he stalked the *Mirror* and other enterprises he owned with all the arrogance of a Tory grandee, he said he was a supporter of the Labour Party—and the Labour leadership glowed with delight.

Now, instead of revelling in his disgrace, instead of exposing it as a disgrace of capitalism like all the other disgraces of recent years—Polly Peck, Ferranti and BCCI—the Labour leaders can only fret and fume and hope the whole thing will go away.

They too are stuck deep in the mud of capitalist corruption.

Socialists need not be mealy mouthed. Maxwell was a great fat capitalist.

His rise and fall reflected the rise and fall of British capitalism in the 1980s. He went up on the backs of workers, and down in the crisis of the market system.

The only good part of the whole filthy story is the spirit of anger and hope which now rushes, like a cleansing wind, through the corridors of the *Mirror* newspaper.

Editors, writers, sub-editors, workers of every description suddenly realise that they don't need Maxwell or anything like him.

This grotesque and apparently immovable statue to modern capitalism has come crashing down, and no one wants to put another remotely like it in its place.

Turning a blind eye to Nelson

Why did he get away with murder?

Brian Nelson has admitted at least four gruesome murders of civilians in Northern Ireland.

He will not stand trial for these murders. Why?

Because when he set them up he was an intelligence agent for the British army.

In a shabby backroom deal clinched last week, Nelson agreed to plead guilty to five conspiracies to murder and a number of other lesser charges.

The murder charges were dropped.

The court case lasted less than a day.

The army and the security services breathed a huge sigh of relief.

The ghastly truth about Brian Nelson would not come out.

Nelson was in court yesterday, but sentence was postponed after a glowing tribute to him from an anonymous colonel. Nelson may end up with a long prison sentence. But before it is fully served it is widely assumed he will be quietly released and found a comfortable job.

In exchange, he will not say a word about his role as a British army agent assisting and encouraging the murder gangs of paramilitary thugs in Northern Ireland.

The story of Brian Nelson

Nelson, 44, a former soldier in the Black Watch, was recruited for British military intelligence in Northern Ireland in the mid-1970s.

He quickly penetrated the inner circles of Protestant paramilitary groups and their murder gangs, such as the Shankhill Butchers.

Daily Mirror 30 January 1992

In 1987 he became head of intelligence for the extremist Ulster Defence Association.

He provided Protestant assassins with names and addresses of IRA suspects. Much of this information came from army intelligence.

The assassins and torturers went out and did their dirty work.

Sometimes they bungled. In May 1988, Terry McDaid, a 30 year old bricklayer, was sitting at home watching television with his wife when masked gunmen smashed down his front door and shot him several times in the chest.

It was all a mistake. They'd meant to shoot Terry's brother, Declan, whose name had been supplied by Brian Nelson.

In 1990 Nelson was arrested by English police officers from the special inquiry into links between the authorities and Protestant paramilitaries under John Stevens, deputy chief constable of Cambridgeshire.

He thought he was completely safe, so he told Stevens everything.

He *admitted* setting up the murder of Terry McDaid.

He *admitted* setting up the murder of another Catholic, Gerard Slane.

He *admitted* knowing in advance of 17 other sectarian murders by the Protestant paramilitaries.

Deputy Chief Constable Stevens was shocked. He insisted on Nelson being prosecuted.

The British army hierarchy was horrified.

If Nelson was punished, they asked, how could they keep their agents among the paramilitaries?

While these arguments raged, Nelson was held for two yeas in the comfortable 'supergrass suite' at Crumlin Road prison, Belfast.

He was charged with the murders of McDaid and Slane.

His case was discussed in the cabinet.

Attorney General Sir Patrick Mayhew insisted the prosecution should go ahead. Then came last week's deal.

The story of James Miller

It has all happened before. In 1970 James Miller, a lift engineer, was recruited by military intelligence in Northern Ireland.

Like Brian Nelson, he became head of intelligence in the UDA, and passed on information about IRA suspects to the Protestant paramilitaries. In a statement published in the *Sunday Times* five years ago, Miller said he had been pressed by his army handlers to push in 1974 for a strike of Protestant workers.

The strike—in the spring of 1974—brought down the Northern Ireland parliament, and all hopes of power sharing between Protestants and Catholics.

After the strike, Miller left Northern Ireland.

The story of Ginger Baker

Like Brian Nelson, Ginger Baker was trained in the British army. In 1972, he deserted his regiment, the Royal Irish Rangers, and went to Belfast where he joined the Protestant paramilitaries and started murdering Catholics. He murdered 14 before he was caught.

Baker at once revealed that he had been working with the police and the army.

If charged with all the murders, he said, he would plead not guilty and denounce his handlers. A deal was done. He was charged with four murders.

He says he was promised a short sentence and accommodation for his family near his prison. In exchange he agreed to plead guilty.

Nothing came out about the disgusting murders Baker had committed, nor about the help he got from the authorities while committing them.

As the years went on, there was no sign of his release. Baker protested.

Now, after 18 years, Baker has been taken back to a prison in Northern Ireland where he hopes soon to be released.

Complicity

The army has been quick to play down the Nelson scandal. They pretend he was out of control.

But the record suggests otherwise. It suggests that ever since the 'Troubles' started in Northern Ireland in 1968 the policy of the British army and the police has been to seek alliances with Protestant paramilitaries and use them in their war with the IRA.

In 1974 army information officer Colin Wallace protested, among other things, about British intelligence complicity with Protestant assassinations.

He was summarily sacked. His appeal against his sacking was nobbled by senior intelligence officers at the Ministry of Defence. After an official inquiry 15 years later, he was awarded £30,000 compensation.

In 1975 military intelligence officer Fred Holroyd complained that the army were involved in assassinations and even in the murderous bomb attack on the Miami Showband pop group. Holroyd was whisked off to a mental hospital, where he had no treatment.

He was forced to resign from the army.

Captain Holroyd was a patriotic, conservative soldier. In his recent book *War Without Honour* he accepts that British troops in Northern Ireland must take sides—for the Protestants, against the Catholics.

But that doesn't mean, he says, that police and troops can cooperate with murder groups.

He concluded: 'If the forces of the state allow themselves to act with the same degree of brutal illegality as those they are commanded to defeat, then in a sense they are shown to be losing the battle.'

Look in the *Mirror*!

After months exposing callous sackings and victimisations across the country, I devote my page today to the astonishing events at the *Mirror*.

Five months ago David Montgomery, former editor of *Today* and the *News of the World*, was appointed chief executive here. Staff protested and occupied the newsroom. Mr Montgomery persuaded us back to work with three written assurances.

(1) 'I have definitely got no plans for job cuts in editorial departments.' How has that worked out? Three weeks later 100 *Mirror* 'casual' journalists were locked out when they reported for work. They were sacked without discussion and without explanation.

Since then the following staff journalists have been 'let go'— almost all of them against their will.

Sacked

John Hicks, Northern Ireland correspondent, Sylvia Jones, crime correspondent, George Thaw, 'Live Letters' and books editor, assistant night editor David Harbord, Alistair Campbel, political editor, Len Greener, pictures editor, David Thompson, leader writer, Terry Pattinson, industrial editor, Marcia Brackett, fashion editor, Pauline McLeod, film critic, Pauline Wallin, TV writer; graphics artists Roy Wright, Sandy Molloy and Steve Latibaudiere; reporters John Jackson, Kevin O'Lone, Robin Parkin, Frank Gilbride, Frank Thorne, Ron Ricketts, Ian Cameron, Alastair McQueen; features subs Irvine Hunter, Trevor Davies, Neil Dunkin, Terry Newell, Kevin Memery, Di Robinson, Neil Sowerby; news subs Simon Clarke, Malcolm Tattersall, Paul Sutherland, Francine Goodman.

(2) 'The editors of all titles remain in their positions.'

But not for long. Nineteen days later, on 11 November, Bill Hagerty, editor of the *People*, was sacked.

Handed out as a leaflet to the public outside the *Mirror* building in March 1993

On 13 November Richard Stott, editor of the *Daily Mirror*, was told by David Montgomery: 'Your job is safe.'

On 15 November Stott was sacked.

(3) 'Union recognition will continue.'

Union recognition means negotiating agreements on pay and conditions with the unions.

The Montgomery management has consistently refused to negotiate any agreement with any trade union.

The National Union of Journalists House Agreement has been ignored.

It states that all sackings must be notified to union officials and discussed with them. None of the above sackings were notified to or discussed with any union official.

Two of the best sub-editors in the country, Irvine Hunter and Trevor Davies, were the top officials of the NUJ at the *Daily Mirror*. They were told they could not keep their jobs and be senior union officials.

Victimised

They refused to resign from their union posts, and a new boss was moved in over them. They were told to work five days a week instead of four. They refused. Their contracts were 'terminated'.

The NUJ chapel elected a new committee. Three of the new members were Terry Pattinson, Neil Dunkin and Kevin Memery. Pattinson was sacked on 8 March, Dunkin on 17 March, Memery on 18 March.

All is gloom and fear. No one knows where next the axe will fall. Last Friday, the corridor where I work echoed to the sound of sobbing. One secretary (27 years service) asked me: 'What have I done wrong?'

Nothing. None of the people sacked did anything wrong. They were sacked because they did not 'fit in'. But who does?

'We need socialist newspapers like never before'

Friends and comrades have been commiserating with me for losing my job on the *Mirror*, and indeed I am sad about it. But my main reaction, looking back on 13 years of Thatcher, Maxwell and Co, is that I have had it pretty good.

For a known and declared member of the Socialist Workers Party to be given a page in a mass circulation tabloid was remarkable. To hang on to it for all that time was pretty well incredible.

The surprise is not so much that I was pushed out, but that it took so long for it to happen.

Ever since 1945 there has been a radical tradition in the *Daily Mirror*. Most of the paper of course wasn't political at all, and the political part of it was pretty firmly controlled by right wing Labour.

George Brown, the very right wing deputy leader of the Labour Party in the 1960s was paid a retainer with the *Mirror*. He was a close friend and political ally of the *Mirror* columnist Jack Connor, who wrote under the pseudonym Cassandra.

Cecil King, chairman of the *Mirror* in the 1960s, was an MI5 agent who tried to lead a coup against the elected Labour government in 1968 and was sacked for his pains.

Still, there was a radical tradition symbolised by an Australian sub-editor who joined the paper in the early 1960s—John Pilger.

When John turned his hand to reporting he quickly revealed an astonishingly evocative writing power. His skill as a writer was entwined with a strong socialist consciousness.

He was outraged by the divisions between rich and poor, and incensed by the violent means by which imperialism, especially US imperialism, sought to preserve those divisions.

Socialist Worker 10 April 1993

John wrote reams of magnificent reports for the *Mirror* which continued all through the 1970s and halfway through the 1980s until Maxwell summarily sacked him.

John turned his skills to television. His contacts with the working class, who followed his reports in the *Mirror* with such enthusiasm, became less frequent.

As Maxwell no doubt anticipated, his sacking was a triumph for the rich.

Chinks of light in the capitalist media were a feature of the 1960s and 1970s. Almost every paper, even the most foul reactionary ones, employed socialists who, with varying frequency, could get their ideas across.

The *Sunday Times*, it is worth recalling, was a marvellous paper of record in those days. The very first act of Andrew Neil when he took over the *Sunday Times* editorship in 1983 was to sack the editor of the investigative 'Insight' column, Christopher Hird, and disband his team.

Other chinks have been shut out as the ruling class has gained in confidence in the last decade.

Even the liberal press has become almost exclusively preoccupied with its own gloom and hatred of people, which drive it to more and more reactionary conclusions.

The bitter turmoil at the *Mirror* over the last few months has been portrayed in the financial media as a desperate attempt to 'restore to profitability' a dying old carcass of a newspaper.

In fact the *Mirror* was making good profits. At every twist and turn in the struggle I got the overriding impression that there was more to this than a greedy management determined to smash the unions.

They were out, at the same time, to extinguish the tiniest flicker of any genuine radical information which might inflame the masses.

When Harold Lind, a media consultant, wrote in the *Times* last October that there were too many good journalists on the *Mirror* and that they should be dispensed with, he meant that, for the masses, any old trash will do.

This was the Wapping school of journalism in full attack, and the new *Mirror* boss Montgomery and his acolytes took up the challenge with a ruthless zeal.

When I started work as a journalist 32 years ago it was possible to imagine some areas where my socialist ideas would be published in the mass media in some form. Now I am not so sure.

The control of the British media has always been in the hands of five or six men, but in the past they have deferred to some semblance of variety and democracy. Now they seem united in their desire to silence every whisper of dissent.

One conclusion for socialists is to hold our heads in despair. Another is more positive: to proclaim the case for socialist papers, openly declaring their socialist ideas.

Such papers by definition cannot circulate in the same market as the capitalist papers. They cannot depend on the same support from capitalist advertisers and distributors. Their economics and their circulation depend on the sacrifice and time of socialists themselves.

This is not just flag-waving for *Socialist Worker*. The uniformity of the capitalist press should not provide anyone with an excuse to make our socialist papers more sectarian and hysterical.

On the contrary. The more uniform the capitalist papers become, the more socialist editors should ensure their papers are open, democratic and varied.

But the developments in the capitalist press, including the union-busting and censorship at the *Mirror* which led to my departure, make a strong case even stronger. We need socialist newspapers like never before.

Ambushing the news

When Rupert Murdoch's Sky Television bid successfully for the right to screen First Division football matches live, the chief executive of London Weekend Television, Greg Dyke, put on a grand display of righteous indignation. It was, he said, shocking that commercial interests should deprive people of the programmes they wanted to watch.

He was right, of course. But is he consistent?

Now he appears in secret conference with other TV bosses, in particular Paul Jackson, the managing director of Carlton TV, which purveys television programmes in London on weekdays.

Jackson, Dyke and all the other commercial TV bosses met recently to discuss the future of the most successful and popular regular television shows ever—*News at Ten*.

News at Ten started in 1967. It lasted for half an hour. From the outset it proved just as popular as the BBC's news.

It has lasted for 26 years, has an enormous and loyal following, and the two minutes of advertising which split it in two bring in nearly £100 million—by far the most profitable regular two minutes for the ITV companies.

The success of television news on BBC and ITV gave the lie to all those who said that the masses were not interested in news.

While the tabloid press published less and less news—and gave more and more space to sport and nudes—the television news, presented on the whole without nudes and without even much sport, proved hugely popular.

Millions of people were gluttons for the news. When Channel 4 introduced its own extended 50 minute ITN news (called *Channel 4 News*) at 7pm, millions tuned in.

Together the two ITN programmes were watched by something like half the adult population. They established minimal standards of fairness and accuracy, which compared favourably with the bias and hysteria of the tabloid press.

Socialist Worker 3 July 1993

The only people who refuse to recognise the astonishing popularity and success of *News at Ten* are the television proprietors.

They don't like news at any time, but they specially don't like it at 10 o'clock at night when it interrupts much more juicy profit making with cheap movies or rotten sitcom shows.

For years now the heads of the ITV companies have been plotting a coup on *News at Ten*.

Last week they finally ambushed it and started to leak plans for putting on a new news programme at 6.30pm.

Everyone agrees that most of the standards of *News at Ten* would be lost in a 6.30 programme—it is too early to develop the day's news, it will compete absurdly with *Channel 4 News*. It will be seen as a demotion, a device to get the news out of the way before getting on with the trivia.

But years of 'deregulation', in television, as in everything else, have made it impossible for the 'watchdogs' to intervene.

Profit-hungry bosses like Greg Dyke, who, with his fellow directors at LWT, has just helped himself to millions of pounds in a scandalous share scheme, are left free to plunder the networks.

Even though she had her own friends on the ITV companies, Thatcher grew to loathe them for their power and their lack of right wing bias.

She waged war to the death with Thames Television over *Death on the Rock*, the exposé of the Gibraltar murders by the SAS.

Her hatred spilled over into *News at Ten*.

The ideological imperative from the right to sweep away anything which can for a moment present the public with some of the facts about the world we live in has engulfed the creations even of the right's own children.

Prey of the Jackal

No one seemed very interested in the revelations on Yorkshire TV's *First Tuesday* that the British army and security services were up to their necks in the worst terrorist atrocity since the war.

The quadruple bombing of main streets in rush hour Dublin and Monaghan in May 1974, which killed 33 people, was the work of a paramilitary Protestant gang, equipped and trained by British army and intelligence officers. The gang was the Mid-Ulster Brigade of the Ulster Volunteer Force and its leader, the man described in the programme as the 'Jackal', has continued murdering people ever since, to the profound indifference of the authorities.

Patrick Campbell, a civil rights leader in Portadown, was shot dead at the door of his house in October 1973 by two men who asked his wife if they could have a word with him. Mrs Campbell later picked out the Jackal from an identity parade as one of the assailants. He was arrested and charged, but the charges were dropped. Nor was the other assailant, Dublin bomber Wesley Somerville, charged.

John Francis Green was assassinated in Monaghan in January 1975 by the Jackal, along with Robert McConnell, a serving officer in the UDR, a British army regiment, and Wesley Somerville. Green's cottage was staked out and his murder planned by an SAS officer, Captain Robert Nairac, stationed at the secret SAS headquarters in Castle Dillon, Armagh.

The Miami Showband, a pop group of no particular political persuasion, was stopped in July 1975 at a roadblock near the border by a group of men wearing UDR uniforms. A bomb was put in the pop group's van. It went off almost at once, killing the man who put it there, Harris Boyle, and Wesley Somerville, both members of the UVF Mid-Ulster Brigade. The rest of the uniformed gang opened fire on the fleeing defenceless pop group, killing three of them.

One of the men arrested for his part in the massacre, James McDowell, revealed in his confession that the gang was accompanied by

Private Eye 16 July 1993

Robert Nairac. That part of his confession was conveniently deleted before the case came to court, and Nairac himself was assassinated 22 months later. McDowell, a serving sergeant in the UDR was sentenced to life, and is still in prison. So was Thomas Crozier, a corporal in the UDR and James Somerville, also a UDR soldier. The Jackal, who supervised and masterminded the operation, was never arrested or charged.

Sergeant Joe Campbell, one of the very few Catholic policemen in Northern Ireland, was shot dead at the door of his house in Cushendall in February 1977. Sergeant Campbell was investigating links between the UVF and Royal Ulster Constabulary Special Branch. He believed Special Branch officers were working with UVF gangsters to rob banks. Sergeant Charles McCormick, a Special Branch officer at Balymena, was arrested and charged with Campbell's murder and a number of armed robberies. He was acquitted of the murder but sent down for 20 years for robberies. He was released in 1984. Yorkshire TV's inquiries among former Special Branch officers involved in the murder have a last revealed that the man who shot Joe Campbell was the Jackal, who was never arrested or charged.

William Strathearn, a Catholic shopkeeper at Ahogill near Balymena, was gunned to death at midnight in April 1977 when he was asked by a group of men in a car if he could get some aspirin for a sick child. In the car were four assassins, including two special patrol group policemen, Sergeant John Weir and Constable William McCaughey, who were duly convicted of murder. Both got life and are now out of prison. In evidence, Weir named the Jackal as the man who pulled the trigger. Asked why the Jackal was not in the dock, the investigating RUC officer, a superintendent, pleaded 'reasons of operational strategy' (*Belfast Telegraph*, 16 June 1980).

Jim Campbell, a reporter for the *Sunday World* investigating Protestant assassinations, was seriously wounded by a gunman who came to his door in May 1984. UVF fanatic Edward McIlwaine, a serving soldier in the UDR, was convicted of the attack and is still in prison. He did not disclose that he had been sent to assassinate Campbell by the Jackal.

The Jackal's gang, whose other two leaders are a Portadown gunman known as King Rat and a son of one of the men who carried out the Dublin bombings, has gone on killing Catholics at random, and with impunity. It was responsible for the appalling murders of Eileen Duffy,

19, Katrina Rennie, 16, and Brian Frizzell, 29, in a mobile sweet shop at Craigavon in March 1991.

The Jackal's gang gets a lot of its weapons from South Africa. In April 1992 two South African military intelligence officers, Leon Flores and Pamela Du Randt, were expelled from Britain after they met the Jackal's gang and discussed the supply of arms to them.

This South African connection has been encouraged by British intelligence. In 1987 John McMichael, a British intelligence informer in the UDA, sent Brian Nelson, a British army intelligence agent in the UDA, to South Africa to seek arms for the paramilitaries.

The arms arrived in December of that year in two batches, one for the UDA, collected by Davie Payne, the other for the UVF. The UDA consignment was seized at once and Payne arrested and imprisoned, but the UVF assignment, which went to the Jackal's Portadown gang, got clean away. No doubt the hand grenades, which formed such a large part of that consignment, are now being thrown by the Jackal's gang at the same police force which let them through.

They're the pits!

So grateful was the government to the Union of Democratic Mineworkers for its help in breaking the miners' strike of 1984-85 that it promised to send a minister every year to address the UDM conference. The UDM was delighted.

In 1986 the minister was David Hunt, who ended his speech with a ringing declaration: 'Mr President, in conclusion, I make it absolutely clear that this government is committed to a secure coal industry that will provide lasting and well paid jobs for its employees.' The conference dissolved in applause and gave Mr Hunt a gold UDM badge.

In 1987 the minister was Cecil Parkinson, newly-appointed Secretary of State for Energy. He emphasised 'the debt the country owes to the UDM'. He was able to soothe delegates' fears about privatisation. 'I can state categorically', he said, 'that...there are no plans in the pipeline for the privatisation of coal at this moment. There are no plans, full stop.' The conference dissolved in applause and gave Mr Parkinson a bowl with the UDM badge on it.

In 1988 the minister was Michael Spicer. He said: 'We do not intend to privatise the industry,' adding, sotto voce, 'before the next election.' The government, he concluded, 'stands shoulder to shoulder with this union.' The conference dissolved in applause and gave Mr Spicer a whisky decanter with the UDM badge on it.

In 1989 the minister was Cecil Parkinson again. He triumphantly announced what he had declared two years previously—he had no plans for...er, coal privatisation. But he promised: 'At a minimum we are determined that everybody working in the industry will have the opportunity to become at least part owners.' The conference dissolved in applause and gave Mr Parkinson a silver tray with his portrait embossed on it.

In 1990 the minister was Tony Baldry. 'I would like', he said, 'to pay tribute to all in the industry for the part you have played in implementing the many approaches to improving productivity that have

Private Eye 4 November 1994

been so successfully put into practice.' The conference dissolved in applause and gave Mr Baldry a table lamp.

In 1991 the minister was John Wakeham, Secretary of State for Energy. He said the UDM 'had struck a historic blow for democratic trade unionism'. He was, he said, 'very confident about the future of the industry' under private ownership, and suggested that the UDM miners themselves might soon own their own pits. 'The future owners of the industry', he said, 'will I hope include many people present in the hall.' The conference dissolved in applause and gave Mr Wakeham a flower bowl.

In 1992 the minister was Michael Heseltine, President of the Board of Trade. 'I have', he trumpeted, 'enormous admiration for the way in which the coal industry has succeeded in transforming its performance.' Much of this, he said, was due to the UDM. 'We promised in our manifesto', he bellowed, 'that one element of the privatisation to which we are committed is to sell British Coal in a way that enables the workers in the industry to enjoy a stake in the future.' The conference dissolved in applause and gave Mr Heseltine a rose bowl.

Four months later the same Mr Heseltine announced drastic pit closures, which have devastated the Nottinghamshire coal field and reduced the Union of Democratic Mineworkers to a rump. Desperately, the UDM leaders clung to the Heseltine pledge that they would get a stake in the few pits which were left. They teamed up with a private company and bid for what was left of the Nottinghamshire pits.

The same Mr Heseltine has decided that the Nottinghamshire pits (and pretty well all the other pits as well) will be knocked down to a company owned by an earth mover and opencast mining director called Richard Budge. He is the only one who will have the 'stake' in the industry which was promised so effusively to the UDM by Mr Heseltine and others.

The UDM and its leaders, effectively wiped out, are devastated. On the other hand, Mr Hunt has been promoted to the cabinet as the prime minister's right hand man; Mr Parkinson is now Lord Parkinson; Mr Baldry has been promoted to the Foreign Office; Mr Spicer is now chairman of the Association of Independent Power Producers; Mr Wakeham is Lord Wakeham; and Mr Heseltine, like all the rest of them, is still making speeches and promises of which no one in the country believes a single word.

Lockerbie: body of evidence

by Paul Foot and John Ashton

Who planted the bomb which blew Pan Am 103 out of the sky over Scotland, killing all 259 people on board? Six and a half years after the Lockerbie disaster, none of the bereaved families or friends of the dead knows the answer. A bewildering array of different suspects has been paraded before them. Even the identity of the airport where the bomb was planted is unclear.

From their governments on both sides of the Atlantic the families have had to put up with paralysis, duplicity and, finally, silence. The current suspects, they are told, are two Libyan airline officials who put the bomb on a flight from Malta. The officials vehemently deny the charge. They refuse to go to court in Britain or the US. Until they stand trial in either of those countries, say the governments and the United Nations, no questions about the disaster will be answered. The whole issue is gridlocked. All further inquiry is officially discouraged.

'The official version,' says Dr Jim Swire, whose daughter died at Lockerbie, 'is no longer credible.' This article follows the Lockerbie story from the point of view of the bemused British relatives and friends of the victims. Drawing on hitherto unpublished documents, it casts doubt on the central thesis of the official version—that the Lockerbie bomb first went on a plane at Malta. It provides new information, until now classified, that Western intelligence knew perfectly well that a Pan Am airliner was in danger from terrorists. It exposes a coordinated campaign by the authorities on both sides of the Atlantic to smear and intimidate investigators who question the official version and their witnesses and sources. And it calls for more investigation and more disclosure on both sides of the Atlantic.

Guardian 29 July 1995

The strange case of Dr Fieldhouse

Weird and inexplicable happenings haunted the Lockerbie disaster on the very night the plane went down—21 December 1988. Dr David Fieldhouse, an experienced police surgeon from Bradford, Yorkshire, heard about it on *News at Ten*. He went straight to the telephone and phoned the police station at Lockerbie. If he could be of any use, he said, he could be at Lockerbie in less than an hour and a half.

The Lockerbie police eagerly accepted his offer, and a few minutes later he was on the motorway to Scotland. He got there before midnight, reported to the police station, and was eventually sent out with a police officer to find bodies and certify them dead. All through the long, cold night, the doctor and his companion slogged through the fields round Tundergarth church. Not stopping for sleep or food, he worked all through the following day as well. When he reported to the police station that evening, he had certified 59 bodies dead and labelled them accordingly. In the following weeks he gave up large chunks of his spare time travelling to Lockerbie and helping the police to properly identify the bodies and where they had been found.

For this selfless effort Dr Fieldhouse received, and expected to receive, no recognition. What was his reward? Nearly two years later, without any warning, he was unjustifiably tarnished by a police officer in official sworn evidence to the fatal accident inquiry into the Lockerbie disaster.

The officer was Sergeant David Johnston of the Strathclyde Police. His evidence was 'led' by Lord Fraser of Carmyllie, the Scottish Lord Advocate. Fraser is a career politician in the ruling Conservative Party, who had served briefly in the House of Commons as a Tory MP for Aberdeen. Sergeant Johnston started his evidence about Dr Fieldhouse as follows: 'On the evening of the disaster,' he said, 'and in the early hours of the following day, Dr Fieldhouse went out and examined a number of victims on his own, pronouncing life extinct, and attached on them his own form of identification. This was not known to us until some considerable time later.'

In fact, Dr Fieldhouse was accompanied throughout by police officers, three of whom he has named. He kept in close touch with the police throughout. The sergeant was completely wrong, but Lord Fraser did not correct him. On the contrary, the Lord Advocate continued with a series of questions which rubbed salt in the doctor's wounds. After asking about the discovery of the body of US businessman Tom Ammerman, Fraser went on:

Q: Would this be another example of Dr Fieldhouse carrying out a search on his own?
A: It would, my lord.
Q: And marking the body of a person who is dead without notifying the police?
A: That is correct.

It was not correct at all. Mr Ammerman's body had been found by Dr Fieldhouse and an accompanying police officer. It was marked in the presence of and with the agreement of the police officer.

When Dr Fieldhouse appeared at the inquiry some weeks later— on 22 January 1991—he quietly disposed of all the allegations which had been tossed about so freely in public. He was puzzled to hear that there were 58 bodies identified in the area he'd worked in—he had identified and tagged 59. He was amazed that all except two of his labels had been thrown away and replaced with others.

Sheriff Mowat, who was in charge of the inquiry, concluded: 'I would record my thanks to Dr Fieldhouse and my apologies for the un- deserved criticism of his activities.'

Nearly two years later, in December 1993, Dr Fieldhouse gave an interview for a film about Lockerbie. A few days after the interview Fieldhouse was summoned to a meeting with two senior West York- shire police officers at Wakefield and sacked as police surgeon. He was given three month's notice—but no credible explanation.

Farmer Wilson's suitcase

The treatment of Dr Fieldhouse is not the only story from the tragic windswept night round Lockerbie which still puzzles relatives of the dead. What is the truth, they wonder, about Farmer Jim Wilson, of Tun- dergarth Mains Farm near Lockerbie, whose fields were littered with the debris of bodies and baggage after the crash? He told one of the rel- atives who visited him soon after the disaster that he had been puz- zled by the police response to a suitcase he had found in one of his fields.

The case, he said, was full of cellophane packets of a white powder, which he thought were drugs. He told the police about it, but they did not react. He had to ring them a second time before they came to take it away. Farmer Wilson, who now understandably refuses to answer questions on the subject, gave evidence at the fatal accident inquiry. To his surprise, he was not asked about the suitcase or the drugs he assumed were in it. The authorities on both sides of the Atlantic continued to insist that no drugs, save a small quantity of cannabis, were found on Pan Am 103.

Some of the relatives carried out further inquiries. They discovered that the name Farmer Wilson had seen on the suitcase did not correspond with any of the names on the Pan Am 103 passenger list.

The invasion of investigators

A senior official at Carlisle airport was astonished at the numbers of officials who arrived by plane from London that night and the following day. At least two coachloads of people arrived before midnight on a Boeing 727. Around 20 of them were Pan Am employees, but there were many other Americans with no obvious affiliation. Another 727 arrived in the early afternoon of December 22, this time bringing people from the US. In it were yet more men in plain clothes. Among their baggage was a single coffin. When they realised that they were being filmed by a cameraman from the local Border TV, they became agitated and demanded that he stop.

Since permission had been granted by the local police, the airport official allowed the cameraman to continue and the pictures were broadcast that night. No explanation has been given about the coffin.

The strange offer to David Johnston

David Johnston, a young reporter from Radio Forth in Edinburgh, with excellent contacts with the Scottish police, was one of the first journalists on the scene of the disaster. In a news bulletin on 2 February 1989 he reported a claim that the bomb had been planted on a crack team of US intelligence agents who were travelling on flight 103 on their way back from Beirut.

Within an hour of the programme being broadcast Johnston was visited in his office by senior Edinburgh police, who demanded to know the source of the story. When he refused to disclose it, he was threatened with prosecution and, simultaneously, made a bizarre offer:

to reveal his source to the prime minister in Downing Street. He turned that down as well.

The strange case of the red tarpaulin

On the night of the disaster, and for weeks afterwards, teams of rescue volunteers searched the area. One volunteer was Ron Smith of Castle Douglas in Galloway. Earlier this year he revealed that fellow rescue workers had come across a large object under a red tarpaulin. As they approached it they were warned off by gunmen in the doorway of a hovering helicopter. One of these volunteers has spoken to us. He confirms that the incident took place just north of the road from Lockerbie to Langholm Road, at map reference 294 818. Farmer Innes Graham was also warned by the Americans to stay away from a small wooded area on top of the hill to the west of his family's farm near Waterbeck, a few miles east of Lockerbie. These strange experiences on that first night worried many of the bereaved relatives. Their worries soon turned into anger.

Was Botha warned?

Almost at once, there was a strong suspicion that the authorities knew the airliner was in danger and passed the information on to selected passengers. The most dramatic example of this was published in the German paper *Die Zeit* on the first anniversary of the disaster. The paper suggested that the South African foreign secretary, Pik Botha, and his retinue intended to fly on 103 but had been warned off. Botha eventually flew on the earlier flight, Pan Am 101, which, unlike flight 103, had special security checks at Heathrow.

Botha and the South African foreign office have denied that he was warned off 103, and no one in South Africa or Britain has been able finally to confirm or refute the *Die Zeit* story. But there were two other crucial pieces of evidence—one of them never before published— that Pan Am 103 was known to be in danger before it took off.

The Helsinki warning

On 5 December 1988, 16 days before the disaster, a man rang the American embassy in Helsinki, Finland, with a message that within the next two weeks a Finnish woman would carry a bomb aboard a Pan Am aircraft flying from Frankfurt to the US. The caller spoke with a Middle Eastern accent and said that the people behind the bomb attempt had links to the notorious terrorist Abu Nidal. The embassy sent a classified cable to the State Department, which was copied to the American consulate in Frankfurt and other embassies. The US President's Commission's report on aviation security and terrorism, which reported in May 1990, reckoned that 'thousands of US government employees saw the Helsinki threat'.

Among the lucky ones were the Americans who worked in the US embassy in Moscow. On December 13, a week and a day before Pan Am 103 went down, an 'administrative notice to all employees' was posted on the board of the embassy, warning of the threat.

At least one civilian in Moscow changed his flight as a result of the posted warning, and another employee changed the booking she had made for a US journalist. Not a single Russian embassy worker took flight Pan Am 103 from Frankfurt on December 21, a standard and popular route home for Christmas.

The US President's Commission on Lockerbie reported that by December 10 the Finnish police had concluded that the warning was 'not a credible one'. Similarly, the British Department of Transport told Pan Am in December that the British intelligence community had concluded that the threat was 'not real'.

Yet the notice went up on the board in Moscow three days after the conclusion of the Finnish police that the notice was not credible. Moreover, the US Federal Aviation Authority did not give an 'all clear' to the aviation authorities. Neither did Pan Am dismiss the warning. Their officials started special screening of Finnish women passengers.

The news of the Helsinki warning broke soon after the disaster and engulfed many relatives in rage and despair. The British Secretary of State for Transport, Paul Channon, reluctantly disclosed that there had been only 16 bomb warnings about aircraft relevant to Britain in 1988, none of them as specific as the one in Helsinki.

Channon and his successors insisted that the Helsinki warning was 'a hoax'. Martin and Rita Cadman were dubious. Their beloved son Bill, 32, a brilliant sound designer, was on the fatal plane. Three and a half years after the disaster, in July 1992, they read in the *Independent* that a man called Stephen Docherty had been sent to prison for four years for making a hoax call to police about a bomb at Victoria station. Martin Cadman wrote at once to the Finnish embassy in London asking who had been prosecuted for the hoax call about the Pan Am airliner and what punishment they received. The answer came back on 17 November 1992: 'The identity of the caller cannot be disclosed, as sufficient evidence has not been assembled to convict the chief suspect, a foreigner who obtained Finnish citizenship.'

Martin and Rita Cadman were vindicated. If the hoaxer could not be identified, who could say for sure that the call was a hoax? They fired off a letter to the Earl of Caithness, junior minister for transport, asking for a further inquiry into the Helsinki warning. Caithness replied that he had 'nothing to add, and had not got the authority to release the name of the hoax caller'.

When the Cadmans pointed out that no hoaxer had yet been identified, they received a couple of testy letters from the director and co-ordinator of transport security at the Department of Transport, Mr Harry Ditmas. 'This warning was a hoax,' echoed Mr Ditmas, without proof or explanation. The Cadmans' irritation at the duplicity of the authorities increased when the 'Helsinki hoaxer' had been named two years before they were told he could not be identified. He was a Palestinian resident in Finland called Samra Mahayoun.

The State Department warning

Today we can reveal another warning, issued by an intelligence source to the US State Department's Office of Diplomatic Security. This warning was issued three days before the phone call in Helsinki. It has recently been released—but not yet published under the Freedom of Information Act. The name of the informant is blacked out, and the message reads: 'Team of Palestinians not assoc with Palestinian Liberation Organisation (PLO) intends to atk US tgts in Europe. Time frame is present. Tgts specified are Pan Am airlines and US mil bases.'

Operation Autumn Leaves

Astonishingly, five weeks before this warning was received, a 'team of Palestinians not associated with the PLO' had been arrested in Germany in possession of a bomb in a Toshiba cassette recorder strikingly similar to the bomb which destroyed Pan Am 103 over Lockerbie.

In the months before the bombing the German police had mounted an anti-terrorist operation under the codename Autumn Leaves. The operation had led to the arrest of a gang associated with a splinter group of the Palestinian movement, the Popular Front for the Liberation of Palestine-General Command (PFLP-GC). The leader of this splinter was Ahmed Jibril, who enjoyed the confidence and protection of the government of Syria and its dictator Hafez al-Assad. Jibril had masterminded several terrorist attacks in recent years, and had, so the intelligence agents reported, taken on an assignment to revenge the shooting down the previous summer of an Iranian airbus by a US warship.

All 290 people on the airbus had been killed. Outrage in Iran was intense and there were widespread demands for revenge. Tehran radio declared that the incident would be avenged 'in blood-spattered skies'. Moreover, the intelligence reports revealed, the leader of Jibril's terrorist gang, Hafez Dalkamoni, had been arrested outside a flat in Neuss, Germany, not two hours drive from Frankfurt, from whose airport Pan Am 103's feeder flight had originated. A bomb with a barometric pressure switch, packed inside a Toshiba radio cassette recorder, was found in his car.

Investigators were in no doubt that the bomb was specifically designed to blow up aircraft. Pieces of a similar model of recorder had been found in the wreckage at Lockerbie. The conclusion seemed inescapable. Pan Am 103 had been blown up by a Palestinian gang, protected by Syria and paid for by Iran. The German police knew the name of the bomb maker they had arrested—Marwan Khreesat. Mysteriously, Khreesat was released soon after he had been arrested with Dalkamoni. The official reason was that there was not enough evidence against him. In April 1989 further police raids in Neuss produced two more bombs designed by Khreesat specifically to blow up aircraft. By then no one was in any doubt that Khreesat had made the bomb which found its way on to Pan Am 103A before it left Frankfurt for Heathrow.

Lunch at the Garrick

One man utterly confident of this conclusion was Paul Channon, British Secretary of State for Transport. On 16 March 1989, less than three months after Lockerbie, Channon lunched in London's exclusive Garrick Club with five of Britain's top journalists.

Channon beamed at the journalists over the excellent food and wine. The 'brilliant detective work of the smallest police force in the country'—Dumfries and Galloway—had, he revealed, uncovered the guilty bombers. Arrests, Channon told his wide-eyed hosts, were imminent. Such conversations, especially at the Garrick Club, are 'on lobby terms': that is, not for attribution.

But the size of the scoop they had been offered was too much for at least one of the journalists. Next morning's papers carried the sensational news that a cabinet minister had revealed that the Lockerbie killers had been identified and would soon be arrested.

Operation 'low key'

Almost at the exact moment as Channon was exciting the journalists over that Garrick lunch, George Bush, the US president, telephoned the British prime minister, Margaret Thatcher. Lockerbie was the subject of their conversation. No doubt Bush too had heard of the success of the Scottish police. His advice to Mrs Thatcher, however, was to 'low key' any excitement over Lockerbie.

The news of this telephone conversation was reported on 11 January 1989 in the *Washington Post* by Jack Anderson and Dale Van Atta. The conversation was denied by both the White House and 10 Downing Street, but Anderson and Van Atta stuck to their story. Whatever was said that March morning, the subject of Lockerbie suddenly slipped from the ecstatic high sung by Channon to a very low key indeed.

The bereaved families, who had assumed after all the publicity for the Garrick lunch that the suspects for the bombing would soon be brought to trial, noticed to their horror that the whole affair seemed to slip suddenly from the public gaze. They stepped up their demand for a proper inquiry. In September 1989, six months after the Garrick lunch, the newly-formed UK Families Flight 103 met Paul Channon's successor as transport secretary, Cecil Parkinson. Parkinson promised the families a full judicial inquiry. To his horror, the cabinet, and especially Prime Minister Margaret Thatcher, Parkinson's close friend and ally, slapped him down. He came whimpering back to the relatives to tell them he had failed.

'Low key' were the words allegedly used by President Bush in that denied telephone conversation with Thatcher in March. In

September, the relatives came to know what 'low key' meant—the refusal of a proper investigation and its replacement by an impotent fatal accident inquiry with no subpoena powers which refused to investigate how the bomb got on the plane for fear of interfering with the police inquiries.

Years later, in 1994, Parkinson took part in a television programme about another disaster—the sinking of the pleasure craft *Marchioness* on the Thames. He confirmed that Thatcher had blocked the Lockerbie inquiry. Parkinson explained:

> I was discussing with the Lockerbie relatives whether we couldn't have some form of public inquiry which would have meant, because the security services were involved, inevitably a certain amount of suspicion—and I wondered whether I could get a High Court judge to look into the security aspects privately and report to me. If I could get the relatives to agree with that, if I got that done, that would satisfy them. Because when you get into the Lockerbie business—how did we find out certain information, how did we know this, how did we know that?—you would have had to recall not only our own intelligence sources but information we were receiving from overseas. Therefore, that had to be a closed area.

This came as close as it could to identifying the real block to a proper inquiry: 'our own intelligence sources'. It was not clear to the relatives then, or now, why the intelligence services on either side of the Atlantic should oppose an inquiry. A month after the Parkinson fiasco, one remarkable answer emerged

The Lebanese connection

On 2 November 1989 the news leaked of a report on the Lockerbie bombing by Interfor, a New York corporate investigative company hired by Pan Am and its insurers. The report suggested that the Dalkamoni gang had got the bomb on the airliner at Frankfurt by exploiting a security loophole. In their desperate bid to free American hostages in Beirut, American intelligence agents had, reported Interfor, struck a deal with Syrian narco-terrorists.

In exchange for information about the hostages, the agents agreed to facilitate a route for drugs from the Lebanon into the United States. The luggage with the drugs was protected by American intelligence.

Normal security restrictions on baggage at the relevant airports were removed and the drugs allowed to sail through. The terrorist gang, with the help of allies at Frankfurt airport, had exploited this security loophole by exchanging a bag with a bomb for one with drugs. The report named a young passenger on the doomed plane, a Lebanese American called Khaled Jafaar, as the 'mule' whose bag of drugs was switched. Jafaar's name had already been mentioned in dramatic circumstances. On New Year's Eve 1988, ten days after the Lockerbie disaster, the *Daily Express* devoted its front page to exposing Jafaar as 'The Bomb Carrier'. The *Express* named its sources as 'the FBI and Scotland Yard'.

Even more fantastically, the Interfor report surmised that Major Charles McKee, the head of the US intelligence team on the plane, was shocked by the deal struck with the narco-terrorists, and was returning on Pan Am 103 to blow the whistle on his colleagues. The inference was obvious, and the report made it plain. Pan Am 103 was sacrificed by the intelligence community in part at least to get rid of the whistleblower.

The Interfor report was greeted with widespread scepticism. Commentators pointed out that Pan Am was being sued by the families for negligence, and stood to duck all responsibility for the disaster if the blame could be shifted to a bizarre intelligence plot. Scepticism about the Interfor report was compounded by new speculation about Lockerbie which switched attention from Beirut and Frankfurt to the tiny Mediterranean island of Malta.

The Maltese connection

As the first anniversary of the crash grew closer, a long series of articles in the *Sunday Times*, which relied heavily on leaks from the Scottish police, reported that the 'net was closing' on the Lockerbie suspects. These articles—by David Leppard—stated as irrefutable fact that the bombing had been carried out by the PFLP-GC under orders from Ahmed Jibril. The gang was led by Dalkamoni, the bomb was made by Marwan Khreesat.

Leppard's articles added a new twist. The bomb, they reported, had first been put on a plane not in London, where Pan Am 103 had taken off, nor in Frankfurt, where its 'feeder' Pan Am 103A had started, but in Malta. The Maltese connection had been detected, the articles argued, because some clothes made in Malta had been found in the suitcase in which, police believed, the bomb had been planted.

The finger of suspicion was pointed directly at another alleged member of the Dalkamoni gang: Abu Talb, a 35 year old Palestinian who was in prison in Sweden awaiting trial for terrorist offences there. Talb, reported the *Sunday Times* on 17 December 1989, had visited Malta and had been identified by a Maltese boutique owner as the man who bought the clothes in the bomb suitcase, including a Babygro. 'The trail to Talb was so strong', wrote reporter David Leppard, that Scottish police had gone to Sweden to interview him. He was, the paper reported, due any moment to be extradited to stand trial for the Lockerbie bombing. The bomb, these articles insisted, had been put on a flight from Malta to Frankfurt for transfer there to Pan Am 103A, which linked with Pan Am 103 at Heathrow. Thus the theory had the bomb surviving two airport switches—at Frankfurt and at Heathrow—before exploding over Lockerbie.

For this remarkable theory the *Sunday Times* (and their informants, the Scottish police) relied on two documents which had not been made available to them until several months after the bombing. These were a computerised list of all the transactions in Frankfurt airport's automated baggage system which related to Pan Am 103, and a hand-written work sheet from one of the several stations where baggage came into the system.

A bag which ended up on Pan Am 103 could be traced to a station where one of the baggage handlers had, in a hurried scrawl, identified it as coming from an Air Malta flight. Yet there were no passengers on the Air Malta flight transferring to Pan Am 103A. It followed, the newspaper argued, that an unaccompanied bag from Malta carried the bomb which blew up Pan Am 103! Together with the Babygro from the boutique, these documents proved the Maltese connection—and the Maltese connection proved the guilt of Dalkamoni and Talb.

Almost all the information which led to these exciting scenarios came through the intelligence agencies. Journalists on their own in such inquiries have very little hope of discovering any information. They go cap in hand to intelligence sources and sift what they are given. In 1989, and most of 1990, the intelligence-based charges against the Jibril gang fitted snugly with American and British foreign policy in the Middle East. Both countries had broken off relations with Syria because of that country's known and persistent support for international terrorism. The long war between Iraq and Iran had ended in the summer of 1988, with the governments of both countries ranged firmly on the side of Iraq. The old hostility to Iran—which dated back to the 1979 revolution there and the seizure of US hostages—lingered on. Though the whole Lockerbie issue had been declared 'low key', both governments were quite 'comfortable' with what seemed at the time the obvious central truth about Lockerbie: that the Jibril gang and the regimes in Syria and Iran were responsible.

The official version was staged again in November 1990 in a long documentary programme by Granada Television to mark the second anniversary of the bombing. Special attention was given to the Maltese connection. A sinister looking Arab was seen to check in his bag at Malta airport and then to slide surreptitiously away to watch the plane take off with the bag in it.

The beauty of 'intelligence journalism' is that it can hardly ever be tested. Granada Television, however, was unlucky. Immediately after the programme, Air Malta sued Granada for libel. A long, powerful and hitherto unpublished document from their lawyers, top City solicitors Norton Rose, demonstrated that there were 39 passengers and 55 pieces of baggage on the Air Malta flight; that all the bags had been checked in by the passengers which flew; that there were no bags on the flight interlined for Pan Am 103 or 103A. So the scenario outlined in the film was, the document insists, quite impossible.

The Norton Rose document proceeds in specific and irrefutable detail to challenge the entire theory that a bomb was put on the flight at Malta. The lawyers carefully investigated the documents— the printout and the work sheets from Frankfurt airport—which had persuaded the *Sunday Times* and the Scottish police that the bomb bag had come from Malta. They concluded, first, that these documents were not designed to identify the flight from which baggage had come; second, that their accuracy depended on the dubious memory of harassed baggage handlers; and third, that even if they were accurate, they did not preclude the possibility that the suspect bomb bag had been planted in the complex of Frankfurt airport.

This comprehensive demolition job on the Maltese connection was never heard in open court. Shortly before the case was due to come on early in 1993, Granada, which prides itself on openly defending libel actions, threw in the towel, and paid £15,005 into court. Air

Malta accepted the money, and, in a statement allowed by the judge, insisted that they had cleared their name. The statement was studiously ignored by the entire British media.

By that time, the whole political situation in the Middle East had been turned upside down. In August 1990, Saddam Hussein invaded Kuwait, threatened to control 8 percent of US oil supplies and to topple the sheikdoms of the Gulf and Saudi Arabia on which Western stability in the Middle East depended. 'A new world order' was called for, with different alliances. If there was to be a Western war with Iraq, Iran had to be seduced into neutrality. More importantly, the Assad dictatorship in Syria had to be courted. If Iran was neutralised and Syria lined up against her old enemy Saddam, Iraq could be defeated without too much upset in the Arab world.

In November 1990 Britain restored diplomatic relations with Syria. Ahmed Jibril, whom everyone assumed was responsible for Lockerbie, was still living there. The same dictator, Assad, was still in charge, presiding over the same terrorism, the same torture in his prisons and the same denial of human rights to dissenters. But now he was an ally of the West. In January and February 1991 Syrian troops joined the Western allies in an assault on occupied Kuwait. Saddam's forces were instantly repulsed. Cheap oil flowed freely again to the US, whose government was eternally grateful to its new allies. Opponents of the dictator Assad were still being locked up and tortured, but President Bush (like President Clinton after him) and Prime Minister John Major covered him with bouquets.

The Libyan connection

As the political allegiances in the region changed, so, at first imperceptibly but with gathering speed, did the official investigations into the Lockerbie disaster. The centre of operations was effectively shifted from the quaint police headquarters in the Scottish Borders to the more sumptuous surroundings of Langley, the base of the CIA. The man in day to day charge of the Lockerbie investigation there was Vincent Cannistraro. Cannistraro had worked with Oliver North in President Reagan's National Security Council. He had been a leading figure in the movement to support the Contras in Nicaragua and UNITA in Angola. He had specialised in the US vendetta against Libya. He had helped mastermind a secret programme to destabilise the Libyan regime which culminated in the bombing of Libya in 1986—an act of international piracy which, for the first time in the history of Muammar Gadaffi's turbulent and dictatorial rule, united the entire Libyan people behind him.

Cannistraro retired from the CIA in September 1990 but by then had helped lay the foundations for a completely new approach to the Lockerbie investigation. This time the chief culprit country was not Iran or Syria—but Libya.

On 14 November 1991, in a blaze of publicity, the American and British governments announced that two Libyan airline officials— Abdel Basset Ali Al-Megrahi and Lamen Khalifa Fhimah—were charged with planting the bomb which brought down Pan Am 103. The official story had completely changed. Gone was any reference to Jibril, Dalkamoni, Talb, Khreesat, Syria, Iran or Palestine. President Bush went out of his way to exculpate Syria which, he announced in a characteristically elegant phrase, had taken 'a bum rap' on Lockerbie.

Simultaneously, like an obedient sheepdog, British foreign secretary Douglas Hurd barked in the British House of Commons that Libyans alone were suspected. Other countries, he said, were not implicated. By amazing coincidence, the only culprits could now be found in the only Arab country besides Iraq to which the US and Britain were openly hostile. Pam Dix, secretary of the UK Families Flight 103, whose brother Peter died at Lockerbie, still remembers her sense of shock on hearing of the indictment against the Libyans. 'In all the three years since the disaster,' she said, 'none of us ever had an inkling that Libyans were responsible. One question I asked myself at once was: why did the American authorities not wait until their suspects left Libya for a country from which they could be extradited? Why did they rush out the announcement when they knew their suspects would not be released for trial?'

To assist confused relatives and anyone else who had followed the story, the US State Department issued a special notice. The 'dominant hypothesis of the early stages of the Pan Am 103 investigation', it conceded, had 'focused' on Iran and Jibril. 'Over time, however, fresh evidence undermined the initial theory linking the PFLP-GC to the bomb.' Four reasons were given:

(1) The radio with the bomb found in Dalkamoni's car 'differed markedly' from the radio bomb in the plane.

(2) The Maltese clothes in the suitcase indicated the bomb went on at Malta.

(3) The bomb in the plane had been set off by a 'sophisticated electronic timer' while the PFLP-GC bomb discovered in Germany had 'relatively crude timers'. Furthermore, such sophisticated timers had been delivered from Switzerland to Libya.

(4) There was no evidence of an altimeter switch in the Pan Am bomb.

None of this was persuasive. Marwan Khreesat made many bombs in many different radios. The 'marked difference' between the radio in Dalkamoni's car and the one in the plane was that the first had one speaker, the other had two. Both were Toshibas. The clothes from the boutique had been used to confirm official suspicion of the PFLP-GC/Jibril gang. The rather subtle distinction between the timers and the switches hardly seemed enough evidence to justify such a dramatic change in the course of the inquiry.

The case of the ubiquitous circuit board

The central plank of the indictment was the alleged correlation between the timers—alleged to have been sold to Libyans—and the tiny fragment of circuit board found near Lockerbie. The timers, the indictment revealed, had been made by a firm in Switzerland. Their circuit boards matched a tiny fragment retrieved from the Lockerbie searches.

This coincidence between the circuit board and the timers has been plagued with questions from the moment it was first mooted. For instance, who found the circuit board and when? It depends what you read. In 1992, American journalist Mark Perry published a book called *Eclipse: The Last Days of the CIA*. This declares that the fragment was found by an unnamed Scottish worker in a field outside Lockerbie 'on a misty morning in early April'.

British journalist Diarmuid Jeffreys, on the other hand, in his book *The Bureau: Inside Today's FBI*, says that the fragment was found 'sometime in 1990' in a 'piece of charred shirt' by the FBI's forensic expert Thomas Thurman. Another recent book on the FBI, by Ronald Kessler, quotes the assistant director of the FBI forensic laboratory saying that the British found the fragment a whole year before Thurman got it. And who identified the fragment as part of the timer?

Jeffreys and Kessler give the credit to Thomas Thurman, Perry to a 'veteran CIA analyst' and David Leppard of the *Sunday Times* to a British military forensic scientist (and hero of the investigation which wrongly jailed the Maguire Seven) Dr Thomas Hayes. The four authors each have different dates for the establishing of the link. They offer a choice between June, August, October and November 1990. It is not hard to imagine the enthusiasm with which a top barrister would expose the history of this crucial 'evidence' linking the bombing to Libya.

And just how firm was the Libyan connection to the timers? To start with, the US State Department claimed that all timers from the Swiss firm had been delivered to Libya. This theory was weakened in December 1993 when the BBC radio programme *File On Four* proved that the Swiss firm had provided the same model of timers to the East German secret police, the Stasi.

The bulk of the indictment asserted without proof that Libyan intelligence had planned the bomb attack, and carried it out through two of its agents. These assertions relied on the say-so of an intelligence team led by a man who once worked closely with Oliver North.

The hidden agenda

None of the active British relatives is convinced by the indictment. In the four years since the indictment was announced, the case against the Libyans has got weaker. The British families continue to be puzzled about the sudden and unexpected change in the Lockerbie suspects. It seems obvious to them that the Dalkamoni gang was responsible for the bombing. So why was the gang not pursued, and why was such a crude official blanket cast over the whole Lockerbie affair? Increasingly, the families hark back to the ghastly theories expounded in the Interfor report. Is there, they wonder, a hidden agenda to Lockerbie, a story within a story, which is the real reason for the 'low key' approach of officialdom on both sides of the Atlantic?

These suspicions were further aroused by the publication in September 1993—in Britain alone—of *Trail of the Octopus* by Donald Goddard, the story of former Defence Intelligence Agency agent Lester Coleman. Like the Interfor report, Coleman concludes there is a connection between the drugs run from Lebanon through Cyprus, where he was based, and Frankfurt airport which contributed to the

Lockerbie disaster. Coleman's detractors accuse him of fleeing his country to avoid charges of falsely procuring a passport. New information published in the *Scotsman* in March this year, however, suggests that the passport charges were trumped up. The FBI claimed that Coleman had asked for a copy of a birth certificate of a dead person, Thomas Leavy, with which to forge a false passport. The relevant authority at New London, Connecticut, however, insists that no person of that name was born at the time claimed by the FBI.

The entire case was invented. But why would a charge of passport fraud be invented unless to intimidate Coleman, and why would the authorities want to do that? Four days before his book was published, Coleman was indicted on another charge: perjury. The first count alleges that he falsely claimed to speak Arabic—which he speaks fluently.

Lester Coleman is not the only sceptic about the official version of the Lockerbie story who has suffered at the hands of the authorities. Juval Aviv, the president of Interfor, who carried out the inquiry for Pan Am and arrived at such extraordinary conclusions, has recently been charged with mail fraud. John Brennan, the president of the insurers for the now defunct Pan Am, has been charged with fraud.

Like Lester Coleman, Aviv insists that charges against him have been trumped up. All three investigations were started by the same assistant US attorney in the Eastern District of New York court—yet neither Brennan nor Aviv have their businesses located in that district, and none of their alleged offences was committed there. All these instances of alleged state harassment came within a few weeks of a 90 minute Channel 4 programme on Lockerbie entitled *The Maltese Double Cross*. Produced by the American film-maker Allan Francovich, it was broadcast on May 11. It featured an interview with a relative of a passenger on the fatal flight called Khalid Jafaar. The relative stated that the boy had been duped by terrorists into taking the bomb on the plane in a bag he believed was carrying drugs. Francovich's film was dogged by continuous official obstruction and resistance.

When it finally got on the air, the Scottish Crown Office and the US embassy took the unusual step of issuing a strongly-worded press release vigorously attacking the programme and the people who appeared in it. For years the same Crown Office had insisted that it was not the job of government to comment on media speculation about Lockerbie.

The 'sub judice' stalemate

In the aftermath of *The Maltese Double Cross*, the stalemate returns. As soon as the indictments were revealed, the British and American governments insisted that the two Libyan suspects should be brought to trial in Scotland or the US. The Libyan government refused to release them. Feeble economic sanctions, not including an oil embargo, were imposed on Libya by the UN in a supposed bid to force the suspects out. Predictably, they have not worked. The Libyan government has, however, agreed to release the men to stand trial in a neutral country, such as The Hague in Holland or Switzerland.

Jim Swire, whose daughter Flora died in Pan Am 103 and who has campaigned ever since to find out what happened, asks: 'What is wrong with a trial in a neutral country? Why shouldn't both sides be treated fairly in Holland or Switzerland? There is talk all the time of the need for international courts—to try Bosnian war criminals, for example. We want these men to stand trial. I've written again and again to British and American governments to ask why the Libyans can't be tried in a neutral country, but haven't had a satisfactory reply. In fact the US government hasn't replied at all.'

There are many precedents in English law for shifting the place of a trial to avoid local prejudice against the accused. Why can't the same argument prevail at international level? One crucial effect of the stalemate caused by the Libyan indictments has been the deflection of all independent investigation into the Lockerbie disaster. 'We have the suspects,' is the official answer to all inquiries. 'The case is sub judice. No comment.'

Many British relatives suspect that this official silence suits both governments. Their suspicions have been confirmed by two recent incidents.

The snubbing of Allan Stewart

No one served the Conservative government more faithfully than Allan Stewart MP. He became a junior minister in the Scottish Office in 1981, and he was still there in 1995. He resigned his post after an incident on a contested motorway site, in which he allegedly brandished an axe handle against the protesters. Out of office, he decided to respond to Muslim constituents who were worried about government sanctions against Libya. He went to Libya and secured the agreement of the Gadaffi government to release the two suspects for trial before a Scottish judge and jury and according to Scottish legal procedures in a neutral country. At last was hope of a compromise, a break in the deadlock. The Libyan government's concessions were substantial. What possible objection could there now be against holding the trial in a neutral country? Back in the House of Commons, Stewart proposed an amendment to the Scottish Criminal Justice Bill then going through the Scottish Grand Committee. His amendment permitted cases to be heard by a Scottish judge and jury outside Scotland. It was voted down by the Labour and Tory members of the committee—only one backbencher, Tam Dalyell, Labour MP for Linlithgow, who for years has challenged the official version of the Lockerbie story, supported him.

The US authorities throw in the towel

Many families now suspect that the British and American authorities would be delighted if the Libyan suspects are never released, and there is never a trial. On 8 June a front page article in the *Guardian* quoted anonymous US officials saying that President Clinton had effectively given up on efforts to bring the two Libyans to trial.

Perhaps the most infuriating effect of the sub judice stalemate is the official silence. In the United States attempts to get information about Lockerbie under the Freedom of Information Act have been constantly thwarted on grounds of national security. Only two important documents have been released, both after a delay of four years. In the prevailing silence the relatives feel they are pawns being pushed around on the chessboard of international power politics. The questions go on forever. Why did the police so recklessly tarnish Dr Fieldhouse? Why did Farmer Wilson's suitcase vanish? Why was there such a prompt official denunciation of the Helsinki warning as a hoax? Why was nothing done to respond to the clear warning issued to the American government about the terrorist danger to Pan Am? Why was the Jibril story, so convincing at the time, brusquely junked? What is there left of the Maltese connection? Why have the British and US governments refused a proper inquiry, and why will the Libyans not be brought to trial on neutral territory? Why, if its hands are clean on the matter, is the US government holding back information about the bombing of a civilian airliner?

Ask all these questions together and it is difficult to avoid the conclusion that someone in authority knows the answers but won't disclose them. On 16 February 1990, a group of British relatives, including Martin Cadman, went to the American embassy in London for a meeting with the seven members of the President's Commission on aviation security and terrorism.

'After we'd had our say,' says Cadman, 'the meeting broke up, and we moved towards the door. As we got there, I found myself talking to two members of the commission—I think they were senators. One of them said: "Your government and our government knows what happened at Lockerbie. But they are not going to tell you".' It is hard to imagine a more serious charge, nor one which more requires the most urgent and relentless probing.

John Ashton was the chief researcher on the Channel 4 documentary The Maltese Double Cross.

Don't back the biggest bully in the Balkans

Bash Serbs! That has been until recently a popular slogan right across the British political spectrum. It came not just from the Thatcherite right but from wide sections of the left. Bashing Serbs, it was argued, was the only way to stop ethnic cleansing in the Balkans. Those of us who refused to take sides in the Yugoslav civil war were denounced as appeasers.

The 'Bash Serbs' slogan has now been taken up with great enthusiasm by the Pentagon and NATO High Command. Serbs have been bashed. What is the result? A lot more ethnic cleansing. How was so much of the left so easily converted to such a disastrous policy? They fell victim to the illusion, so prevalent during the Gulf War in 1991, that the only way to stop a bully is to get a bigger bully to knock him down: only the US government was strong enough to knock out a dictator like Saddam Hussein or a fanatic like General Mladic.

The problem is, however, that the US government's only interest in the Middle East or Yugoslavia or anywhere else is to preserve cheap oil and a safe 'free market' for the big corporations. Any 'solution' imposed by this big bully is invariably worse for the ordinary people in the area than the crimes of the small bully. The UN (US) attack on Iraq killed at least 100,000 innocent people—and the dictator is still in power.

Many on the left do not openly support the NATO blitzkrieg of the Serbs, but they took sides with what they saw as the weaker combatants, declaring themselves 'with Bosnia' or 'with Croatia'. All this has proved futile. The Bosnian-Croatian army is every bit as savage in victory as were the Serbs, and the alliance which holds it together will certainly burst, as it did in 1993, into yet more terrible violence.

The only possible hope comes from those in the Balkans who reject all the nationalisms, and campaign against the war and all

Guardian 25 September 1995

ethnic divisions. This used to be a substantial minority, which has grown smaller as the war grew more ferocious. But they have been isolated where they should have been supported. At least some of the responsibility for the victory of nationalist reaction lies in the collapse of so many left wingers in Yugoslavia into one of the nationalist camps.

These are old lessons, but not outdated. The Balkan Wars before the First World War were reported with great insight by the Russian revolutionary, then in exile, Leon Trotsky. His theme bears up well:

> Unity of the Balkan peninsula can be achieved in two ways: either from above, by expanding one Balkan state, whichever proves strongest, at the expense of the weaker ones—this is the road of wars of extermination and oppression of weak nations, a road that consolidates monarchism and militarism; or from below, through the people themselves coming together—the road of revolution that means overthrowing the Balkan dynasties and unfurling the banner of a Balkan federal republic.

Bombs away—let's kill a few children

Opponents of the Vietnam War devised a slogan in the form of a question to the then president of the United States, Lyndon Baines Johnson: 'Hey, Hey, LBJ, how many kids have you killed today?' The slogan needs to be adapted slightly to fit the current crisis in the Gulf: 'Hey, Hey, Blair and Bill, how many kids do you plan to kill?' Killing thousands of children and other civilians is the only certain consequence of the bombing of Iraq by British and US warplanes.

All the claimed justification for the mass slaughter of Iraqis last time—in 1991—have vanished. There is no mandate for the bombing from the United Nations, no mandate from the other Arab states, no invasion of territory by Iraq, no explanation of how the use of weapons of mass destruction can annihilate weapons of mass destruction without the casualties leaping from thousands to millions.

So what is the only argument left to Blair and Clinton? It is that Saddam Hussein is a brutal dictator, that we must 'stand up to him', 'keep him in check', and that only US armed forces are capable of doing so. Leave aside the long list of brutal dictators heroically supported by post-war US governments—Trujillo, Duvalier, Marcos, Pinochet, Galtieri, Noriega, Sukarno, the House of Saud.

Perhaps Saddam Hussein is worse than all of these. The point is, however, that Saddam himself would not be where he is today without support from the Pentagon and Whitehall.

No less an authority than Oliver North has told us how the US government, from the very start of the war between Iran and Iraq in 1980, 'quietly sided with Iraq' under its new dictator, Saddam Hussein. When the war ended eight years later, bequeathing to both countries a mountain of debt and a million corpses, the US and British governments rushed to sell arms to the dictator of Baghdad.

In an ecstatic paper on Iraq, William Waldegrave, 'moderate'

Guardian 9 February 1998

Minister of State at the Foreign Office, could not contain himself:

> I doubt if there is any future market on such a scale anywhere where
> the UK is potentially so well-placed if we play our diplomatic hand
> correctly, nor can I think of any major market where the importance
> of diplomacy is so great to our commercial position.

He and his fellow ministers relaxed the guidelines on the export
of arms to Iraq and a great river of British 'defence equipment' flowed
into Baghdad.

When, two years later, Saddam used the equipment to invade
Kuwait and threaten the supply of cheap oil to the USA, he quickly
became a 'brutal dictator' and was crushed. In the moment of military defeat, he seemed doomed. At last the way was clear for the
people of Iraq to throw off their hated oppressor. But then US policy
switched again. The deployment of the victorious allied forces was devoted not to toppling Saddam but to keeping him in power. The fear
of popular revolution was far, far greater than the continued regime
of a brutal dictator. The whole region might be 'destabilised'! The Iraqi
Kurds might win their autonomy, and inspire Kurdish communities
elsewhere. What would happen then to the 'stable' regimes in Turkey
and Syria? Thus Saddam survived, not by accident, as some suggested,
still less from some perverse compassion, but by design.

Why are Saddam's saviours now abusing and threatening him
again? The answer is that they expect their dictators to behave. Like
Noriega, Saddam refused to curb his vainglorious ambitions in the interests of the Pentagon. He sulks, and constantly lashes out.

So he has to be 'taught a lesson'. And if the lesson has to be learned
in blood and starvation not by the dictator, but by children and civilians who detest the dictator anyway, who cares?

I was intrigued to hear defence secretary George Robertson listing
the awful weapons hidden in Saddam's arsenals. On such matters,
genial George cannot always be relied upon. On 6 March 1988 three
unarmed IRA members were shot and killed in Gibraltar by the SAS.
BBC news the next morning 'reported' that the trio were trying to
escape after planting 'a huge car bomb in the centre of the colony'.
Every one of the 11 daily newspapers carried the 'fact' of the 'huge car
bomb'. The fact, however, was fiction. As foreign secretary Geoffrey
Howe revealed to the commons that afternoon, there was no bomb
in the car.

The truth came so late that Howe didn't have time to brief his 'shadow' on the Labour benches, George Robertson. So Robertson proceeded eloquently to denounce the bomb in the car which the foreign secretary had just revealed did not exist. If the attack on Iraq is allowed to continue, we can expect a lot more such factual reporting.

The system

The great society

The main point about the building societies when they started out was that no one should make a profit from them.

They were 'mutual societies' into which people who wanted to save money to buy a house or on the security of a house they already owned could do so in the certain knowledge that no one would rip them off.

The societies were patronised in the early years by better-off working class people (or worse-off middle class people, which is pretty well the same thing).

They developed most strongly in northern cities like Halifax, Leeds, Bradford and Bingley, from which they took their names.

Most of their patrons subscribed to what could be called the 'liberal tradition' of the last 25 years of the last century, the sort of 'decent, sturdy' folk much patronised by bourgeois social historians.

The societies had nothing to do with socialism. On the contrary, the money they collected was assiduously invested in capitalist industry and services.

As time went on, and more and more people built houses, so more and more people deposited their money in building societies.

By the end of the 1960s, when the balance of surplus value from housing tipped away from rent (council housing) to interest (so called 'home ownership'), the building societies' vast funds were an important marker on the capitalist landscape.

Hunger

As the Thatcher administration released more and more of society to the unfettered control of capitalists, gentlemen at the top of society turned their eyes with ever increasing hunger on the building societies.

If only the outdated restrictions which made it impossible to profit from the societies were removed! What endless riches this opened up!

Socialist Worker 22 July 1989

It wasn't just a question of owning shares. Nor was it even a matter of raising top peoples' salaries, though that of course was a crucial factor.

The real treasure would be the release of the societies' funds from the strict legal controls which had existed when the societies were mutual.

It was, in short, a treasure hunt of unfathomable wonders for the ruling class. Slowly, surreptitiously, they started to woo the investors, whose vote was required if the change was to be accomplished.

The investors were bribed. They were promised the vast sum of £100 in free shares which they could convert, if they were lucky, into about £116 if they sold them on the first day.

Sweetened by this bribe, the investors in the Abbey National voted by a huge majority in favour of the change. So now it is legal to make profits out of the Abbey National. All the old, decent, 'sturdy' restrictions have been swept away, and the free market reigns.

It is hard in the whole grim history of Thatcherism to imagine a more cynical or foul development than this one, which was of course enthusiastically applauded all over the newspapers, including the sturdy liberal ones.

Hitches

There were, however, some hitches in the flotation. Because they had to send out millions of bribes, the managers boobed.

Tens of thousands of people got two lots of bribes. Many more thousands didn't get their bribes on time, and so couldn't cash them in on the stock exchange casino. Such people were convulsed by fury.

They felt they had 'right' to their little bribe. None of them even for a moment thought where their little bit 'extra' was coming from.

Did privatisation suddenly open up a pot of money that wasn't there before? Or wouldn't it come, as it always does, from a worse service, a cut in office workers' pay, an attack on the unions and all the rest of the reality of Thatcher's dream?

The managers were shocked by the stampede which their own bribes and bungling had caused. Sitting as they are on a fortune, they scoffed at the investors they had fooled as the latter rang up (burning out the switchboard), and shouted or swore their indignation.

Mr John Fry, general manager of the Abbey National, told the press haughtily:

'There is an enormous greed factor out there'.

I like the phrase 'out there'. The 'greed factor' in the building societies is not 'out there' at all, but right 'in there', with Mr Fry and his shortly to be enriched colleagues.

Why the world is eating less

In the *Independent* newspaper I read the following headline: 'World Appetite For Grain Still Fading'. I expected the article under it to be about diet; about the shifting food fads of the kind of people who read the *Independent*.

Perhaps some homeopathic doctor has been working on the consciences of the rich and persuading them to eat less grain so that there can be more for the poor.

Indeed, I recall as a child in a rich home being persuaded by a stern nurse to eat everything on my plate. 'Think of the starving millions,' she would say, as though they benefited from my full stomach, or were insulted in some way by my leaving bits of gristle on the side of the plate.

But no, this is not an article about diet. This is written by Lisa Vaughan, the *Independent*'s financial correspondent. Her main point is that 'growth in world grain consumption may continue to slow this decade'.

She produces figures from the International Wheat Council to show that the amount of bread consumed by the world's population has hardly grown at all during the Glorious Eighties. Indeed, wheat consumption since 1982 has gone up by only 2.4 percent a year, while world population in the same period has gone up by just under 2 percent.

Bread

Consumption of coarse grain (maize, barley, rye, oats, etc) has risen even slower than population—1.3 percent to 1.9 percent.

Now let's go back to that headline, 'World Appetite For Grain Still Fading'. Can it be that all over the world people are sick and tired of eating bread and are turning to a more tasty substitute?

In the tortured language of the financial correspondent, Lisa Vaughan gives us the answer: 'Instead of being driven by demographics, grain use is now primarily determined by financial restraints facing governments.'

She quotes directly from the report of the International Wheat Council:

> Financial and economic factors are likely to remain the chief influence on grain usage for many years to come. Because of debt repayment or foreign exchange obstacles, many countries have been obliged to restrain grain imports even when prices are low.

In plain English, what does this mean? It means that people are eating less because they are poor. It is not, as the *Independent* so coyly puts it, people's appetite which is fading—on the contrary their appetite is growing.

More and more people, especially children under the age of five, are dying of starvation. Their appetite is growing as rapidly as the capacity of the rich farmers of the world to produce the food they need to keep them alive. It is not their appetite but their ability to pay for the grain which is fading.

Flood

Their governments, even when food prices are low, are so stuffed up with debt imposed on them by multinational companies and bankers that they cannot buy the food to feed their people. And if they have the good fortune to produce any home-grown food, for the same reason, they must sell that to the rich!

Over the last few weeks there has been a flood of reports and statistics about the widening gap between rich and poor. Like Lisa Vaughan, the authors all seem surprised; as though they have come across something which is clearly wrong and must instantly be put right.

They dare not draw the conclusion which stares them in the face, namely that the cause of all this totally unnecessary distress and absurdity is their beloved market system.

If 'money talks', as all these commentators insist it must, then the logic of a society cut into classes will drive all production towards the rich and away from the ever multiplying poor.

It used to be fashionable to describe the result of all this as Doomsday.

But when we discover the results already—when we discover, for instance, that 72 percent of the babies born in Peru last year are stunted or deformed because of the malnutrition of their parents— we realise that, for four fifths of the world's population, Doomsday came long ago.

Ever since Malthus

Once there lived a man called Malthus who was worried that so many people in the world didn't have enough to eat.

He came up with a very simple answer. There were too many people in the world.

The whole calculation could be reduced to the level of a New Testament parable. There were two loaves of bread and there were 5,000 people. If you were Jesus Christ you could divide up the loaves between the 5,000.

But if you weren't Jesus Christ all you could do was ensure that somehow 4,994 people weren't there any more—leaving six people for two loaves, which is about right.

Ever since Malthus had this brilliant idea he has been followed by all sorts of earnest people who want to solve the problems of world poverty.

The same argument keeps cropping up in different guises. For instance, you often hear, 'There are too many people in this country for the jobs available.'

Formula works

Get rid of some of the people, or stop allowing so many in, and then we can share out the jobs. If the formula works for jobs, what's more, it can work for hospital beds and houses and every social facility.

These are the 'rational arguments' with which racists spread their prejudices. And isn't it funny how often 'too many people' means too many black people?

This week—200 years of so after Malthus—there's a big conference in Cairo. Various governments are gathering with United Nations experts to discuss ways of keeping the population down.

Some of the governments have had a good shot at population control already. For instance, the government of Indonesia, which is heavily represented at Cairo, tried out a fascinating new method of population control in East Timor.

It wiped out a third of the population by shooting and burning them to death.

But why, if starvation and poverty are the result of too many people, are people starving even more horrifically in East Timor than they were before President Suharto engaged in his own special brand of the Final Solution?

In the industrial countries of the West the most prosperous years in all history were the years when large numbers of people flooded in from other countries.

Malthusian monstrosity

Mass immigration coincided with a better standard of living not just for the people previously living in the country but for the immigrants as well. Mass immigration coincided with full employment.

There were more people and more jobs. The whole Malthusian monstrosity was turned on its head.

People are not just consumers, empty vessels waiting to be filled from finite quantities of food and drink. They produce food.

The more they come together and pool their resources, the more they can produce.

Five thousand can make many more loaves per head than six.

The problem is not too many people. If people could decide what they produce, there would be more than enough food and accommodation for three times the world's population.

The problem is that only a minority decide—a minority who want to organise production for their own benefit and for no one else's.

That's why they promote people like Malthus—to prove that hunger and poverty are not the fault of the rich for deciding not to produce what people need, but the fault of the poor and hungry for being too many.

Capitalism is stripped bare

Here is the capitalist argument in all its bare beauty.

Private enterprise breeds competition. Competition forces firms to cut prices, and this leads to an endless spiral of cheaper goods and services. It also leads to variety, since capitalists are always looking for ways of doing something new.

Born again Christians Brian Souter and his sister Ann Gloag believe in capitalism. They are a dream—Dick Whittington capitalists who started off in Dundee with a couple of old buses and now run the second biggest bus company in the country.

The very name of the company, Stagecoach, has a romantic ring about it. It follows, of course, that they got where they are today by dint of hard work and competitive free enterprise.

Well, no, actually. They got where they are today chiefly because of the government's obsession with flogging off the old publicly-owned bus companies.

Predatory

The Monopolies and Mergers Commission is a very sedate and moderate body composed almost exclusively of Tories and entrepreneurs.

In its report just out on the activities of Stagecoach in Darlington, however, the commission has resorted to regrettably extreme language. 'Predatory, deplorable and against the public interest' were the exact words used.

What happened in Darlington? After studying the Tory bus laws, the Labour council decided to privatise the municipal bus company and called for bids. By far the lowest bid came from a firm called Yorkshire Transit, which employed a lot of the bus drivers from the old publicly-owned company. The council made it quite clear that Yorkshire Transit, according to the basic rules of free competition and tendering, had won the contract.

Socialist Worker 12 August 1995

At once Stagecoach recruited the best and most hard working of the council drivers on fantastic bonus rates of up to £1,000 and a guarantee of three years work.

For the first few weeks in which Yorkshire Transit struggled to meet its new obligations, Darlington was flooded out with Stage-coach buses from all over the country.

The drivers had instructions to watch out for the scheduled buses and to nip in front of them at the bus stops and nick their custom. If the drivers weren't quick enough it didn't really matter—because the Stagecoach services were entirely free.

Even the most principled supporter of public ownership in Dar-lington was reluctant to pay for a bus ride when another was offered along the same route with no conductor and no fare.

In five weeks flat Yorkshire Transit was smashed and Stagecoach, which had lost the tender on the first call, was awarded it. Ever since it has hardened and toughened its monopoly in Darlington—and of course now (since there are no competitors) Stagecoach charges high fares.

This is the eighth time either the MMC or the Office of Trading has slammed Stagecoach. From northern Scotland to eastern Kent, its companies have gobbled up the former public bus undertakings, driven the competition off the road, cut wages, smashed the unions and sacked loyal drivers.

None of its fantastic growth is due to competition or free enterprise.

On the contrary, Stagecoach used its strength in numbers of buses and in cash in the bank to knock out the competition.

The privatisation of the bus industry has had exactly the opposite effect to that promised by the Thatcherite think tanks in the 1980s.

There are now less people travelling by bus—because the fares are higher, there are less bus routes in the unpopulated areas and much less accountability.

State of terror

As we contemplate the horrors of Death Row we're inclined to write off capital punishment as a peculiarly American barbarism, a throwback to the distant reactionary past, unthinkable in civilised social democratic Britain. In fact, between 1900 and 1949 some 632 people were murdered by the British state because they had allegedly committed murder.

In 1949 there was a Labour government in office. In the (Tory) Federal Republic of Germany capital punishment had just been abolished. In Holland and Scandinavia there had been no capital punishment for more than 50 years. British Labour, true to its radical traditions, could not make up its mind. It ducked the question by appointing a Royal Commission, which took four years to report. In the interim, with Labour still in office, Timothy Evans, a young Welsh worker, was brutally done to death by the hangman for murdering his beloved baby daughter—a murder to which Reginald Christie confessed several years later.

The Royal Commission report in 1953 saw arguments on both sides, and its recommendations were equivocal. The (Tory) government happily decided to do nothing. But the argument would not go away. It was taken up enthusiastically by reformers of every description. Influential books by the socialist publisher Victor Gollancz and by Arthur Koestler put the case against. In 1957 capital punishment was abolished for most murders and retained only for murders of policemen or with firearms. Under this law James Hanratty, a young worker from north London, was hanged for a murder near Bedford on the A6 when (as later evidence proved) he was 200 miles away in Rhyl at the time.

The argument for abolition got angrier. In 1965 the new Labour government allowed time for a private member's bill which finally abolished it.

Through all those years the argument on both sides of the Atlantic was rational. The case for capital punishment was based almost exclusively on its effectiveness as a deterrent. It was widely agreed by people on both sides of the argument that capital punishment was wholly indefensible unless it prevented murder on a substantial scale.

The more the argument for capital punishment depended on a rational case for deterrence, the more it was lost. The Royal Commission found no conclusive evidence of deterrence. Especially impressive were the statistics from the United States, where capital punishment had been abolished in some states, not in others. In North Dakota, for instance, where capital punishment was abolished in 1915, the murder rate was slightly lower than in South Dakota, where the social composition was very similar and where capital punishment was still in force. In Maine, capital punishment had been abolished in 1876 and reintroduced after a right wing hullabaloo following an especially nasty murder. The murder rate, however, went up even faster, so capital punishment was abolished again in 1887—after which the rate subsided.

The truth was that there was no correlation at all between the incidence of capital punishment and the incidence of murder. Murders were mainly personal or domestic crimes, immune from deterrence. Moreover, there were plenty of American 'mistakes' similar to the tragedies of Timothy Evans and James Hanratty. Capital punishment did not deter murders, and if a 'mistake' was made there was no way of putting it right.

In the 1950s and 1960s the possibility of such a mistake was widely dismissed in polite society. Lord Chancellor Lord Kilmuir, discussing the Evans case, told parliament that the idea that a judge, jury and the Court of Appeal could convict the wrong person was 'in the realms of fantasy'. Those realms of fantasy have been visited again and again in recent years as an enormous stream of prisoners wrongly convicted for murder have emerged from the High Court after years of wholly unjustified, and not at all fantastical, imprisonment.

As long as the argument remains on a rational level—does hanging deter?—capital punishment doesn't stand a chance. The most remarkable feature of the recent enthusiasm for the rope and the electric chair, however, is that it casts all reason aside. It is founded almost entirely on medieval incantations about 'retribution' ('an eye for an eye') and on a belief in violent punishment as a means of keeping the 'criminal classes' (that is, the lower classes) in order.

The loonies who swept into the US Congress and Senate in last year's right wing backlash couldn't care less whether capital punishment deters or not. They are like the lynch mobs in those westerns where justice for a (usually white) victim of crime is the instant murder of someone who might (or might not) be responsible.

Guilt and deterrence are not really relevant provided the anger of the mob is assuaged in blood.

There is a grim logic behind this abandonment of logic. It was summed up for me when I was asked recently to take part in an episode of the BBC's *Moral Maze*. The issue was the state murder of some poor British man who had been on Death Row for as long as anyone could remember. I came armed with the legal statistics about deterrence and mistakes by the legal system. They were brushed aside. An American professor in London declared, 'I am with Thomas Hobbes. I want people to live in permanent fear of the laws.'

This assertion, which I dare say is a bit hard on Hobbes, explains what is happening. As the lunacies and unfairnesses of the market system become more and more obvious, as the precious market fails more and more ostentatiously to deliver the even handed, civilised, rational society it promises, so the people who benefit from it seek to escape from rational thought altogether. Unable any longer even to pretend that the system can erode the poverty and inequality which create crime, they search for slogans which will satisfy the rage of the victims of crime and keep them in order at the same time. 'Kill the murderers!' is a fine slogan for both purposes, especially as almost all the alleged murderers due to be killed are poor or black or both.

It matters not an iota that killing murderers does nothing to stop killing or murder, or that the people being executed may not be murderers at all. What matters is the immediate satisfaction of blood lust. The feeling that something is being done is far better than the reality of doing something, especially when doing something means dismantling the inequalities on which class society depends. It follows that politicians and businessmen who clamour for these state murders are far, far more guilty of violence and social chaos than any of the victims of their society whom they want to murder.

Giving power back to the rich after 350 years

I hope the playwright Caryl Churchill will not mind me pointing out that by far the most exciting act in her play *Light Shining In Buckinghamshire*, currently revived at the Cottesloe Theatre, was not written by her. It was not written by anyone. It was an argument in the general council of Cromwell's army 350 years ago. The council was debating the form of government which should be set up after parliament's victory over the king. Most of the soldiers' representatives argued for a new democracy in which all men voted. 'Every man that is to live under a government ought first by his own consent to put himself under that government,' said Colonel Thomas Rainborowe. After all, he argued, why should people obey laws made by a parliament for which they couldn't vote? These arguments were brushed aside by Cromwell and his son-in-law General Henry Ireton. They explained that wealthy people like themselves could not contemplate giving the vote to everyone. The majority, they observed, had no property. So any government elected by that majority would at once pass laws to swipe the property of the rich. The argument sways back and forth, passionate and intense on both sides. It is persistently absorbing, not just for the fine acting and skilful editing, but also for its painful relevance to the contemporary contortions of New Labour.

For 200 years, Ireton's primeval fear of democracy—'the majority will take my riches'; 'one man one vote will lead to one man one estate, one salary, one job'—inspired his rich descendants to reject all demands for universal suffrage. They were terrified by the Chartist revolt of the 1830s and 1840s. The Chartists wanted the vote not for its own sake but to make life easier for the workers and the poor. This meant spreading political democracy to economic democracy. Their 'schoolmaster', the journalist Bronterre O'Brien, demanded 'democracy not only in government, but throughout every industrial

Guardian 21 January 1997

department of society'. Political democracy on its own without changing an economic system whose purpose was to keep rich people rich and poor people poor was a sham; a talking shop parliament with little or no relevance to the lives of the people who voted for it.

Naturally, the rich who controlled parliament denied the vote to such subversives. They waited 20 years until the government was secure in the hands of two rich men's parties, Tory and Liberal. Even then, the vote was conceded gingerly, drip by drip, over another half a century. The formation of the Labour Party to represent the trade unions, and 'to secure for the workers the full fruits of their industry' seemed like Ireton's nightmare come true.

Here was the prospect of democracy extending from politics to economics, from parliament into the real bastions of oligarchy and hierarchy—the bunkers of the rich. Despite the lamentable failure of Labour governments this century to penetrate those bunkers, their leaders were mostly committed to the idea that they were in charge. Their political power, which derived from the ballot box, brought with it, they believed, a measure of economic power as well.

They might not want to dictate to the rich, but they at least imagined themselves able to do so.

The pronouncements this week from Blair and Brown dispose of any such illusions. Brown pledges that 'as Iron Chancellor' he will not interfere in any way with the free flow of the market system. He will not deduct a single penny from the grotesque fortunes of the rich. Blair calls the trade union laws of the 1980s 'reforms'—'reforms' which he and his colleagues angrily and rightly opposed because they were not reforms, but handcuffs on the trade unionists Labour is meant to represent. He cannot wait to make pledges to uphold the inalienable rights of pension fund millionaires, supermarket kings and dirty tricks specialists at British Airways. Even before New Labour takes office, its leaders are abjectly surrendering economic power to the people who already have it, and, in the process, polluting the political power they seek from the votes of people most of whom have no wealth at all.

Wigs and Tories

If the enemy of my enemy is my friend, it follows that the enemy of Michael Howard is my hero. So awful was Howard's long reign at the Home Office that many liberals sought democratic relief from the most blatantly undemocratic section of the establishment: the judiciary. It was the strange sound of Law Lords denouncing Howard's preposterous insistence that 'prison works' and the widespread jubilation at his many snubbings in the courts that led to liberal hosannas for the judges. And the judges in turn were happy to see themselves as Supreme Keepers of the Public Liberties. On the right, Mr Justice Laws called for a 'higher order law' under which judges could overrule elected governments in the interest of the people's 'fundamental freedoms'. On the left, Mr Justice Sedley wrote: 'Modern public law has carried forward a culture of judicial assertiveness to compensate for, and in places repair, dysfunctions in the democratic process.' In the centre, Lord Woolf: 'I myself would consider there were advantages in making it clear that ultimately there are even limits on the supremacy of parliament which it is the courts' inalienable responsibility to identify and uphold.' Common to all three was the notion that the judges are the obvious people to intervene wherever 'dysfunctions in the democratic process' emerge.

Joshua Rozenberg tells the story of the 'trial of strength'—'petulant squabble' might have been more accurate—between the judges and Tory ministers in the final years of the Major administration. At huge length he regurgitates the argument that attended Howard's plans to extend sentences for serious crimes. This argument was a sham: the statute law is full of minimum and maximum sentences set down by government. Howard sought ruthlessly to increase sentences, and the senior judges publicly attacked him. Their conclusion—that sentencing is best left to democratic and compassionate judges—was greeted with hollow laughter throughout the prisons. Last January at Leicester Crown Court I sat dumbfounded as Judge Hammond sent

London Review of Books 18 September 1997

Fred Whelan to prison for a year. Whelan was 65 and had never been in trouble with the police. His 'crime' had been to take a lump of cannabis into Gartree Prison to afford some comfort to his desperately ill stepson, Michael Hickey, who was serving his eighteenth year in prison for a murder which we now know he did not commit. In vain, witnesses (I was one) tried to explain that Whelan was not a man even to consider taking drugs himself: that his so called crime was a typical act of generosity. In court that day, as in the courts every day, the judge showed no compassion and no common sense, but coolly proceeded, at enormous public expense, to cause further distress to a family already distressed beyond imagining by judicial recklessness.

The reason that the judges campaigned against Howard's sentencing proposals had nothing to do with humanity or common sense, as they pretended. They saw the government, which had only recently dared to suggest a relaxation of the barristers' closed shop, as a poacher on their patch who had to be shooed away. Rozenberg disagrees. 'The senior judges', he asserts, 'are a modern and liberal-minded group of people' who 'seek to act in the broad public interest.' As proof he chronicles the staggering growth in applications for 'judicial review' of government decisions, up from 491 in 1980 to 3,293 in the first ten months of 1996. It is undoubtedly true that a great many injustices have been righted by judicial review—hundreds of paupers wrongfully imprisoned for not paying fines have been set free, for instance. More important, the authorities have been forced to disclose information which they wanted to keep secret—the Hickey case was among many bust open by this process. But these blessings flowed as much from the fact that injustices could be aired in public, and from all the resulting campaigns, articles and petitions, as from any judicial tendency to justice or mercy. Rozenberg praises the achievement under judicial review of his 'modern and liberal-minded' people, while apparently forgetting the endless line of injustices which have disfigured the courts of justice over the last two decades.

Lord Bridge, we are reminded here, was forthright in his opposition to the gagging order on *Spycatcher*. Excellent. But it was Mr Justice Bridge who presided at the 1975 trial of the Birmingham Six, and declared in a judgement groaning with bias that the evidence against the defendants was the strongest he had ever heard. Lord Donaldson is quoted here fervently defending the judges' right to fix sentences. But it was Mr Justice Donaldson who presided at the trial of the Guildford

Four. The only politician respected by the former Lord Chief Justice Lord Lane, we are told, was Douglas Hurd. But was not Hurd openly attacked by the same Lord Lane in his monstrous judgement at the first appeal of the Birmingham Six, which he dismissed? In the cosy, cautious style of a BBC correspondent (one of Rozenberg's most radical proposals is that the judges should appoint a public relations officer; and he twice quotes approvingly from an *Observer* columnist called Melanie Phillips, without revealing that she is his wife) we are introduced to two other urbane and reforming senior judges, the late Lord Chief Justice Taylor and Lord Goff. But it was Messrs Justice Taylor and Goff who, with Lane, refused even a proper appeal to the Bridgewater Four when, with overwhelming new evidence of their innocence, they first went to the Court of Appeal in 1981.

Rozenberg quotes 'a brave and decent judgment' from Mr Justice Collins: 'I find it impossible to believe that parliament intended that an asylum seeker who was lawfully here, and who could not lawfully be removed from the country, should be left destitute, starving and at risk of grave illness and even death because he could find no one to provide him with the bare necessities of life.' This as Rozenberg points out, was naive in the extreme. The precise and only purpose of the new government rules withholding benefit from asylum seekers was that they should be starved out of the country and back to the repressive regime whence they came. Hoorah for the brave and decent Mr Justice Collins. Yet Andrew Collins QC was sharply criticised by the Scott report for not disclosing documents vital to the defence of six men charged with illegally exporting fuses to Iraq. Another judge who simply could not believe that parliament, in the shape of Peter Lilley, could contemplate starving asylum seekers to death and thus violating the 'basic human rights' was Lord Justice Simon Brown. But it was Simon Brown QC who appeared in the divisional court for the government in 1982 in an initially successful attempt to deprive Mr Ron Smith of Leeds of his basic right to an inquest into the death of his daughter who had been found dead in strange circumstances in Saudi Arabia. The law at the time was clear—everyone had a right to an inquest into any dead body they bought to Britain. But Simon Brown argued that parliament could not possibly have meant what it said, and successfully asked the judges to contradict it. For that matter, how many fundamental freedoms did the latter-day champion of 'fundamental freedoms' Mr Justice Laws curtail in his long stint as John Laws QC, the Thatcher government's chief court lawyer?

Joshua Rozenberg's not entirely original view is that elected politicians should make the laws and judges should administer them. He advises the two sides to stop attacking each other: politicians should be respectful of judges and judges respectful of politicians. He admits that this separation of powers is very difficult to define or to act on, and he seems to think (though he hates to commit himself) that we would all be better off with a Bill of Rights which would override all other legislation. One surrogate Bill of Rights which he commends is the European Convention of Human Rights, which New Labour is committed to incorporating into British law. He lists the growing number of judges who are so much in favour of a Bill of Rights that they are threatening to bring one in through the back door by means of the common law if the government doesn't do so by statute. There is nothing surprising about mounting judicial enthusiasm for a whole new area of law which will give lawyers yet more lucrative work and at the same time empower judges to overrule an elected parliament. With a Bill of Rights to pick over, the judges would be much more active and much more powerful. Another advantage of a Bill of Rights is that it doesn't need much democracy to sustain it. Rozenberg earnestly discusses as 'limited judicial entrenchment' the Bill of Rights Ordinance in Hong Kong, which, he says, 'preserves parliamentary sovereignty', while overlooking one rather important right denied by this sovereign parliament—the right to vote for it.

So, after a rather pointless chapter on *Spycatcher* and the Scott inquiry, the book concludes—without a conclusion. We are left gazing at the same old scales with an elected legislature on one side and an 'independent judiciary' (independent, that is, of the electorate) on the other, and listening to Rozenberg's lecture on the supreme importance of keeping the balance between them. 'It is one of the strengths of the common law', Lord Woolf wrote in 1995, in a passage admiringly quoted here, 'that it enables the courts to vary the extent of their intervention to reflect current needs, and by this means it helps to maintain the delicate balance of a democratic society.'

What a relief that Rozenberg's book was followed so quickly by the fifth edition of John Griffith's classic, *The Politics of the Judiciary*, and to see Woolf's pompous dictum written off for what it is—'a pleasing conceit'. Griffith explains that the notion of a balance of power between legislature and judicature 'derives from ships of state on even keels'. There is no 'objective hidden hand which holds the constitution in perpetual equilibrium'. On the contrary:

> Political power, the power of government, is exercised by a...small number of people, consisting of ministers, senior civil servants, a few heads of industry, banking and commerce and some influential advisers... Until recently, the most senior judges have been part of this oligarchy...they have today lost that high status...and part of the reason for their present robustness is to be found in their attempt to regain what status they have lost.

Griffith had started by asking who the judges are and where they come from. Even if the judiciary has recently lost a bit of ground, his conclusion holds good:

> Judges are the product of a class and have the characteristics of that class. Typically coming from middle class professional families, independent schools, Oxford and Cambridge, they spend 20 to 25 years in successful practice at the Bar, mostly in London, earning very considerable incomes by the time they reach their forties. This is not the stuff of which reformers are made, let alone radicals.

In other words, the judges are not a brake on the excesses of the controlling oligarchy: they are part of it.

We need to keep that oligarchy accountable and in check, and our parliamentary institutions are woefully inadequate for the task. Griffith (not Rozenberg) has some suggestions as to how we might do it:

> Far more than on the judiciary, our freedoms depend on the press, politicians and others to publicise the breach of these freedoms and on the continuing vulnerability of ministers, civil servants, the police, other public officials and private interests to accusations that these freedoms are being infringed. In other words, we depend far more on the vigilance of those members of society who...make it their business to seek to hold public authorities within their proper limits.

First published as a review of Trial of Strength: The Battle Between Ministers and Judges Over Who Makes the Law *by Joshua Rozenberg (Richard Cohen 1997) and* The Politics of the Judiciary *by J A G Griffith (Fontana 1997).*

Hammered on the Pacific Rim

As part of his campaign to rewrite Clause Four of the Labour Party constitution and remove the party's commitment to public ownership, Tony Blair used to point to the 'continuing success story' of the 'tiger economies' of south east Asia.

The future for the world, he said, was being hammered out on the 'Pacific Rim'.

The governments and peoples of these countries, he argued—and he singled out Singapore, South Korea and Hong Kong—had no truck with old fashioned ideas such as nationalisation or strong trade unions.

Often without unions and always without nationalisation, the vibrant people of these nations were building new, young, modern economies which were piling up the profits and spreading prosperity for all.

Blair took his cue, as ever, from the Tories. Ever since the early 1980s Tory free marketeers pointed eastward. The Thatchers, for instance, were in love with Hong Kong, where Denis had substantial business interests.

Prime Minister Thatcher sponsored and led several high powered business delegations to Singapore, Jakarta and Kuala Lumpur.

The grand corruption of the Pergau Dam affair flowed from Thatcher's fascination with the tiger economy of Malaysia and the wonderful market it opened up for the booming British arms trade.

Tigers' mouths

On all sides the story was the same. In the 'old democracies' growth was frustrated by trade unions, by public ownership, by busybody parliaments. In the new countries these brakes on growth were being removed and, hey presto, the free market worked.

Socialist Worker 1 November 1997

The money followed the propaganda. By the beginning of 1996 British pension funds had thrown about 5 percent of their entire assets—about $50 billion of other people's pension money—into the tigers' mouths. In between 1993 and 1996 a fantastic $33 billion went from the United States and into the stock exchanges of Hong Kong and south east Asia.

Then suddenly last year the whole picture changed. The British pension funds started selling 'tiger' stocks. US inflow into these fashionable stock exchanges all but dried up.

The chorus, 'invest, invest, invest', has suddenly changed to 'liquidate, liquidate, liquidate'. The booming stock exchanges of the tiger economies became bust stock exchanges.

Last Saturday's *Financial Times* had a headline which told the whole story: 'The Pacific's Grim Rim'. Not only has the great success story changed almost overnight into the great failure story, but the commentators are now earnestly discussing whether the collapse will drag the 'older democracies' down with them.

Fuddy duddy

In a trice, Blairite confidence about world growth has changed to doom and gloom. In the same trice, the remedies are rather different. Last week the South Korean government acted to save its biggest private car firm from closure. How? By good old fuddy duddy nationalisation.

Why has all this happened now? The fundamental point about capitalism is that no one knows these things. The system depends on not being planned. It depends on the vagaries of a market economy based on stock exchanges.

These exchanges are no more or less than casinos in which the stakes are people's jobs and living standards. They go up and down at random with the most devastating consequences for human beings who have no control over the process. The alternative is not some other set of stock exchanges in some other part of the world, but socialist planning.

Taken for a ride

This is a David and Goliath story. David is Frank Wheeler, a 70 year old retired bus worker with perforated eardrums who lives with his wife in a council bungalow on a joint pension of £100 a week. Goliath is the Department of Transport, represented by secretaries of state from both major parties and advised by Allen & Overy, the City's most expensive lawyers. The argument is about £200 million which Frank Wheeler says the government has stolen from him and about 40,000 other pensioners who once worked on the buses. After ten years battling against hopeless odds, David has Goliath on the ropes. Frank Wheeler was born in 1927. In 1944 he was called up for active service in France. Some months after VE day in 1945 a mine exploded under him. He recovered consciousness in an army hospital in Uttoxeter and was told both his eardrums were perforated. Thanks to some expert NHS treatment at the Royal Victoria Hospital, Blackpool, his hearing was eventually saved. By that time he was driving buses. He drove for the Ribble bus company for 25 years. He was for all that time an active trade unionist. He became chairman of the Blackpool bus branch of the Transport and General Workers Union. He had had little or no formal education, and was taught by the trade union movement. He regularly attended weekend schools and seminars arranged by the union. His bungalow walls are festooned with certificates of merit from his union. He was always thinking and acting against the stream. He joined the Communist Party for a few months in the mid-1970s, chiefly in protest against the TGWU's 'black circular' banning Communists from office. He thrived in the golden years of British trade unionism, the late 1960s and early 1970s. When the Ribble company was nationalised, along with some 70 other private bus companies, by the Labour government in 1968, trade unionists got free time to organise, and made the most of it. He remembers only one long strike which was victorious.

In 1974 the National Bus Company started a pension scheme for

Guardian 15 November 1997

its 40,000 workers. The scheme was run by representatives of the company and the unions. Frank Wheeler, like many trade unionists of his time and ilk, took a lasting interest in the pension scheme and carefully studied its reports and accounts.

All this was thrown into reverse by the Tory governments after 1979. Frank Wheeler watched in dismay as the profitable and successful National Bus Company was privatised in 1985. He argued in Blackpool that the workers should buy up the Ribble company, but was defeated by his colleagues, who voted instead for a management buyout. Before long the new directors had enriched themselves by selling out to an ambitious new company called Stagecoach whose directors applied themselves energetically to selling off many of Ribble's property and assets. One afternoon in April 1986 over a cup of tea in the depot, Frank saw a report on the company noticeboard. It revealed that the National Bus pension fund was in surplus to the tune of £114 million: 'I thought, that's good, that will come in handy. And I remember thinking, there's 200 men affected by that—and yet there's only one report stuck up on the board without any advance notice. Why hadn't we all been told this good news?'

Two months later, in June 1986, all 200 men got a set of documents from the National Bus Company. An agreement had been reached between all the parties about what should happen to the Bus Employees Superannuation Fund, the pension fund. The money in the fund would be used to buy annuities for all its beneficiaries from the Standard Life insurance company. These annuities would guarantee pensions at the rate then being paid, and would rise each year with the retail price increase and a little bit extra. When the annuities were bought, the fund would then be wound up. 'The very last paragraph', Frank remembers, 'said that any surplus in the fund would be paid to the National Bus Company. But there was no indication of how much the surplus would be. Most of us assumed it would be just a few coppers. But I kept remembering that notice on the board— £114 million. What had happened to that?'

He sat down, and on his ancient typewriter battered out the first of many hundreds of letters he has written on the subject since. He wrote to Mr W A Walker, managing director of the defunct National Bus Company, asking how much was the surplus on the fund, and what had happened to it. Walker replied with what Frank calls 'an anodyne letter'. All the parties to the pension committee which advised the fund, he said, including all the trade union representatives, had agreed the terms of its distribution and winding up. All present and future pensioners, he promised, would be no worse off with their new annuities than they were under the previous scheme. 'He kept answering questions I asked,' says Frank. 'I still wanted to know what was the surplus and how and why it had been handed back to the company.' Some answers came with the publication of the trust's accounts in 1987. They showed that the surplus of £114 million had been handed back to the company.

Shortly before he read these accounts, just before his sixtieth birthday, Frank Wheeler suffered a stroke. He was told he could never drive a bus again, and retired on his annuity from Standard Life. He now had more time to try to unravel the mystery of the £114 million which, he believed, had been wrongly taken from him and his fellow busmen.

He wrote to the Occupational Pensions Advisory Service and was put in touch with Chris Lewin, who was then working as a pensions expert at Associated Newspapers. Lewin wrote to the transport department. He discovered that shortly before the £114 million had been transferred the rules of the pension scheme had been altered. Frank Wheeler wrote off at once to NBC asking if he could see the old rules before they were amended. No, he was told, he couldn't. In that case, he wrote again, could he see a copy of the rules once they had been amended? No, he was told, he couldn't. Back he went to Chris Lewin, who managed to wrest from the department a copy of the old rules and the amended ones. The old rules stated quite clearly that if the fund was wound up any surplus had to be used to pay pensioners. Moreover, they stated that the rules could not be changed if they adversely affected any pensioner unless all the beneficiaries were consulted and most agreed to the change. Frank Wheeler knew that he had not been consulted. The full force of the scandal came home to him. An enormous sum of money from the fund had been taken by the government. Obviously, this decision adversely affected pensioners. Yet the rules had been changed to allow the surplus to be taken without anyone being consulted as, according to the rules, they should have been.

Who could help him put right this wrong? Chris Lewin, who is now director of pensions at Guinness, remembers Frank Wheeler well. 'When I looked at the rules of the scheme, it was obvious there was something strange,' he says. 'I took advice from the legal panel of OPAS, a set of lawyers who give their time pro bono (for no payment—as Mr Lewin did). They agreed with me. There was something wrong here. Mr Wheeler had a clear prima facie case. The problem was, what could he do about it? His only course was to go to court, but this would have been extremely expensive, in fact impossible for him unless he was backed by his trade union.'

His trade union, however, was distinctly unhelpful. In October 1989, a few days after hearing from Mr Lewin that he should seek the help of the TGWU, Frank wrote for help to the national bus officer at the union, Stevenson. The reply came from the union's legal officer, A C Blyghton: 'I thought I had made it clear to you that the trustees of the scheme are those responsible for making decisions as to how the particular scheme is adopted, and as long as the benefits of the scheme are guaranteed and paid no claim can be pursued against them'. Mr Blyghton then added a warning: 'You now say that you are going to apply for legal aid. In due course will you please produce this letter to whoever solicitors you decide to instruct to the effect that if they apply for legal aid we would want to make representations to the Legal Aid Authority immediately, because we believe that any action that you contemplate would be ill-founded.'

Frank was dumbfounded. Here was his union, which he had served faithfully and without any sort of reward for 30 years, threatening to stop him getting legal aid to sue the trustees of the pension fund. Mr Blyghton's letter exactly expressed the union's attitude to Frank's campaign. The union had, after all, agreed with deal which allowed the pension surplus to go to the government, and at that stage were not prepared to risk any action which might put the deal in jeopardy.

A further blow came soon afterwards when Frank applied in the county court at Runcorn, where he was living, for an order forcing the trustee of the pension fund to disclose the relevant rules and minutes. Soon after the Department of Transport heard of his application, Frank got a letter from Allen & Overy, who declared their intention to fight the case with no expense spared and to appear at Runcorn County Court with an expensive QC, his junior and a reserve army of well-paid solicitors from Allen & Overy. The letter reminded him that if he lost his application he would be liable for many thousands of pounds in costs. Frank recalls this episode with disgust. 'All I wanted was information to which I was entitled. Yet they threatened to bankrupt me.' Frank could work no longer because of bad health. He and his wife Cath were for the first time in their lives finding out about the poverty of the elderly undemployed. They could not even consider consulting a solicitor to take on the Department of Transport. He withdrew his application, but nothing would stop him writing letters. When in 1991 the BEST pension fund was wound up, and the directors of the trustee company replaced by two officials from the Department of Transport without any funds, he redoubled his efforts to provoke some sort of official inquiry into the pension fund surplus which he calculated, with interest, was now worth at least £200 million.

He was incensed by the report on the privatisation of National Bus by Sir John Bourn, the Comptroller and Auditor General of the National Audit Office, which was published in November 1990. 'Overall', Sir John reported, 'the department believe that the sale represents a very creditable achievement'; a view from which he did not differ. 'A very creditable achievement!' Frank snorts. 'They got £45 million for the whole industry, and yet they pocketed £114 million from the pension fund. It may have been creditable from the point of view of the government, but what about the pensioners?' In a long correspondence which followed, Sir John stood firm on the government's inalienable right to take the surplus. Throughout 1989 and 1990, Frank continued his steady flow of letters. Michael Portillo, Minister of State for Transport, was the chief recipient—and the most dismissive. Where else could Frank turn? He continued to write to Chris Lewin, who in March 1991 had some good news. The government had set up a Pensions Ombudsman, with powers to investigate complaints from the public and to recommend restitution for wronged pensioners. The big difference from anything which had gone before, explained Lewin, was that anyone could complain without spending more than the cost of a postage stamp. There was no need for legal representation. Lewin recommended that Frank take his complaint to the ombudsman, a former social security commissioner called Michael Pratt, whose office opened on 1 April 1991. Pretty well the first envelope opened in that office contained a long complaint from Frank Wheeler.

But Mr Pratt did not err on the side of eagerness. 'He sat on this for three years,' claims Frank. Nor was there any joy from the Wheelers' Tory MP, Chris Butler. 'After a couple of letters he told me he didn't want to waste my time, and he didn't want me to waste his,' scoffs Frank. He was delighted when Butler lost his seat in the 1992 general election and was replaced by Mike Hall. Hall is one of the few people to emerge from Frank's account with any credit. 'He was great,' interrupts Cath Wheeler. 'Every letter we went to him brought two replies.' Hall was shocked at the Department of Transport's refusal to give Frank basic information. In February 1994, under a new code for access to information, he complained to the Parliamentary Ombudsman, William Reid, about the failure to give Frank the minutes of the meetings where the rules were changed to allow the surplus to be taken. Despite furious objections from the department, this complaint was upheld, and the department heavily criticised for behaviour 'inconsistent with good practice for dealing with requests for information'.

In spite of this finding in 1995, Frank Wheeler was still a long way from his goal. He seemed to be blocked on all sides. Though Mike Hall continued to bombard the authorities with letters and inquiries, the House of Commons never debated the issue. The union had, apparently, thrown in the towel, and the whole pensions industry seemed ranged against him. In 1995, he and his wife left Runcorn for the small sleepy town of Moffatt in Dumfriesshire, where Cath's stepson worked for the St John's ambulance service. He was further away from London, and, it seemed, further away from any sort of success for his lone campaign.

His only hope was a new Pensions Ombudsman. In 1994, Michael Pratt was replaced by Dr Julian Farrand, who immediately started to take a keen interest in Frank's complaint case. Farrand's approach was much brisker and more determined than his predecessor's. In his first year he decided 83 cases, compared to 47, 59 and 49 in the three years Mr Pratt was in charge. In 1995-96, Farrand's decisions jumped to 326 and the following year to 374. Many of these prompt 'determinations' upheld complaints and ordered restitution. They infuriated the expensive pension lawyers who made a good living assuring employers that 'their' pension funds basically belonged to them, and preferred long, drawn-out, expensive legal battles to quick and cheap decisions from someone who wasn't even a proper lawyer. Ensconced at Moffatt, Frank Wheeler noticed a change of attitude from the ombudsman's office. The case worker assigned to his complaint, Tony King, was actually ringing up and asking questions. He seemed to be listening where no one in authority had listened before.

The breakthrough came on 6 September 1996. Typically, Frank read about his triumph first in the *Observer*. He rang the following day, and the news was confirmed. The ombudsman had 'determined' that Frank had been right all along on the two main points. The trustees in 1986 had no right to change rules which plainly affected the pensioners adversely without balloting all the beneficiaires. Moreover, the trustees should have resisted the 'improper' pressures imposed on them by the bus company to bully them into a settlement which included handing back the surplus. Dr Farrand's language was clear. By proposing the change of rules, the bus company directors 'were offering a bigger carrot, wielding a new stick and seeking a further advantage'. The employers had threatened to withhold their contributions unless the surplus was returned to them. This was not only 'a breach of the duty of good faith' but 'constituted an improper use of the power'. The 'appropriate remedy' for the trustee was 'to recover the monies paid to the company on winding up, with interest at an equitable rate', and for the money to be used for buying enhanced pensions for the scheme's beneficiaries. The awful truth slowly dawned on an unsuspecting ministry and pensions industry. The lone busman who they had written off for so long as a demented deaf old lefty pest had been right all along. The government had unlawfully walked away with £200 million which rightfully belonged to impoverished pensioners. It had been a robbery conducted in broad daylight of which Robert Maxwell would have been proud.

Ever since the previous April (1996), when Dr Farrand had told ministers of his provisional determination upholding Frank Wheeler, the normally placid corridors of the Department of Transport were infected with panic. The trustees who had been so clearly instructed by the ombudsman to 'recover the monies' illegally seized by the government were two directors of a defunct company which had no assets. They were both senior officials of the Department of Transport. Despite their lack of funds, however, these officials were able to commission a legal opinion from one of the top commercial barristers in the country. Who paid for that opinion? Why, the Department of Transport (the taxpayer). Frank Wheeler is on first meeting a careful man who measures his words. But it soon becomes clear that he is driven by a sense of outrage which merges all the time with a sense of humour. He has a short mocking chuckle which erupts again and again as he recalls the official Bumbledom of the time. 'We were told the trustees were wholly independent of the ministry (chuckle). But they were senior officials of the ministry (chuckle). We were told they had no funds—so they had to go to their minister, independently, and say: "Please, guv, can you give me £70,000 for a barrister's opinion?" (chuckle) "Of course—here you are," says the independent minister (chuckle). And then I think, well, it's all absolute bloody rubbish.'

The counsel's opinion so independently acquired stuck to the legal advice which Allen & Overy had always given the department. The transfer of the surplus, in their view, was perfectly legal. However, the ombudsman did have the power to adjudicate and order the trustees to recover the money. What should the government do? Should they pay the money to the pensioners or should they appeal against the ombudsman in the High Court? After consulting with his colleagues in the government, the Secretary of State for Transport, Sir George Young (a name Frank Wheeler loves to pronounce, with a not entirely lilting sound on the word 'Sir'), decided to do neither. The bicycling baronet, as he was known, was determined to hang on to his £200 million. As he sensitively put it in the Commons, 'payment of such a sum would involve serious accounting issues'. But he was not very keen either to appeal to the courts against the government's own appointed ombudsman. He lit on a brilliant compromise. He (or rather the taxpayer) would pay the trustee company (whose directors were his own officials) to sue his own department. The taxpayer would pay the costs of both sides. In order to make the lawsuit sound slightly less crazy, ownership of the trustee company was shifted from the two ministry officials to the Official Solicitor. This was done without any public announcement in August 1996, a couple of weeks before Dr Farrand's adjudication.

The Official Solicitor is, in Sir George's words, 'a wholly independent official appointed by the Lord Chancellor'. The Lord Chancellor is a senior member of the cabinet and the office of the Official Solicitor is paid by the government. His most famous appearance on the public stage was his representation of five dockers jailed for breaking picketing laws in the summer of 1972. The dockers refused to give an undertaking not to repeat their illegal acts, and the general council of the TUC called a general strike. The Official Solicitor, described by Labour leader Harold Wilson as a 'fairy godmother', jumped into court in the nick of time to 'represent' the sacked dockers and secure their hasty release.

As soon as Mike Hall heard (in a letter from Sir George Young) that the Official Solicitor now owned the trustee company of the bus workers' pension fund, he fired off an angry letter: 'Given the fact that you are a direct employee of the government and are contemplating legal action against another arm of government, how do you intend to reconcile the obvious conflict of interest?' The Official Solicitor, Mr Peter Harris, insisted that he was wholly independent of government. To prove it, he appointed two directors and a secretary to the trustee company which he now owned. They were Mr William Macbryde, who worked in the Official Solicitor's Office, Mr Bob O'Mahoney, who worked in the Official Solicitor's Office, and Ms Sheila Pearson, who worked in the Official Solicitor's office. All these directors were appointed without the slightest reference to anyone who had ever worked on buses. Further proof of Mr Harris's independence was his choice of lawyers to represent his case against the Department of Transport. He chose Allen & Overy, who had advised the Department of Transport on the issue and had since the very first day of privatisation strongly supported the transfer of the surplus to the government. They had issued to interested parties a long and highly questionable memorandum opposing the ombudsman's determination line by line. For *seven months* after taking over the trustee company for the fund, the Official Solicitor, in his bid to secure £200 million from the Department of Transport for the pensioners in his trust, used the same solicitors as the Department of Transport. It was only in March 1997, after Mike Hall and other MPs pointed out the grotesque conflict of interest involved, that the new trustees changed their solicitors to another City firm, Taylor Joynson and Garrett.

The ombudsman's determination had, meanwhile, entirely changed the political atmosphere on the issue. The one-man band in Moffat was joined by all kinds of players. On 15 January 1997, ten years after the rules of the fund were changed and the surplus taken by the company, came the first ever debate on the subject in the House of Commons. It was led off by the veteran MP for Hull North, Kevin McNamara, who denounced the government's actions as 'theft'. He was followed by a string of angry Labour MPs: Gwyneth Dunwoody, Eric Martlew, Eddie Loyden, Max Madden, and Glenda Jackson, Labour front bench spokeswoman on transport, whose rhetoric reached a high level: 'The activity defined in the ombudsman's report would actually be associated with the cut-throat City takeover tactics of billion pound multinationals. Fraud, breaches of trust, threats and unlawful activity should have no part in the pension arrangements of men and women who, having worked hard all their lives, seek nothing more than security in their well-earned retirement.' To this barrage of indignation the wretched minister, John Watts, had no real reply. Most of the Labour MPs who spoke that day were sponsored by the Transport and General Workers Union, whose interest in busworkers' pensions had been awakened by the ombudsman's report. Cheerfully putting behind them their predecessors' efforts to shut Frank Wheeler up, the union legal officers now approached him, begged him for his papers and even paid the £250 legal costs he had incurred while trying to get a solicitor to enforce Dr Farrand's determination.

In March Bill Morris, the union's general secretary, went to the House of Commons transport committee with a huge dossier on the case, most of it made up of Frank Wheeler's letters. Morris reckoned that the money taken by the government would provide an extra £1,000 a year for each bus pensioner. During the general election campaign in April, the TGWU ran a powerful campaign demanding immediate payment of the bus pensioners. Advertisements were taken out in most mainstream newspapers featuring a cartoon of the Tory prime minister. 'John Major once wanted to be a bus conductor,' ran the caption. 'He didn't make it. So what's he doing with a busman's pension?'

When a Labour government was elected on 1 May with a mighty majority, the hopes of the 40,000 bus pensioners must have soared. Gavin Strang, the new Secretary of State for Transport, had his constituency expenses paid by the TGWU. Glenda Jackson was Parliamentary Under-Secretary for Transport, Mike Hall was PPS to Ann Taylor, leader of the House of Commons. Surely now the money unalwfully swiped by the government would be paid to the pensioners? In a press release on 29 May Taylor Joynson Garrett, solicitors to the trustees, announced that they they were issuing a writ against the Department of Transport demanding the £200 million unlawfully taken from the national bus pensioners. Their press release reported: 'The change of government has apparently made no difference to the Department of Transport's attitude in this matter.' Less than a month after taking office the ministers who had unleashed such fury on the previous government for refusing to pay back the money they took from the bus pensioners were now following precisely the same path. The campaigners of a few months back suddenly fell silent. Asked to comment on the BEST case by the BBC's *Face the Facts* programme, Glenda Jackson refused. The Transport and General Workers Union retired to the place where friends of all governments conduct their campaigns: behind the scenes. Union leaders met the trustees and their lawyers and agreed not even to demand an extra trustee from the union. Instead another trustee was appointed to join the officials from the Official Solicitor—Sheila Gleig, a pensions expert.

What about Frank Wheeler? Was he not the ideal person to be a trustee for the pensioners? Was it not entirely due to him that any legal action was taking place at all? 'I would like to be a trustee', he says, 'because I want access to the information the lawyers are getting. I think I would know as well as anyone how to use it best for the pensioners.' I asked Mr William McBryde of the Official Solicitor's Office and Mr Christopher Belk of Taylor Joynson Garrett why they had not appointed as trustee the only man in the country who had fought against the taking of the pension surplus from the moment it was taken. Both men insisted (a little unctuously, I thought) that they had 'great admiration' for Frank. McBryde emphasised the practical difficulties of 'getting him down from Scotland once a month—we couldn't put that burden on him, quite frankly'. Belk concentrated more on the 'need to appear independent'. The impression I got from both men was that they believed that high matters of law were best left to the lawyers. They were looking forward to arguing their case and they really didn't want to have to bother answering to anyone, let alone someone as insistent and on top of his subject as Frank Wheeler. The truth is, however, that allegedly independent lawyers were responsible for making the mess in the first place. As the case drags its expensive and weary way to court, and no doubt to yet another shabby compromise, the pensioners would be much better served if there was one of them to protect their interests among the trustees—and who better than the little David from Moffat with the irrepressible chuckle and the undying suspicion of wealthy Goliaths who pretend they know what's good for him?

Free market forecasters don't know their boom from their bust

City boffins wrong again

Marx says somewhere that capitalism is always booming until the day it is in crisis. He might have added—and even during the crisis the spectre of the boom lingers on. No service industry is more heavily subsidised by capitalists than economic forecasting. The best brains of our generation are set to work to tell us what will happen next. Yet no industry has a worse record. Absolutely no one predicted the collapse of the Russian economy in the summer.

Professor Richard Layard of the London School of Economics and John Parker, European editor of the free market's top propaganda sheet, the *Economist*, has just published a book entitled *The Coming Russian Boom*. No one predicted the sudden progressive collapse of the 'tiger' economies of the Far East.

When the tigers and the privatised Russian bear suddenly disintegrated, something like panic swept the financial journals. 'Does Anyone Have The Answers?' pleaded the usually very cocksure *Far Eastern Economic Review*. After 80 pages, the answer was no.

'Not since the 1930s has a financial crisis appeared to pose such a threat to the world as a whole,' wrote Martin Wolf in the *Financial Times*.

Then, miraculously, nothing very terrible seemed to happen. A few thousand workers lost their jobs. But the stock exchange rallied a little. Perhaps the 'storm' has passed, the 'contagion' has been cured. Last Saturday's *Financial Times* editorial was entitled 'Cruising Nicely Past Recession'. 'The reefs and shoals of recession are past,' it said. But hold on.

Guardian 17 November 1998

There was a two word proviso: 'with luck'. All the best brains are transfixed on the wheel of fortune. Nobody plans the free market and therefore nobody can predict it. It runs on two engines: the greed and fear of the rich, neither of which has anything to do with rationality or predictability. The only certainty is uncertainty, the only sure thing insecurity. If City boffins want to predict the economy, they will have to plan it. But there are plenty of other people, less well-heeled and less choked with jargon, who could do that job much better.

On a glorious spring morning 31 years ago I wandered down to the Round House to hear a young speaker from the States who had provoked the outrage of the right wing press. I was in superior mood. I thought I was in favour of workers' power, not black power, but after an hour listening to Stokeley Carmichael, the two ideals came together.

His theme, which he pursued with the most ferocious wit, was discovery: 'Columbus discovered America, but what about the people who were already there?'

All of us lucky to be there that morning discovered a new black America, angry, funny, intransigent, determined to be free. He died of cancer on Sunday, but anyone who heard him speak will never forget him.

Democracy and socialism

Century of the great hope

Margarethe von Trotta's fabulous film about Rosa Luxemburg opens on New Year's Eve 1899 with a huge centenary party ball organised by the German Social Democratic Party. The scene throbs with gaiety, ribaldry and, above all, hope. All the great leaders of the rising new movement were there to celebrate the dawn of a new era, the start of another hundred years, which everyone assumed would be incomparably better than the century of wars and dictators which was drawing to a close.

What was the chief cause of this great hope? It was not just that the German Social Democratic Party was increasing its influence throughout the country, but that everyone expected that before too long the mass of the German people would win the vote, and that vote would lead inevitably to a prolonged period of democratic government. The essence of that new democracy was conveyed by the word 'social' in the party's name. Of democratic bourgeois parties, ever since 1848, the workers had had their fill. Now at last their place was to be taken by a socialist party whose democratic qualifications were millions of workers' votes. Now at last the travesty of democracy would give way to a government committed to measures which would be passed through parliament and at last put a stop to the rulers' interminable exploitation of the working class.

Two characters dominated that tumultuous celebration: Karl Kautsky, the doyen of German Social Democracy, unbending in his insistence on Marxist politics in the party, and Rosa herself, fresh from a furious argument with Eduard Bernstein. Bernstein had argued against the idea that social change could only come about through social revolution. This was understandable in an age of tyranny, Bernstein argued, but plain silly when the workers, without risking either the violence or the unknown future course of revolution, could change society by electing deputies to parliament and therefore, through the majority they were certain to win in those parliaments, change the country's laws, customs and inequalities. Rosa replied that capitalism would never consent to being reformed into another system, and would certainly resist every measure that threatened to take the country and its industry towards socialism. Those who worked from the top of society to change it from the top wanted, she argued, merely to reform the capitalist system, while she and her comrades wanted to abolish the system altogether and replace it with socialism. It was quite wrong, she concluded, to pretend that this was an argument about ends and means. Those who wanted to reform capitalism rather than replace it were seeking 'a different goal'.

The argument was still raging when the SPD luminaries gathered for their New Year Ball in 1899. Many guests, including Karl Kautsky, responded to the Marxist language favoured by Rosa Luxemburg, though the more practical politicians among them, again including Karl Kautsky, were secretly impressed and even excited by Bernstein's parliamentary perspective. In the film the argument hovers lightly, almost frivolously, over the celebrations without spoiling them. Whatever happened, all the guests assumed and rejoiced that under the auspices of the mighty new party life would get better.

Two decades later the SPD was elected to national office after the defeat of the German Revolution. Rosa Luxemburg, a leader of that revolution, was fished out of a river after being murdered by troops under the orders of the new SPD government. Karl Kautsky and most of the other SPD leaders had voted for the unspeakably murderous First World War, and the intellectual heirs of Bernstein were all in high office. In 1933 the right to vote, the very basis of their power and the essence of the celebrations at the centennial ball, was abruptly usurped. No sooner was Adolf Hitler elected chancellor than he banned all future elections, wiped out trade unions and opposition parties, and installed himself as fascist dictator. The century of the great hope became the century of the Holocaust.

The British experience was similar, if slower and less dramatic. British Labour leaders were far more reluctant than their German counterparts to form an independent party. They did so gingerly, and still glancing nostalgically back to the days when they were welcome in the Liberal Party. The clinching argument was the need for an independent party which would represent the working masses and fight for those masses against the rich and powerful. The new Labour Party ushered in a new era of democracy. Until then the choice for British electors was between Tories and Liberals, two parties which drew their leaders and policies from the propertied minority. The notion that by voting Labour the British people could elect a government which would then pass laws in the interest of labour and the working class was a million times more democratic than anything which had gone before. For the first time democracy meant something more tangible for the workers: a chance to choose a friendly government which could reverse the oppressive balance of class forces and immeasurably improve the lives of working people. In a speech in 1923 the Labour leader, Ramsay MacDonald, explained that these changes would come through elected Labour governments which would, by persistently passing reforming laws, bring about a 'gradual supercession' of capitalism.

Almost at once MacDonald got his chance. The general election of 1929 returned Labour as the largest party. Less than two years later, in conditions of mass unemployment and economic crisis, neither of which had been expected, let alone predicted, MacDonald and his close colleagues proposed a plan to cut the dole for millions of unemployed workers. The plan was intolerable to the rank and file of the Labour Party and to the TUC. Rather than accept the majority view of the party they had built and led, MacDonald, chancellor Philip Snowden, and Jimmy Thomas, whose special ministerial responsibility was unemployment and under whose term of office unemployment had tripled, crossed the floor of the House of Commons and joined the Tories in what they called a National Government. At the subsequent general election Labour lost 3 million votes and all but 50 of its MPs.

Shocked and angry, Labour Party members rallied to calls from the left never again to allow such a betrayal. The newly formed Socialist League argued that the only effective antidote to such a betrayal was a thoroughgoing socialist policy and a ruthless determination by the next socialist government to pass that policy into law. The League's policies were designed to breathe some life into the democracy so humiliated by the MacDonald betrayal. But, by the time Labour was re-elected in 1945, on the crest of precisely the wave of popular socialist conviction which the League had anticipated, the Labour leaders had lost any enthusiasm they may have had for replacing the power of capital. Despite its nationalisations and the National Health Service, the post-war Labour government stuck firmly to the old rules of parliamentary government, and before three years were out had become, for all to see, the servant of capital, not the master of it.

The same wretched process, greatly exaggerated, dogged the two other periods of majority Labour government after the war—under Harold Wilson from 1964 to 1970, and Wilson and James Callaghan from 1974 to 1979. Both succumbed to the 'continuity of policy' which Stafford Cripps of the Socialist League had castigated as the harbinger of compromise and betrayal. Both accepted the dictation of reactionary foreign policy priorities from the United States and blatantly anti-union decisions from the judiciary. Above all, both governments trailed helplessly behind the economic priorities of capitalism: if the market called for high unemployment, the government conceded it; if the market called for low investment, the government conceded it; if the market called for cuts in public services, the government conceded them. Yet no one elected the market and each time the elected government conceded to the market another slice of democracy was lost.

Nor was the power of capital to dictate policy restricted to periods of Labour government. In the autumn of 1992 the newly elected Tory government was proceeding happily along its carefully chosen path with Britain as a member of the ERM, which set the European rate for the currency. Massive speculation by wealthy gamblers, none of whom were elected or had any concern about public policy except to make the swiftest buck for themselves, forced the government, against its declared will, to abandon the policy and leave the ERM. Interviewed about this six years later, Kenneth Clarke, who was home secretary at the time, said the ERM debacle proved the fantastic political power of market forces. 'We as government were totally out of control,' he revealed. Nor was the Tory government alone in that humiliation. Membership of the ERM was the declared policy of the Labour and Liberal Democrat parties.

The combined effect of this relentless drain of democracy has been to convince the professional politicians that there is no real scope for any substantial change in the social order. For formerly bourgeois politicians, Liberal and Tory, this new mood represented no change. They always stood for capitalism, and are quite content to continue to do so. For Labour, which stood for at least a gradual supercession of the capitalist order and a slow, gradual march to socialism, the new pessimism required a sharp change in direction. The election in 1994 of the openly Liberal politician Tony Blair to replace the social democrat John Smith as Labour leader was the first sign of this change. Then, in quick succession, came the removal from the party constitution of Clause Four, which had committed it to public ownership, and a string of watered-down commitments whose combined effect was to ensure that under a Labour government the rich get richer while the workers and their unions are held firmly in the judicial grip which Margaret Thatcher had fashioned for them. As the coup de grace in this slaughter of former commitments, Blair, almost as soon as he was elected, held meetings with the Liberal Democrats to offer them seats in the cabinet. He yearned for the day when British democracy would once again hold out a glorious choice between a Tory party committed to capitalism and an anti-Tory party committed to capitalism. Labour's huge 1997 majority in the Commons—itself a sign of the growing wrath against years of Thatcherism—made it impossible for Blair to clinch his cherished Lib-Lab dream, but he is determined to keep trying. The conclusion at the end of the century of the great hope is that the highest aspirations of the modern Labour Party reach no further than those of the Democratic Party in the United States: that social democracy can now be dispensed with, and that any true meaning of the word 'democracy' will vanish with the 'social'.

One reaction to this sad story is to proclaim the invulnerability of capitalism, and to limit politics and political action to the reactionary vistas of Tony Blair. This is the reaction of people who believe either (a) that there is no working class with common wants and common interests, or (b) that the working class has no power to make its presence and its interests felt in high society. Coincidentally, this sort of pessimism was rife in Britain 100 yeas ago when a Tory government was in apparently unshakeable control and the voters were about to be seduced by a juicy war in South Africa. That pessimism was soon shattered in the great burst of agitation by workers, women and Irish Republicans in the years leading up to the First World War. It was shattered still further in the Russian Revolution and the burst of workers' confidence which it inspired all over the world. The plain fact is that as long as society is split into classes, as long as the rich try to get richer by bashing the poor, there will inevitably be periods of mass protest as the workers and the poor organise to hit back.

The class struggle, in short, is not over. It will show itself again and again. As it does so, another temptation will distract workers. So sick will so many of them be of the long periods of passivity, or of the hideous betrayal of socialist principles by the Stalinist counter-revolution in Russia, that they will urge their followers to abandon politics to professional politicians and do their best to batter down the ramparts of capitalism armed only with strikes and demonstrations. Such a strategy leaves the rich class with their strongest weapon intact. They know, as they did in 1911 and 1921 and 1972, that workers' militancy can fall as fast as it can rise, and that great explosions of militancy can dissolve like fireworks in the night. They know that as long as militancy can be confined to its own borders it can be contained and eventually defeated.

Socialist politics, based on the aspirations of rank and file workers, can bind that militancy together and arm it with answers to the inevitable questions. Why should better off workers go on strike—why not redistribute the wealth of richer workers among the starving millions? Is it really true that one man's wage rise is another man's price rise? Above all, what is this socialism and why should it be any better than what we have at present? The very questions themselves are unanswerable by those who support a society ruled by a bureaucratic state capitalist tyranny or by a grasping ruling class. The answers can only come from a militant working class movement in revolt against capitalism.

The case emerges clearly for socialist organisation whose strength and potential come from its links to workers' militancy and their readiness to use their power to fight. The enduring political lesson of the 20th century is that socialism and social democracy through the ballot box have failed on both counts, and that there is no short cut to socialism from the rulers of class society, however enlightened or socialistic those rulers claim to be. There is no socialism, and because of that no true democracy. Those who believed that either or both could be achieved through the ballot box alone have been confounded. Roll on the next century, not only of the great democratic hope but also of the greatest possible democratic achievement: the emancipation of labour.

Index

Gadaffi, Muammar 256
Gale, Detective Chief Inspector 157
Galtieri 265
Gardiner, Samuel Rawson 63, 66
Gentles, Ian 64, 66
George III, King 25
George, Prince
German, Lindsey 15
Gibbings, Sir Peter 173
Gilbride, Frank 230
Gissing 93
Gittings, Robert 42, 44, 46
Giuliani, Rudy 174
Gladstone, William Ewart 211
Glazebrook, Richard 168
Gleig, Sheila 303
Gloag, Ann 279
Goddard, Donald 258
Godwin, William 62, 78
Goff, Lord 288
Gollancz, Victor 92, 281
Gooch, G P 63
Goodman, Francine 230
Goodman, Geoffrey 222
Gordon, Tony 160
Gould, Bryan 193
Graham, Innes 246
Graham, S T 142
Gray, Peter 160
Grayson, Victor 37
Green, John Francis 237
Green, Peter 139-140
Greener, Len 230
Greenslade, Roy 11, 13
Griffith, John 289-290

Haas, Beatrice 41
Haggerty, Bill 230
Hain, Peter 150
Hall, Mike 298, 301, 302
Hall, Peter 55, 56
Hamilton, Archibald 110, 139, 140
Hammond, Judge 286
Hand, Michael 150
Hanratty, James 281-282
Harbord, David 230
Hardie, Keir 51-52, 98, 210
Harker, Elsie 35-36
Harman, Chris 15, 50
Harp, G J A 157
Harriman, Jane 114-115
Harris, Peter 301
Harris, Robert 199
Harrison, Tony 96
Hastings, Max 15
Hattersley, Roy 193
Hayes, John 105
Hayes, Thomas 258
Hazlitt 192

Healey, Denis 181, 183, 184
Heanan, Pat 115
Heath, Edward 107, 185
Hedouville 31, 33
Heiser, Sir Terence 160
Heseltine, Michael 164, 196, 241
Heyhoe, Barney 152
Heyhoe, David 111
Hickey, Michael 118-125, 287
Hickey, Vincent 118-125, 126, 127
Hicks, John 230
Higgins, Terrence 110
Hill, Christopher 58-59, 203
Hird, Christopher 233
Hislop, Ian 13-14
Hitler, Adolf 91-92, 307
Hobbes, Thomas 283
Hogg, Jefferson 43
Holcroft 74
Hollick, Clive 173, 199
Hollis, Patricia 246
Holmes, Richard 42
Holyrod, Fred 109, 229
Horne, Graham 156
Hoult, Tim 148
Howard, Michael 124, 286-287
Howe, Darcus 50
Howe, Geoffrey 266
Howick, Nigel 156
Hunt, David 240, 241
Hunt, Leigh 43
Hunt, Doug 172
Hunt, Sir John 185
Hunter, Irvine 230-231
Hurd, Douglas 123, 256, 288
Hussein, Saddam 14, 142, 146, 255, 263, 265, 266
Hyndman, H M 37-38, 100

Illsley, William 130, 131
Ingrams, Richard 13, 14
Ireton, Henry General 65, 284-285
Irving, George 124

Jack, Judge Raymond 159
Jackson, Glenda 301-303
Jackson, John 230
Jackson, Paul 235
Jafaar, Khaled 252, 259
James, C L R 32, 50, 93
James I, King 39
James, Gerald 141
Jeffreys, Diarmuid 258-260
Jenkins, Roy 211
Jibril, Ahmed 249, 252, 253, 255-257, 261
Johnson, Ben 97
Johnson, Lyndon Baines 144, 265
Johnson, Dr 72
Johnston, David Sergeant 243